AF365901

LEAN MANUFACTURING
Step by step

Luis Socconini

Collection: Gestiona
Director: David Soler

Lean Manufacturing. Step by step
1st edition, 2021
2nd edition, 2024

© Luis Vicente Socconini Pérez Gómez
© of this edition, ICG Marge, SL
Original title in Spanish: *Lean Manufacturing. Paso a paso*

Publisher: Marge Books
Brutau, 160 – 08203 Sabadell (Barcelona)
Tel. 931 429 486 - marge@margebooks.com
www.margebooks.com

Translator: Henry O'Donnell
Make-up editor: Mercedes Lara

ISBN printed edition: 978-84-10238-11-4
ISBN digital edition: 978-84-10238-10-7

The paper used in this book has not been bleached with elemental chlorine (CI_2).

Index

The author 7
Acknowledgements. 9

Part I. The basis for world-class leadership and culture

Chapter 1. Introduction 15
Chapter 2. Productivity constraints 29
Chapter 3. Diagnosis and implementation 52
Chapter 4. Hoshin kanri strategy 75

Part II. Detailed knowledge of the processes

Chapter 5. Value mapping 93

Part III. Basic tools

Chapter 6. Kaizen events to apply process improvements 115
Chapter 7. The 5S of good housekeeping 129
Chapter 8. Visual control 142

Part IV. Tools to improve team effectiveness

Chapter 9. Total Production Maintenance 155

Part V. Tools to improve delivery time and capacity

Chapter 10. Cellular manufacturing 171
Chapter 11. Quick product changeovers 184

Part VI. Tools to improve quality

Chapter 12. Prevention with FMEA 197
Chapter 13. Poka-yoke error proofing 206
Chapter 14. 8 D problem solving 214
Chapter 15. Six Sigma for variation reduction 223

Part VII. Tools for materials and production control

Chapter 16. Kanban for material and production control 235
Chapter 17. Heijunka for production sequencing 244

Part VIII. Integration and control of information

Chapter 18. Standard work 251
Chapter 19. Lean accounting for decision making 260

Part IX. Tools for energy reduction

Chapter 20. Energy saving 283

Glossary of terms and definitions 295

The author

Luis Socconini

Is an industrial engineer of ITESM, Guadalajara campus. Luis has a master's degree in quality and productivity and is a Master Black Belt.

Luis holds certification in Strategic Management from Stanford University, *Leading Product Innovation* from Harvard University, and *Industry 4.0* from MIT.

He has worked for the Wharton business school (Pennsylvania) as a business consultant, at Grolsch Brewery in the Netherlands as a pro-cess engineer, and at IBM as a manufacturing engineer.

As director of Lean Six Sigma Institute, he runs high impact projects in companies such as Abbott Laboratories, Kraft Heinz, Coca Cola, BMW, Bimbo, and Fender, among others. He constantly develops productivity applications in sectors such as construction, mining, agri-culture, public administration, energy, services, etc.

He has been a distinguished professor at several prestigious universities in Mexico.

He is author of the books:

- *Lean Manufacturing. Step by step.*
- *Lean Six Sigma Yellow Belt. Certification Manual.*
- *Lean Service. Certification Manual.*
- *Lean Company. Más allá de la manufactura.*
- *El proceso de las 5´S en acción.*
- *Lean Six Sigma Green Belt. Certification Manual.*
- *Lean Six Sigma Black Belt. Certification Manual*

He is also co-author of:

- *Lean Six Sigma. Management system for Leaders.*
- *Lean Energy. Guía de implementación.*
- *5S Practical guide to improve quality and productivity.*

Acknowledgements

To my mother, who showed me the path of righteousness and has supported me in all my projects.

To my wife Marce and my daughter Sofi for being my sources of inspiration and supporting me at all times.

To Áurea Delgado, Marco Barrantes, Javier Masini, Roberto Hernandez and many other people who have taught me and helped me with their knowledge to better understand how to apply many of the concepts described in this book.

To my colleague and friend Juan Pablo Martín Gómez for providing very valuable information on the subject of energy saving.

To Diego Reyes and Francisco Zaldívar for supporting me in the review.

To my clients for trusting my advice and allowing me to enter a world of challenges and new knowledge for me.

To my teachers for having the patience to teach and show me the way to learn for myself and especially to all my students in different universities for keeping me learning constantly and for giving me the opportunity to share unforgettable moments of reflection and knowledge.

To my work team for giving me the opportunity to live together in a competitive environment, full of challenges and responsibilities.

To the following companies and individuals who allowed the use of photographic and graphic materials for the production of this book:

Javier Masini.
Rexroth de Bosch Automation.
Flexim Mexico.

To chambers and associations such as Careintra, Canaco, Coparmex, Cintra, Cámara del Tequila, Cadelec, etc., for allowing me to approach companies and for their strong commitment to improving competitiveness.

To the universities that have allowed me to grow and have given their recognition to historic achievements: Tecnológico de Monterrey, Universidad Panamericana, Universidad del Valle de Mexico, Universidad Autónoma de Guadalajara and Universidad del Valle de Atemajac.

LEAN MANUFACTURING

Step by step

Part I

The basis for world-class leadership and culture

Chapter 1

Introduction

Manufacturing background

The beginning of the evolution of modern manufacturing was marked by James Watt's invention of the double action steam engine in 1776. With this development the Industrial Revolution was starting. Later, in 1798, Eli Whitney's design with its ingenious machinery of interchangeable parts gave greater impetus to mass production, thereby laying the foundations for what is now known as standardization.

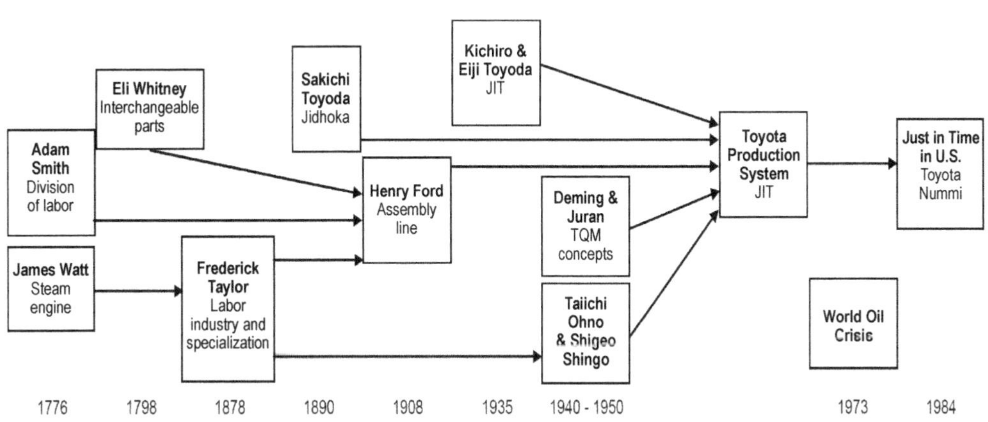

Figure 1.1

Frederick Taylor (1856-1915) completely changed the approach of manufacturing by turning its management into a science. With his detailed work studies, he institutionalized the batch production system and proposed the division of labor into departments that focus their efforts on very specific activities. This system was named Scientific Management and became a model for Western industry. Taylor proposed the standardization of work.

For his part, **Henry Ford**, originally from Greenfield Township, Michigan, built his first automobile, the quadricycle, and drove it through the streets of Detroit in 1896. In 1908 he began manufacturing his famous Model T, of which 15 million units were manufactured. Then, applying the principles set forth by Adam Smith in the 18th century, in which he stated that work should be divided into specific tasks, in 1913 Ford created the assembly line and revolutionized how products were manufactured.

Brief history of Toyota production system

Toyota's history begins with Sakichi Toyoda, a Japanese inventor and thinker born in 1867 near the city of Nagoya, Japan. As a child he learned the trade of carpenter handed down from his father and later, in 1890, he applied that knowledge in the invention of his automatic looms.

On this long journey of effort and hard work, Toyoda worked long and hard and came up with several inventions. There was one notable invention in this story, which consisted of a mechanism that caused the loom to stop if a thread broke, warning the operator with a visual cue that the machine had stopped and needed attention. This invention is named *jidhoka,* which means autonomization of defects or automation with a human approach; the original word is *jidoka* which means automation and the "h" is added to denote that it influences people (human). This invention was one of the most important he came up with. All this meant Sakichi Toyoda was considered a great engineer and the king of inventors in Japan.

In 1894 his son Kiichiro Toyoda was born, who later began working at Toyoda Loom Works' Sakichi factory where he applied a very technical approach

Looms at Toyoda Loom Works.

to the improvement of his father's looms and managed to keep the machines running uninterrupted without stoppages for long periods of time. So, in 1924, Kiichiro completed the design of the G-type spinning machine which could work several shifts without interruption.

In 1929, Kiichiro traveled to England to negotiate the sale of patents for his "fail-safe" invention to the Platt brothers, who paid £100,000 for the invention. With this capital, Kiichiro started the Toyota Motor Corporation in 1933 (Fujimoto, 1999).

Toyota's production system, popularly known as *just in time*, has its origin in Japan, given the great need to run a post-war economy in a nation devastated by World War II. By the end of the war, the Japanese replaced their efforts to stand out and impress the world by their military strength with a new twist in the "battle" for global competitiveness and the resurgence of a new fighting spirit, this time for economic leadership. It was then that the Japanese industrialists set out to direct their efforts towards competitiveness in their companies.

Kiichiro Toyoda, then president of Toyota, realized that the competitiveness of Japanese workers was almost three times lower than that of German workers and almost ten times lower than the Americans, so he decided to start a path to competitiveness by creating a system that would ensure profitability and healthy participation in a highly competitive market.

Toyota City, located in Nagoya, Japan.

After Kiichiro, Eiji Toyoda took over the company and alongside Taiichi Ohno led it to international success, relying on its ingenious *just in time* production system. Eiji was the son of Heihachi Toyoda, the brother of Sakichi Toyoda, founder of Toyoda Loom Works. He was a prominent industrialist, largely responsible for the development of *just in time*, as well as the successful take-off of the Toyota Motor Company in profitability and international recognition. Historically, what stood out in his strategy was the establishment of a partnership with GM, and together they created the Nummi plant in Freemont, California (USA). In this plant, cars are still assembled for both companies with an interesting hybrid management system of Japanese and Americans. Eiji remained CEO of Toyota until 1994.

Western influence

After World War II, Japan would face enormous difficulties in rebuilding its cities and businesses. The United States and the Allies did not want the military forces to resurface. Under this condition, General Douglas MacArthur, commander of the U.S. forces, set the goal of rebuilding the economy and infra-

General Douglas McArthur. commander of the U.S. forces.

structure whilst making sure that the military force did not do so. MacArthur got some experts to help with the reconstruction and invited personalities like Homer Sarasohn, an engineer at the Massachusetts Institute of Technology (MIT). He was responsible for rebuilding the communications system in Japan at a time when the Japanese society viewed the United States as a hostile entity for continuing to occupy Japanese territory.

Unfortunately, there were no radio sets to send these messages to the Japanese people, thus the manufacturing of radios was promoted. The first devices were of very poor quality and unreliable. A testing laboratory was then established to inspect their quality. While this helped, it was not a long-term solution so the strategy of training Japanese managers in management techniques was adopted, including statistical control of the work-based process devised by Walter Shewhart.

The Civil Communication Section (CCS), together with the Union of Japanese Scientists and Engineers (JUSE), was responsible for technical and vocational education. The JUSE wanted more training in statistical control and asked the CCS to recommend an expert to continue the learning. Walter Shewhart was the best option, but he was not available; the next option was a professor named Edwards Deming from Columbia University who had learned and applied Shewhart's methodologies. So, on the recommendation of Homer Sarasohn, Deming entered the history of Japanese manufacturing. Deming was already known in Japan since in 1947 he made a visit on a census mission. In 1950, the JUSE asked Deming to conduct a very thorough training for two months in which he taught many people from engineers to managers.

Joseph M. Juran was also invited to give some lessons and emphasized management's responsibility to lead quality improvements. A key element was defining the quality policy and ensuring that everyone understood and supported it.

Taiichi Ohno and Shigeo Shingo: the pioneers of Lean Manufacturing

In the days of Eiji Toyoda, Ohno said he wanted to turn a winery into a machine shop and wanted to see everyone working and being re-trained for that purpose. He did not say how to do it, he simply laid the foundations and gave the orders. Since he had the power and authority, it was understood that what he said had to be carried out. He was unquestionably a leader with a lot of character and determination and faced the huge challenge of turning an automobile factory into one of the most profitable businesses. This proved to be a fundamental pillar in the creation of what is now *Lean Manufacturing*.

Taichi Ohno was born in Manchuria, China in 1912 and graduated from the Nagoya Technical School. He started working for Toyota in 1932. In the 1940s and early 1950s, Taiichi Ohno served as assembly line manager and developed many improvements. In those years Toyota was on the verge of bankruptcy and could not make big investments, which made it use its ingenuity to achieve the major advances that were made, given the need to improve without much financial resources.

From the 1940s, Taiichi Ohno and Shigeo Shingo shared unforgettable experiences in transforming the plant and creating its manufacturing strategy; what we now know as Lean Manufacturing. Ohno's career grew thanks to the major successes demonstrated in the assembly plant and he was promoted to executive vice president in 1975. In the early 1980s, Ohno retired to become president of Toyota Gosei, a subsidiary of Toyota and supplier of Toyota Motors. He died in 1989 in the city of Toyota.

For his part, Dr. Shingo was possibly one of the most brilliant manufacturing geniuses the world has ever seen as he was able to solve any manufacturing problem put before him. Taiichi Ohno recognized three great masters in his life: Kiichiro Toyoda, who instilled in him a great vision of the future and business; Henry Ford, who showed that he could build a car from steel and make a finished product in just four days; and, finally, Dr. Shingo, who was his consultant, companion, and teacher.

Dr. Shingo was an industrial engineer who studied Frederik Taylor thoroughly in relation to the scientific management of work as well as Frank Gilbreth and his time and motion studies. He was able to understand the differences between processes and operations and to study them as a flow that can be transformed into continuous streams with minimal interruptions in order to provide the customer only what they needs without the need to make large batches or generate unnecessary inventories. He understood perfectly that processes are flow streams that can be optimized by taking care of some details such as the standardization of work and the measurement of capacity and demand, in addition to making continuous flows without interruptions so that they make the production flow only when the customer requires it and at the speed that demand dictates.

Furthermore, to pave the way for continuous improvement, Shingo developed a need in people, based on the idea that improving at work also helped them as people. He showed openness in his philosophy by stating that there are many ways to improve and solve problems, just as there are many ways to climb a mountain.

His contributions to manufacturing include the creation of Poka-yoke devices which eliminate defects by eliminating errors. These mechanisms were formerly known as *baka-yoke* (foolproof) but Shingo claimed that the term offended people and moreover, it had to be recognized that all people, even the most intelligent ones, make mistakes; for this reason the name was changed to Poka-yoke, which means "error proofing".

In 1955 he began his relationship with Toyota as a consultant, a position he also held in other companies. In 1959 he founded his own consulting company and managed to reduce the setup times for 1,000 ton presses used to change from one product to another from 49 hours to 3 minutes, thereby creating what we know today as SMED (Single Minute Exchange Of Die) or "die changes in single digit minutes". In the 1970s he traveled around the world to teach his techniques. He wrote 14 books, and in his honor, the Shigeo Shingo award is currently given to those involved in manufacturing excellence, as a tribute to his genius and creation. He died in 1990.

Shigeo Shingo was born in the city of Saga, Japan in 1909. He studied at the Saga Technical School. He initially worked for the Taipei Railway Company and in 1943 worked for the Amano manufacturing plant in Yokohama. He was associated for many years with the Japanese Association of Managers and worked to improve the industry at many manufacturing plants.

What is Lean Manufacturing?

Lean Manufacturing is the name given to the *just in time* system in the West. It is also called world-class manufacturing and Toyota production system.

It can be defined as a continuous and systematic process of identification and elimination of waste or excess. The term "excess" meaning any activity that does not add value to a process but rather results in incurred costs and labor. This systematic elimination is carried out by working with teams of well-organized and trained people. We must understand that Lean Manufacturing is a tireless and uninterrupted task to create more effective, innovative, and efficient companies (Bodek).

The real power of Lean Manufacturing lies in continuously discovering the opportunities for improvement that every company hides because there will always be waste that can be eliminated. It is about creating a way of life that recognizes that waste exists and will always be a challenge for those who are willing to find and eliminate it.

> Hiroshi Okuda, CEO and Director of Toyota Motors said: "I want everyone in Toyota to change or at least not be an obstacle to others to change. I also want everyone to write their plans for change for the year."

A lean, slim, or agile company which wants to make the most of the changing conditions in a globalized world must be able to adapt quickly to change by using the excellent improvement, prevention, problem solving, and management tools available and have habits that influence culture and management congruent with leadership that motivates change and self-growth. Therefore, in this book, we will deal with subjects that not only serve to implement improvements, but we will also deal with tools that have been shown to strike a balance between the different common needs of organizations and that should be part of their toolbox in order to achieve outstanding performance.

Strategic model

It is commonly mistaken that the main subject of study in the *just in time* system is inventory and reducing it its final goal, even going so far as to use synonyms such as "zero inventory" to simplify this idea. This is nothing more than a myth originated by a misunderstanding, as can be seen in the model that Toyota itself designed for the system. Note that, in any business activity, the goal to be achieved is customer delight and sustained profitability. This message about the company's goal denotes a clear interest in ensuring customers obtain not only their requirements but goes much further by seeking true satisfaction.

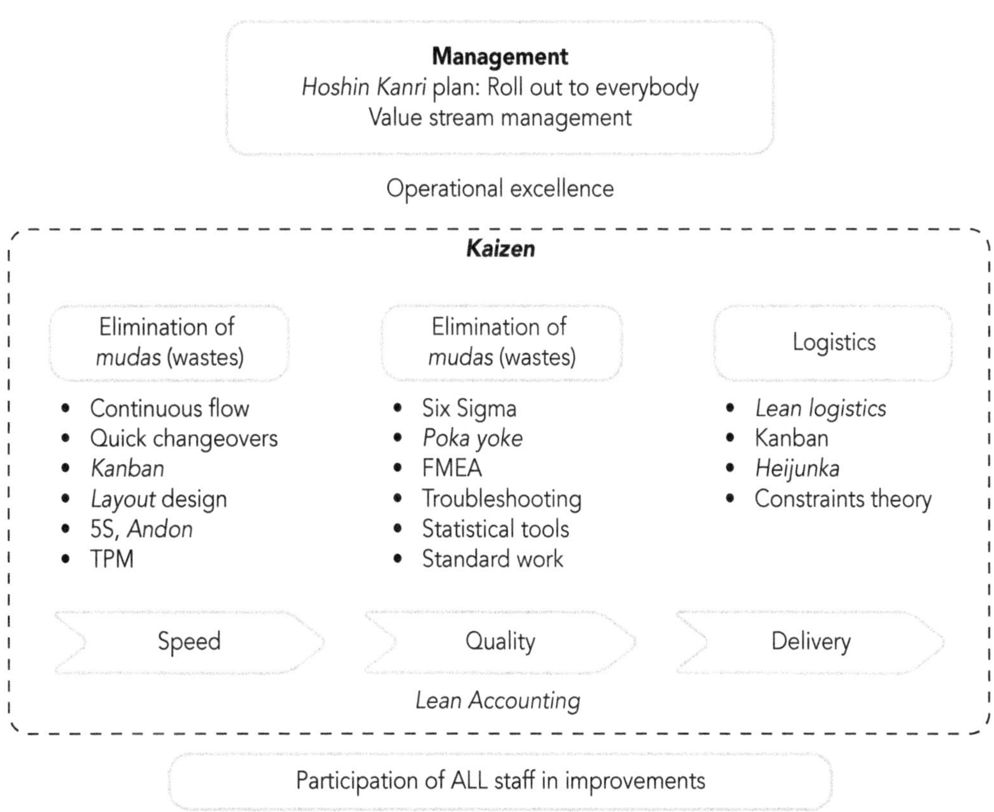

Figure 1.2

Moreover, this customer satisfaction must be achieved economically, without wasting the resources that the company's shareholders have deposited in it. Therefore, profitability means that all those related to both the product and the brand as well as customers, suppliers, workers, and shareholders, are looking for the company's activity to generate profits.

Effectiveness in operations and production processes must be part of a strategy. There are many cases of companies that have implemented very simple tools to complex management systems or expensive information systems, without it being part of a medium to long term strategy. When tools, improvements, training, machine purchasing, and other implementations are not part of a strategy, history has shown that such efforts, in the vast majority of cases, are doomed to fail.

In the management table we can see a strategic approach based on the company's philosophy which is deployed at all levels using policy management and communication by means of Hoshin kanri; sending each person their part of the plan and strategy in order to achieve the company's objectives. Management is based primarily on the value generated for customers and the processes to carry it out; here lies the importance of carrying out a value analysis (see chapter 4).

In today's markets, customers and consumers require increasingly more agile solutions to meet their needs. From waiting for a pizza delivery to the time a bank takes to authorize a customer loan, the market is less and less willing to wait. Alongside this reality, as will be seen throughout this book, Lean Manufacturing has identified a strong relationship between response speed and business profitability. In other words, it is understood that a process that takes a long time may be concealing a series of costly wastes, such as waiting or errors in production planning, machine breakdowns, large batch production, transport, etc; most of them invisible to management. These hidden wastes almost always leave a footprint that can help find them: time. Long response times will normally be clear evidence of the presence of other types of recurring problems, so in manufacturing we must look for processes with minimal cycle times, i.e. with less waste and with a continuous flow production system.

For its part, the quality of products and processes must be achieved in the very operations that produce them and not just measured or evaluated at the end by sampling. Such sampling can only discover part of the defects, but it hardly prevents defects. Quality at source means that operators and their teams contribute by their processes to achieving excellent quality from the first time the work is done.

It is not enough to be capable of doing excellent quality work if the machine being used is out of order, so, in this lean manufacturing system maximum efficiency in machinery is essential to optimize its effectiveness too. This is achieved by having the operator take care of his machine through daily cleaning, lubrication, general servicing, and minor adjustments. This is a fundamental part of Lean Manufacturing which bases the system on active staff participation and improvements on own initiative. This approach is achieved by empowering people to participate in improvements and enabling them to make decisions about what, in production and its processes, is relevant to creating value.

Finally, visual control is an important part of Lean Manufacturing as it allows anyone to detect anomalies and make decisions about them simply with visual aids such as warnings, lights, guides, and procedures. The challenge is to create factories for "deaf-mutes" where it is not necessary to shout, search, explain, etc. but to be an organization dedicated to creating value with the minimum of waste.

The oil crisis

With the oil crisis of 1973 many companies around the world had to close their doors due to low profitability caused by the high costs of energy, their main raw material. However, despite the adversity, there were some companies that managed to survive in these conditions, which focused the attention on them.

As Japan was not an oil producer but a consumer, Japanese companies suffered this on a much larger scale than their American counterparts. However, the special case of the Toyota Motor Company drew world attention, not only was it not suffering major problems in the face of this restriction on the world economy, but on top of that it was still making profits. It was this fact that led the Japanese government to ask Toyota to "open its doors" to the world of industry and show what techniques and strategies it was using. This is how Toyota began its commitment to international industry by demonstrating the techniques that led it to amazing results in productivity and competitiveness.

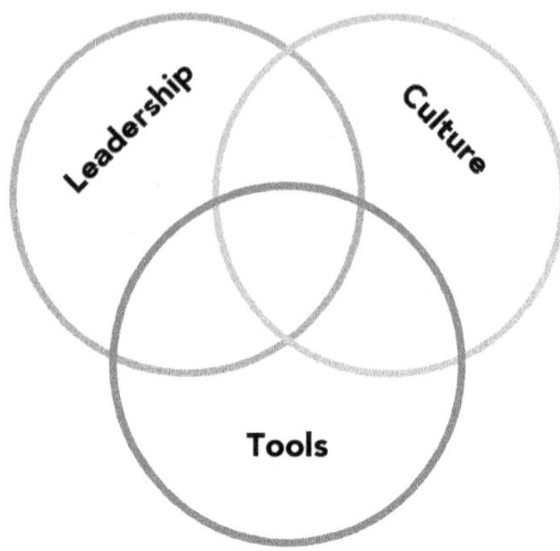

Figure 1.3

Implications of success

Sometimes we think that only by introducing new methodologies and tools will companies achieve significant changes but when it seems that these efforts have not yielded the desired results, we ask ourselves: what was missing to get the expected results?

In a world-class company it is valid to consider that it is not only about implementing tools but rather a leadership attitude in working to create a new culture.

The challenge really is to change the culture positively, not just to introduce new strategies, tools, or plans.

The leadership undertaken by management is essential because it sets short, medium, and long-term goals and objectives, provides the means for implementation, creates and monitors work plans, and ensures that these plans are known and carried out, providing the resources and monitoring the implementation.

The tools are very valuable but are not enough if they are not implemented under good leadership; this determines whether people are committed and not just involved. Leadership is the fuse that ignites the vigor of radical change in organizations.

Culture is simply the way of being, thinking and acting of a society, this can be a nation, a company or a family. At the base of culture are habits and these, –although they may be good or bad (virtues or vices)– are formed on the basis of constantly performing actions. There are two things that are really difficult when it comes to forming habits: starting them and stopping them.

Within the concept of habits lies the essence of resistance to change that many people have towards new ways of doing business; this resistance is a way to express fear of the unknown or the fear of what takes them out of a comfort zone they have reached by doing no more than what is absolutely necessary to keep their job.

Why can some and others can't?

Companies that make changes have a winning combination of efforts such as:

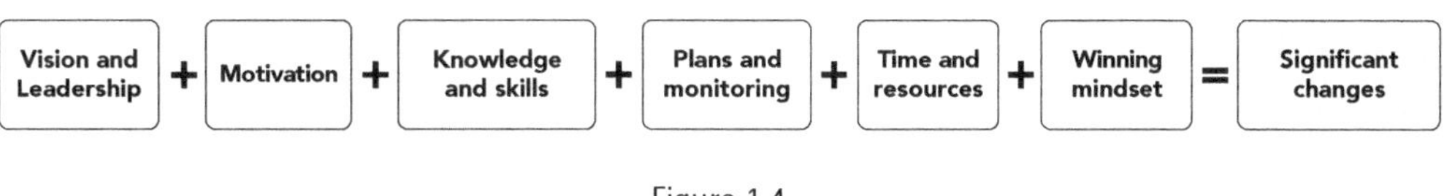

Figure 1.4

In the absence of any of these components it is very likely that the changes will not last long or will not achieve the expected results.

If there is no vision and leadership, there will be uncertainty about the new challenges facing the company; without motivation, the changes will take a long time to arrive; without the knowledge and skills to launch the initiatives, a feeling of frustration arises from having all the elements but not knowing how to materialize them; without plans and proper follow-up, we'll only have false starts and sooner or later the programs will be dismissed as just another project; without the time and resources, we will only see good intentions but will not have the power to change things; and, finally, without a winning mindset with which we can imagine the future of the company before starting significant changes, it will be difficult to achieve extraordinary results. It is necessary that a winning mindset be imbued in everybody and that the projects carried out be supported by people who believe in themselves and feel it.

Personal quality

This is the basis of all qualities. To be able to think about the quality of our products, first we need quality in the people, with that there will be quality in the departments and with this we will achieve quality in the processes. So, the quality of the products or services will be the result of this whole cycle. We will only have quality if we demand it and that is why this enormous effort must start with people.

If we want winning companies, we need to hire people with that mindset; healthy and strong managers who give off that vitality to others. Experience is a necessary component, but even more so is common sense and the ability to make good decisions with the information available. Age is not important but rather creativity and the enthusiasm to learn and give your best to the major undertaking that is work, where we spend a third of our lives.

Applications of Lean concepts

Various applications have been developed, not only in manufacturing but also in services.

Success stories are currently being developed in the following applications of all these concepts and tools:

- Lean Manufacturing.
- Lean Government.
- Lean Office.
- Lean Healthcare.
- Lean Hotel.
- Lean Design.
- Lean Logistics.
- Lean Accounting.

Specific applications aim to improve processes, whatever they may be, and eliminate wasteful practices that exist in almost every process.

Commitment

We are in an age of high competitiveness in business activities, where large corporations disappear just by being off guard in their way of thinking or doing, and where small companies find a way to be the best thanks to that mindset and work method. We realize that only speed with quality can really build strong and solid economies which are born out of creatively designed products and services. That is why the commitment of those who make decisions every day, decisions that mark the course of our companies and our countries, is fundamental in this competitive and global world.

Chapter 2

Productivity constraints

Productivity

Although productivity is quite the buzzword nowadays, many fail to know its meaning and above all, how to measure it in order to improve it.

In a global world where competitiveness has become the biggest strategic weapon, many companies strive to increase their sales, lower their costs and improve their image but few are achieving tangible results.

In this chapter we will analyze the main productivity constraints and determine ways to detect and fight them off. It will also examine how constraints in a production system limit the achievement of objectives.

Productivity model

In any business activity, be it a processing or service company, there are several inputs that can be summarized in five broad basic groups: materials, machinery, manpower, methods, and environment. Many authors have agreed to refer to them as the 5M. It is important to recognize that each of these groups is very different from the others but there is a common factor inherent in all of them: money. It is obvious that all the above incur costs, as a result many companies with liquidity problems try to reduce that cost by "cutting back" the 5M: laying off personnel, reducing the quality of materials, reducing the maintenance of machinery, etc. However, it has been fully demonstrated that these cutbacks to 5M only have an immediate impact on the profit and loss account but do

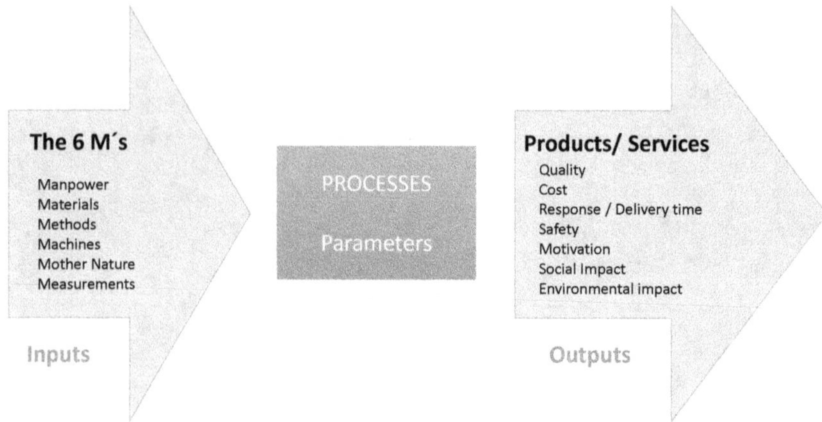

Figure 2.1

not solve the problem in the medium term. Remember that the main source of loss comes in the form of waste and this problem is not solved simply by laying off personnel; on the contrary, sometimes this generates new waste and the corresponding costs.

If we follow the value stream within the company, the 5M's (let us say "what enters the business") are combined and transformed into products or services through defined processes. These processes should be standardized by means of specific parameters that clearly describe how to obtain the desired performance of each process. As a result of the processes several outputs are created (i.e., "what leaves the business"): the products that are produced, the quality of them, their cost, the time required to produce them, the accidents or non-accidents that occur as a result of the processes, the motivation of the people, as well as the impact of the processes on the environment. The relationship between these outputs and inputs is what we know as productivity. Productivity improvement is the achievement of better results in a process. In a nutshell: "do more with less".

According to this model, the importance of processes in productivity and, therefore, in the implementation of Lean Manufacturing is evident. Productivity, as we saw, is the relationship between results and inputs, and in processes inputs are transformed into results. It is here that the importance of mastering processes becomes evident, understanding that achieving that mastery involves knowing, controlling, and improving them.

How to measure productivity

$$\textbf{Productivity} = \frac{\text{Outputs}}{\text{Inputs}}$$

In this formula, the outputs correspond to the products that are created, and the inputs correspond to the number of resources that enter the system.

Productivity is an important indicator and must be measured constantly in order to know the true state of the improvements.

Example

We want to know the productivity in a company that produces 332,650 pieces per month and whose costs are as follows:

Manpower = $50,000.
Machinery = 10,000 $.
Methods =   2,000 $.
Materials = 20,000 $.

$$\textbf{Productivity} = \frac{332\ 650 \text{ units}}{82\ 000\ \$} = \textbf{4,05 units/\$.}$$

If in the next period the company produces the same or more, but by investing less resources, then productivity will be increasing.

The main wastes and their sources

"There is nothing more useless than making something efficient that shouldn't be."

Today's markets are being strengthened by the formation of large trading blocs, in many cases removing tariff barriers between countries and improving the costs and response time of freight transport and information transfer. In short, changes in economies are taking place at breakneck speed. In these competitive environments, "wasting time" is unthinkable. For this reason, it is vital that management and employees invest their efforts every day only in activities that add value to customers, leaving aside what represents costly waste.

For many it will come as a surprise to know that in most cases only 5 to 10% of all activities carried out in companies add value; the rest is waste. If we are able to phase out this waste, we will understand the success of companies that make the difference in terms of competitiveness.

The big problem is that this waste is the main reason for the low competitiveness of those companies that are currently closing down and they don't realize it. They seek to overcome their liquidity problems by laying off staff or changing the quality of their inputs but they do not attack waste. The cause of this waste usually lies in policies and ways of thinking anchored in the past that have not been reviewed and much less improved.

Once you learn to observe and discover waste, the company culture will gradually eliminate these wastes of time, delays, additional efforts, and high costs. For this reason, those who begin this major task will be greatly rewarded, both in the future of their companies and in their personal lives.

As a result of waste in processes, it is common to derive other losses, the latter being more evident than the waste itself. Among the most common losses are the loss of time, the loss of capacity, the loss of resources and, finally, the loss of opportunities.

Requirements for the elimination of waste

- Have strong leadership.
- Be convinced that ongoing training should be supported.
- Have the right management team for the current reality.
- Have a clear vision of the future of the organization.
- Have a participatory management.
- Have well-defined plans and strategies.
- Disseminate strategies among all staff.
- Be aware of which wastes affect the company.
- Recognize the impact that such wastes have on the company.
- Fully convince all staff of the importance of systematically eliminating wastes.

Three productivity constraints

A process uses materials, people, natural resources, technology, and financial resources that result in a product or service. In any process, certain transformation activities are carried out, the effectiveness of which is measured by their productivity indicators, as explained above.

However, in business, productivity is not infinite. This is affected by a very wide range of problems that limit the results that can be obtained from the available resources. Japanese engineers have classified these constraints into three groups called the 3 "Mu", because they all start with the syllable "mu":

MURI = Overload

MURA = Variability

MUDA = Waste

Figure 2.2

Overload or muri

The productivity of business activities and people decreases when the workload they are given exceeds their capacity. If operators are required to produce above their normal limits or if machines are made to produce above their capacity, the organization's most valuable resources are depleted, thereby reducing productivity.

Figure 2.3

Variability or mura

This refers to the lack of uniformity created from the input elements of the processes, such as materials, specifications, training, skills, methods, and machinery conditions; this in turn produces a lack of uniformity in the processes, which translates into the generation of products or services that are not uniform either, i.e. they exhibit variability. This variation may or may not cause problems for our customers, so it is important to recognize the type of variation and whether it is natural. When the variability of a certain process and its results is natural,

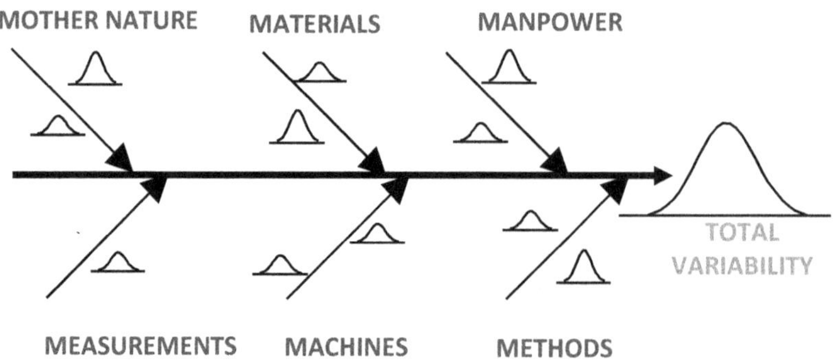

Figure 2.4

the process is said to be controlled. But if a new source of variation is introduced into the process, then the process is said to have gone out of control. Variability is the main subject of study and control by statistical methodologies like statistical process control or Six Sigma.

Waste or mudas

The best translation of the Japanese word *muda* is "excess". The seven types of waste that negatively affect productivity must be well understood, detected, and eliminated or minimized every day in businesses and institutions. One of the main objectives of Lean Manufacturing is to systematically know, detect, and eliminate all wastes in the industry as they reduce the capacity of companies on a daily basis and pose a challenge for directors, managers, and employees in general.

To understand what waste is, it is best fit to first explain what activities add value (VA). VAs are those that directly produce a change that the customer wants, to the extent that he is willing to pay for that effort. Waste or excess will be any other effort made in the company that is not essential to add value to the product or service as required by the customer. These efforts increase costs and lower the level of service, thus affecting the results achieved by the company. Toyota classifies waste or *mudas* into seven main groups:

1. Overproduction *muda*.
2. Excess inventory *muda*.
3. Defective product *muda*.
4. Transport of materials and tools *muda*.
5. Unnecessary processing *muda*.
6. Waiting *muda*.
7. Unnecessary worker movement *muda*.

1. Overproduction

Overproducing basically means:

- Producing more than necessary.
- Producing faster than required.
- Manufacturing products before they are needed.

Characteristics of overproduction

- Accumulated inventory.
- Excess large capacity machinery.
- Unbalanced material flow.
- Excessive storage space.
- More manpower than necessary.
- Complex inventory management.
- Too much installed capacity / investment.
- Large spaces on the floor.
- Hidden problems.
- Feeling of unsafe work environment.
- Obsolescence of materials.
- Manufacturing batches of excessive size.
- Manufacturing in advance.

Causes of overproduction

- Production is accelerated. "Just in case" mentality.
- Communication between departments or with the customer is poor or non-existent.
- Machine optimization is done individually without having a global view of the value stream.
- Automation of operations that do not require it.
- Very slow changeovers and repairs.
- Inadequate cost accounting practices for in-plant decision-making.
- Insufficient preventive maintenance.
- Lack of consistency in production scheduling.
- Focus on optimistic expectations of sales forecasts.
- Processes with very low potential capacity.

2. Excess inventory

Excess inventory is any material, product in process or finished products that exceeds what is needed to meet customer demand.

In general, inventories are generated to avoid the following inefficiencies:

- Erroneous forecasts of expected demand.
- Production imbalance.

- Low confidence in there being no breakdowns in the machinery used for production.
- Lack of knowledge of actual production capacity.
- Produce to increase the efficiency of individual teams or areas.
- Processes or machines separated by large distances.
- Division of labor into batches, which slows down the process.
- Defective products that must be replaced by an increase in production.
- Massive rework campaigns when defects pop up.
- Very high product changeover or machine setup times.
- Inadequate plant layout.
- High buffer stocks with no production plan between processes, thereby hiding the problems.

Characteristics of excess inventories

- Large spaces on raw materials reception platform.
- Permanence of first arrivals instead of applying the principle "first in, first out".
- Large quantities of product waiting to be processed.
- Large areas for product storage (raw materials, materials, product in process and finished product).

- Lengthy process times when engineering changes are implemented.
- Need for additional resources for materials management (personnel, equipment, shelves, warehouses, spaces, systems).
- Low inventory turnover.

Causes of excess inventories

- Poor knowledge of the speed of real or current demand.
- Inadequate processes to meet customer requirements and specifications.
- Uncontrolled bottlenecks.
- Insufficient capacity of supplier companies.
- Excessive scheduling of overtime.
- Bad management decisions.
- Optimization of people's work and workplaces is not achieved.
- Poorly applied productivity bonuses.

3. Defective products

This *muda* refers to the loss of resources used to produce a defective item or service, since materials, machine time, and most importantly, a person's time were invested to perform work that ultimately did not add value to the customer. It is similar to what happens when a cake burns while baking: the ingredients, gas, and baker's work are wasted; everything ends up in the trash, including the time and money invested.

Repeated tasks also fall under this category because, while the defects can be corrected, repetition involves performing one or more tasks two or more times, thus incurring more expenses and the loss of availability of company resources.

Characteristics that cause defects

- Over-staffing to inspect, rework, or repair.
- Inventory accumulated specifically to be reworked.
- Complex product flow within the plant.
- Product or service of questionable quality.
- Errors in shipments and deliveries.
- Little interaction between customer and supplier companies.
- Low profits due to repeated tasks, waste and costs of urgent freight premiums and returns.
- The organization becomes reactive: "putting out fires".

Causes of defects and repetition of tasks

- Inefficient processes.
- Excessive variation in the production process.
- Incapacity of supplier companies.
- Lack of process control.
- Lack of control of staff errors.
- Incorrect management decisions.
- Inadequate training.
- Inadequate equipment and tools.
- Inadequate plant layout or excessive material handling.
- High inventory levels.
- Poor environmental conditions.
- Lack of quality culture.
- Lack of leadership on the subject of quality.
- Lack of knowledge of the causes of problems.

4. Transport of materials and tools

This *muda* consists of all those material transfers that do not directly support the production system. Moving products from one side of the plant to the other does not translate into a significant change for the customer but it does imply a cost and even puts the integrity of the product at risk. It should be clarified that we refer to transportation as the movement of materials within a company and not to the delivery of the product to customers or distribution centers.

Transport features

- Excess equipment for transporting materials on trucks or forklifts.
- Excess conveyor belts, ramps, or pipes.
- Too many storage sites.
- Excess shelves for materials.
- Poor inventory management.
- Inadequate design and use of facilities.
- Poor inventory control.
- Too many personnel to transport materials.
- Long distances between processes and warehouses.

Causes of transport

- Manufacture of very large production batches.

- Inconsistent production schedules with many changeovers.
- Lack of production schedules.
- Lack of organization in the workplace.
- Inadequate layout of facilities.
- Changes in products without making the corresponding changes in processes.
- Acquisition of machines more efficient than necessary.
- Excessive inventory of products in process.
- Investment in production overtime without having a defined schedule.

5. Unnecessary processes

While many well-standardized processes can always be found within the company, they do not always directly add value to the customer. Many of the tasks are the result of shop floor needs (such as a press die changeover), manufacturing quality (such as inspecting an item before shipping it to the next station) or poor delivery planning (such as unpacking raw materials before starting production). Proper management of this type of waste includes its total elimination, its combination with another process that does add value, its reduction or even its simplification. Plant engineers refer to this process as ECRS (elimination, combination, reduction, simplification).

Characteristics of unnecessary processes

- Presence of bottlenecks in the process.
- Lack of clear specifications on the part of the customer.
- Excessive inspections or verifications.
- Lack of machines with fail-safe mechanisms.
- Some workstations are at a standstill while administrative work is being done.
- Excessive information (in the process there are many documents that are not used).

Features of unnecessary processes

- Poor understanding of processes.
- Engineering changes are made without making the corresponding changes in the process.
- Misused new technology.
- Decision-making at wrong levels.
- Inadequate policies and procedures.
- Lack of information on customer requirements as well as their specifications.
- There is no definition of the production process or process flow.

6. Waiting

This *muda* refers to the time wasted when an operator is waiting for the machine to finish the job, when the machines are stopped and waiting for the operator to make some adjustment or even when both the operator and the machine are waiting for materials, tools, or instructions. All of this means a consumption of time that does not add value. Waiting is the most common of all wastes in the industry.

Waiting characteristics

- The operator is waiting for the machine to complete its processing cycle.
- The machine is waiting for the person to finish his cycle.
- The time required for a product changeover or machine set-up obliges people to wait.
- One person is waiting for another to start or finish their work.
- The person and machine are waiting for instructions, a schedule, or materials.
- Unconcern for equipment errors.
- Unexpected machine stoppages.

Causes of waiting

- Poor production scheduling.
- Little production control.

Unproductive waiting.

- Imbalance in operations.
- Lack of product changeover scheduling.
- Inadequate scheduling of overtime.
- Proper machinery is not available.
- Too many staff employed.
- Work is organized by departments and there is too much specialization.
- Lack of multi-skill training programs.
- Lack of operator training.

7. Unnecessary movements of people

This *muda* refers to the transfer of people from one point to another in their workplace or throughout the company, without it being essential to add value to the product and without contributing to the transformation or benefit of the customer. If you carefully observe each cycle of a worker, you will easily find this kind of waste: if you count the steps or follow the paths (something we are not used to doing) you discover that the person often walks more than is necessary. Another very common example of this waste is the search for tools, materials, or information. All those movements, as well as the ones that are essential for the customer, waste time and, therefore, reduce the productivity of the processes.

Muda of unnecessary worker movements.

Characteristics of unnecessary movements of people

- It takes a lot of time to locate materials.
- It takes a lot of time to locate people and instructions.
- It takes a lot of time to locate tools.
- Unnecessary movements are made when crouching or walking.
- Efforts are made to reach the tools or materials in each work cycle.

Causes of unnecessary movements by people

- Inadequate plant layout.
- Poor organization of the work area.
- Work methods poorly defined or not updated.
- Large production batches.
- The machines or people do not work at their maximum capacity.
- Little production control.

Other major wastes

In addition to the seven major waste groups posited by Toyota, it is important to introduce others whose detection can also be useful for companies, be they industrial or service-based.

- Waste of energy (be it electricity, fuel, or steam).
- Excessive expenditure due to lack of leadership and control.
- Financial mismanagement.
- Waste in design: products are produced that have more functions than necessary.
- Poor communication.
- Waste of talent.
- Erroneous or obsolete policies.

Waste of energy

It is very common for companies to waste energy without realizing it. Energy is usually a fluid that is transformed into work and can be electricity, gases, fuels, etc.

Characteristics of energy waste

- A lot of air leaks in the plant.
- Incorrect installation of machines, wiring, networks, etc.
- Badly installed or missing foundation.

- Poor timing in machinery startup.
- Poor lighting of work spaces.
- Use of electric light on sunny days.
- Indiscriminate use of equipment.
- Water leaks that require constant pumping.

Causes of energy waste

- Deficient or obsolete facilities.
- Lack of maintenance in the power distribution system.
- Lack of maintenance in the support team and process machinery.

Excessive expenditure due to lack of leadership and control

Lack of control due to poor leadership generates a huge waste of talent, resources, etc. For this reason, leaders are required who really know how to listen to customers, employees, and suppliers. These leaders know the processes and problems of companies, and, above all, they provide knowledge, motivation, and trust.

Excessive expenditure due to lack of leadership and control

- Staff without defined jobs.
- Poor selection of competent staff.
- Poor results in operational and financial performance.
- Dissatisfied staff.
- Zero knowledge.

Causes of excessive expenditure due to lack of leadership and control

- Lack of ethical and professional quality in the company's leaders.
- Poor overall health of managers.
- Little training in decision making.
- Unreliable information for decision-making.

Poor financial management

At times, traditional accounting is only used to meet the requirements of the tax authority or managers and shareholders, so the crucial importance of financial, administrative, and operational indicators for decision-making is not recognized.

Characteristics of poor financial management

- Little knowledge of processes and their variants.
- The feeling that more is being sold but less earned.
- Accounts payable exceed accounts receivable.
- Incomplete information for decision-making.

Characteristics of poor financial management

- Incompetent staff in the areas of administration and finance.
- Cumbersome or non-existent information system.

Waste in design

Characteristics of design waste

- There are too many product changeovers in the production phase.
- Very complicated process due to a non-manufacturable design.
- High process costs due to poor design.

Causes of design waste

- Lack of design techniques for manufacturing.
- Design conceived just for looks, not for manufacturing.
- Little interaction between engineers, customer, and designers.

Poor communication

In many organizations there are various technological means to improve communication such as the internet, mobile phone, etc. However, this does not necessarily guarantee good communication as it may be observed that the work done to obtain results is often based on incorrect, incomplete, or false information and, in many cases, direct contact with people has been lost and it is no longer possible to interact with them.

Characteristics of poor communication

- Staff who are not clear about their duties.
- Objectives not known to all members of the organization.
- Bad human relations.
- Uncertainty in decision-making.
- Lack of information for decision-making.

Causes of poor communication

- Little managerial ability to communicate goals.

- Poor media design.
- Inadequate means of integrating communication.
- Little direct communication between people (only technology is used).

Waste of talent

People's knowledge, the valuable experiences they have accumulated throughout their professional life, their creativity, or their innovative ideas are not always adequately exercised.

Characteristics of talent waste

- Staff feel neglected.
- Insecurity in proposing new ideas.
- Few or no suggestions for improvement by staff.
- Unstable environment and high rotation.

Causes of talent waste

- People's opinions are not taken into account.
- There is no adequate system for suggestions.
- Leaders take suggestions personally, which turns them into complaints.
- Low leadership capacity in management.

Erroneous or obsolete policies

This is one of the largest and least expensive areas of opportunity for business improvement, as constantly reviewing labor policies prevents them from becoming obsolete or constraining productivity.

Characteristics of erroneous or obsolete policies

- Decisions based on established policies and not on actual needs.
- Staff make decisions without being fully convinced that they are the best.
- Too much time is required to solve problems.
- Management staff spend too much time on meetings.

Causes of erroneous or obsolete policies

- There is no fundamental review of policies or the reason for their existence.
- Managers fall into workplace habits and blind spots.
- Lack of interest in changing the way of doing things.
- There is little analysis of industry best practices.

The worst of all wastes: overproduction

Lean Manufacturing started from the premise that the worst of all wastes is overproduction. This can be exemplified by a river where there are large rocks at the bottom, as shown in figure 2.5. This example displays the impact of overproduction and excess inventory on the results of business activity. The figure shows a boat crossing the river. In order for this boat to sail to the lighthouse, the depth of the water measured from the bottom must be greater than the height of the rocks. Well then, offering a satisfactory level of service to the customer is equivalent to the boat being able to cross the river, because each rock represents a productivity problem. In other words, to prevent productivity problems from affecting customer service levels, it is necessary to keep an inventory that cushions the impact that a machine breakdown or forecast error, for example, might have on service levels.

Although the logical solution seems to be to keep the river deep enough, it actually has at least two drawbacks. The first –but not the most important– is that keeping inventories (the depth of the water) is quite expensive, besides

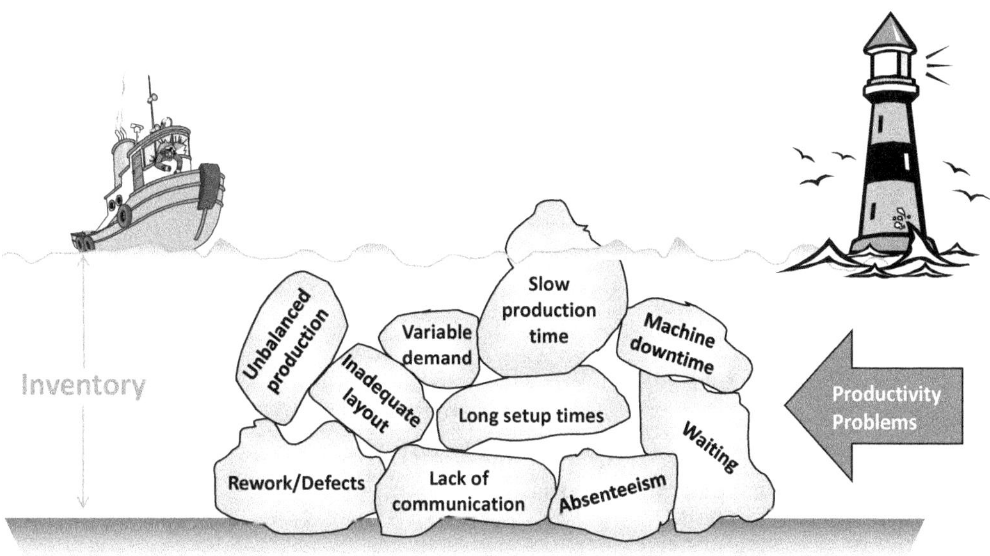

Figure 2.5

stagnating the company's resources, it increases financial leverage and requires space, insurance, management, and handling of the items. But that list, according to Toyota engineers, is not the main problem. The main problem caused by overproduction and excess inventory is that in the long run they hide the important problems.

It is natural for companies to consider the existence of a certain level of inventory as "normal". If we continue with the example of the river and the rocks, a navigator who has always crossed the river without ever colliding with the rocks will, after a certain time, stop paying attention to them (if he ever did) and will end up considering them as a natural part of the landscape. The same occurs with productivity problems because, by not directly impacting on customer service levels, the false idea is created that there are no problems in the company or that these are a natural part of the business "landscape". What needs to be kept in mind is that these productivity problems (rocks, involve a high economic cost as well as opportunity costs).

This model presented by Toyota was the reason that many authors misinterpreted just in time as an inventory management system that seeks to reduce stocks to zero. If we analyze the model properly, we see that inventory is only an indicator of the number of problems present in the processes, but it is not the object of study in the system. The object of study are the problems themselves, i.e. the rocks. It is about improving productivity by eliminating the problems present in the processes (removing rocks from the river) which will result in lower costs, better quality, and faster customer response.

What to do to eliminate these wastes

To detect the wastes generated, the company needs to do a thorough analysis of each waste, using the waste detection guide to determine the areas of opportunity in a general way. This must be done by directly visiting the actual place where the work is done (the Japanese call it *gemba* which means "crime scene"). The guide will serve to document the wastes found with the naked eye and in collaboration with staff working in each area. Therefore, it is very important that the analysis to be carried out is explained to everyone.

Suggestion scheme for all employees

In order for a process of eliminating wasteful practices and the effect of Lean Manufacturing to start showing cost reductions and be successful, it is necessary that all the organization's employees provide ideas for improvement in all areas of the company and that the responsibility be shared.

To better understand this concept, it would be useful to ask ourselves how many improvements each employee proposes per year, month, or week. This is where the real secret lies for organizations that grow beyond the limits established by common business management practices. It's enough to implement a suggestion scheme in which each employee makes at least one suggestion for improvement per month during the first year, two per month in the second year, and so on. Let's say we have a company with 1,200 employees. If we multiply 12 suggestions by our 1,200 employees, we'll have 12,000 suggestions per year. that's 12,000 opportunities per year to improve our company.

It is important to ensure that the proposed improvements do not necessarily involve costs and are motivated by creativity and self-satisfaction in bringing something good to the workplace. This will result in greater satisfaction for the worker who will not have the feeling of performing monotonous work without challenges.

To put this suggestion into practice, we recommend implementing a visual system that allows one to observe the suggestions in the very place where they are located. This is done by using an opportunity card and placing the corresponding stub on the suggestion board shown in figure 2.6.

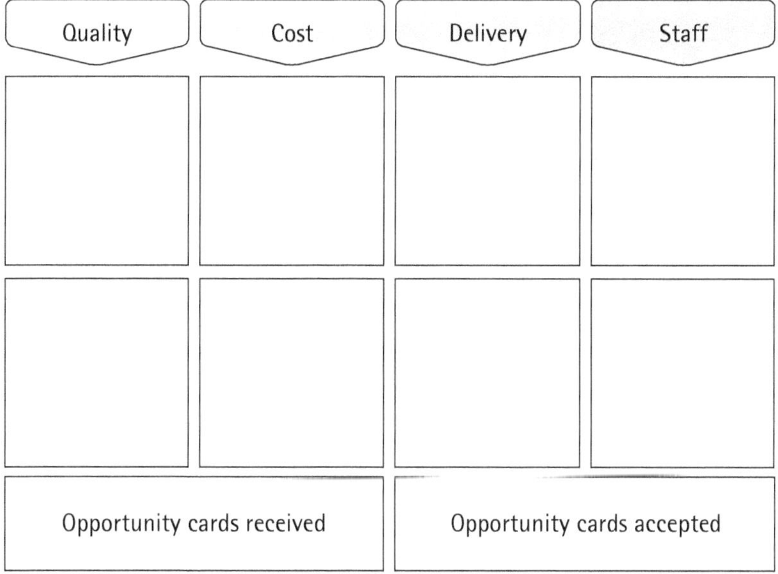

Figure 2.6

This example consists of a scoreboard that contains sections for quality, cost, delivery, and personnel-related activities. There is also a space to stick the opportunity cards received and another slot where the approved ones are placed.

The principle of cost reduction

In most companies that use a traditional work model, it is normal that only 3 to 5% of their activities add value. The above represents a great opportunity to create high-value projects. As pressure to reduce costs is known to be a management priority and is easier said than done, the traditional cost-cutting process is limited to laying off staff and reducing supposedly superfluous expenses.

In the traditional system for setting the price, one usually starts with the cost and adds on the desired profit margin. When the cost increases, we simply increase the price and the profit margin is maintained.

In the case of World Class Manufacturing, it is not the company who decides on the price, it's the current market that determines them, and instead of increasing, they tend to decrease. That is why it is necessary to design a powerful cost reduction program that can improve profit without raising prices. The only way to keep a company competitive is to have detailed control of costs and continually strive to reduce them or at least not allow them to increase.

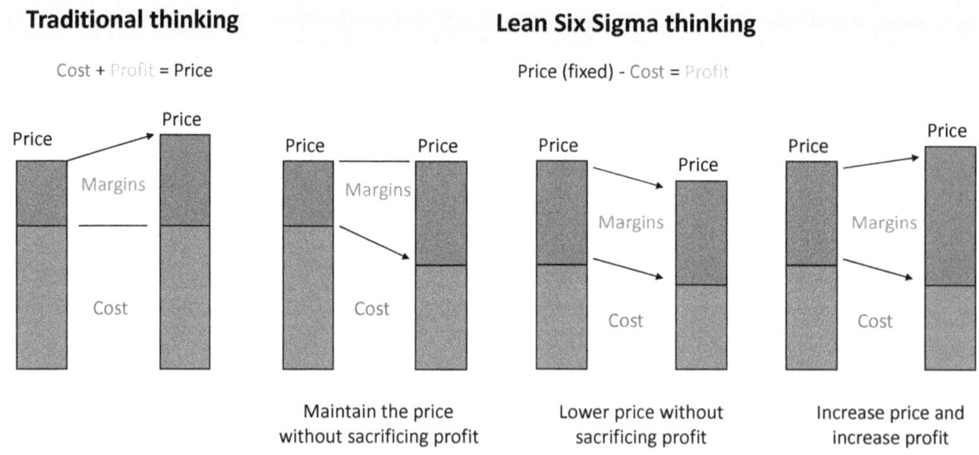

Figure 2.7

Application exercise

To detect and document large wastes and opportunities we suggest using opportunity cards (see table 6.2 in Chapter 6) which detail the type of waste and document the classification (A, B, C).

It is advisable to form multidisciplinary teams and make regular crime scene visits in the company of those teams to identify the wastes and sources of variation and risk described above.

Once the team members identify the wastes, a plan is made for their elimination. Activity sheets can be used for this purpose (see table 6.3). The most valuable thing about this exercise is that it becomes a habit through which everyone contributes to the detection of productivity constraints.

Chapter 3

Diagnosis and implementation

Presentation

In this chapter we will analyze the process of implementing Lean Manufacturing in manufacturing companies, since it's more likely to fail than succeed, the purpose of this chapter is to clarify the implementation landscape, the success factors, and risk factors.

Usually, companies that decide to implement Lean Manufacturing activities have the firm intention of achieving a successful transformation or at least of obtaining significant results that make it possible to assess whether these efforts will be useful to the company.

It is very important to consider three key elements for successful implementation:

1. Lean Manufacturing is a strategic project.
2. The organizational structure must be prepared to work with Lean tools.
3. All employees must be committed to the implementation.

1. Lean Manufacturing is a strategic project because it will have a strong impact on expenses and therefore, on the financial results of companies. Therefore, it must be included in the company's strategic plan. Also, in order to develop a good plan, it is necessary to thoroughly understand the level of maturity of the processes relating to a Lean company. Normally, companies try to implement lean projects as a one-time project or maybe label it as the project of the month or of the year. This type of thinking is not linked to the strategic objectives or the objectives of the company. For this reason, those companies that are not managed strategically will inevitably end up being just another failed project.

2. The organizational structure represents a major implementation challenge because companies usually have a functional-type organization, i.e. by departments, each of which is responsible for performing certain functions unrelated to those of another department. In production processes, the areas are divided up according to their processes, so the lines of authority must be respected so as not to affect the interests of other areas. Departmentalization generates too much bureaucracy, this creates competition between departments rather than competition between companies. Moreover, people focus on the results of their departments and on getting along well with the heads of the areas rather than on achieving overall results for the company.

3. All employees must be committed to the implementation. When the implementation only takes into account managers, heads, or engineers, it will very likely take too long to be completed since the responsibility for it is assumed by only a few people and not by the entire staff. While starting implementation with a core group of staff is very important, consideration should be given to the gradual integration of all levels in the organization.

The need to understand the numbers

When starting up a business improvement project, sometimes it's hard to know if the efforts are really accomplishing their goal because it's difficult to understand everything that happens in an organization given the large number of variables involved and the diversity of methods used to interpret the data. It is therefore very important to define the indicators that will be used to interpret what is most important in an organization. A method for developing strategic plans will be presented in the next chapter. By defining quantifiers for the guidelines and strategies of such plans, we will be precisely defining the key indicators that will allow us to understand the performance of our actions, projects, decisions, etc. Therefore, the correct definition of a key indicator table will be the beginning of a process of continuous learning and decision-making through the short-term interpretation of the meaning of the measurements made. This process is outlined in figure 3.1.

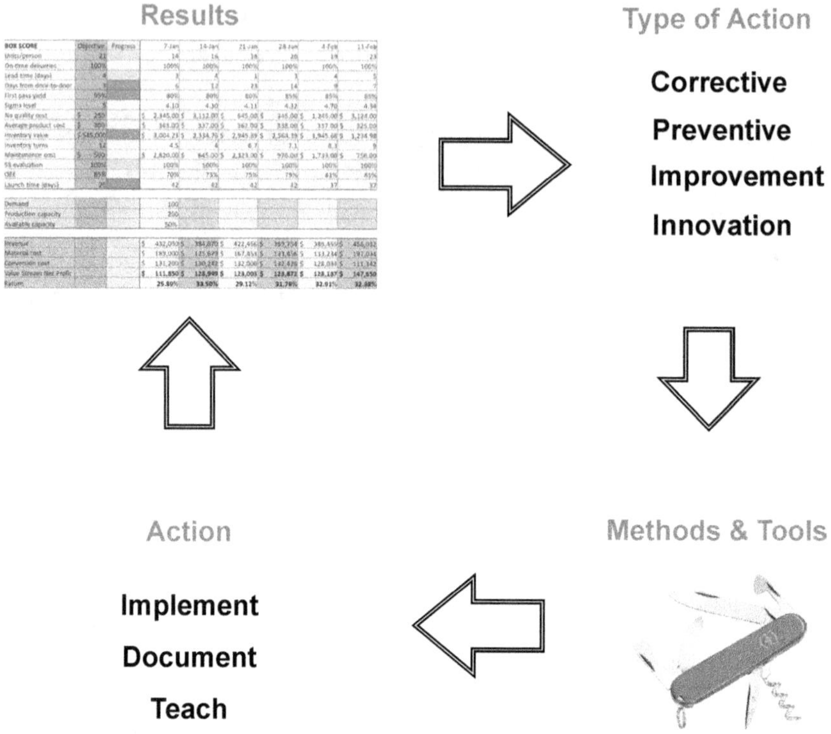

Results

Type of Action

Corrective

Preventive

Improvement

Innovation

Action

Methods & Tools

Implement

Document

Teach

Figure 3.1

In this model we can see that key business indicators (see Chapter 4) will allow decision making based on relevant and current information. Take as an example one indicator: on-time deliveries (see figure 3.2). This indicator shows the trend and in the period from Week 8 to Week 11, there was a problem as deliveries were outside the trend and several delays occurred.

In this case, the corrective action mechanism is applied first; since there is a deviation in deliveries it is necessary to restore the situation to normal. For this, the 8 disciplines (8 D) methodology can be applied. Once the deviation is corrected, a preventive mechanism can be used to prevent it from happening again.

The improvement action is used when it is observed that the goal has not been achieved and additional effort is required to achieve it. In this case, Lean tools are used to improve performance levels. The management action is to support improvements or results.

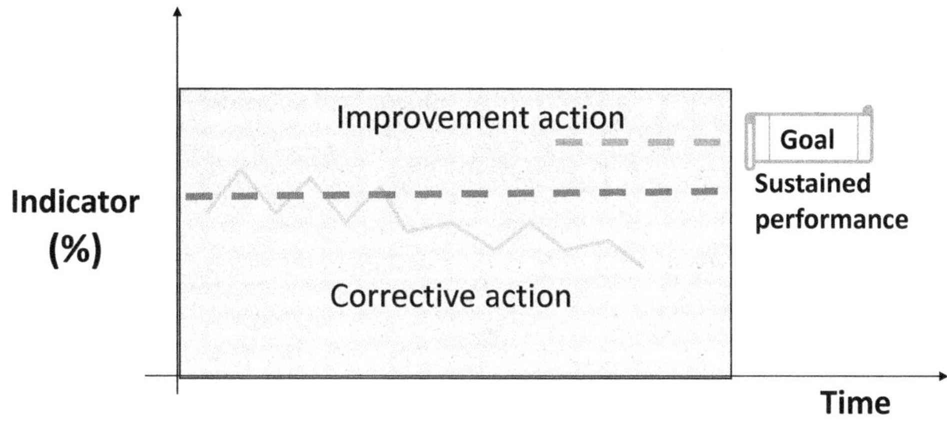

Figure 3.2

Once the methodology and tools have been chosen, the most important thing will be to implement them following a plan, working as a team, documenting the activities and their results and teaching what has been learned to those responsible for monitoring these actions. Then one must go back to the indicator to find out if the results obtained through results table indicate the existence of changes and new behaviors.

Lean Diagnosis

Before making a plan for the implementation of Lean Manufacturing, it is very important to determine the current conditions of all key processes in the organization through a diagnosis that includes the following steps:

1. Company strategy.
2. Structure.
3. Design.
4. Logistics.
5. Operations.
6. Accounting and finance.

This diagnosis must be made by company managers and key personnel who know in depth the reality of each of the scenarios presented. There will be several people participating who will check their concerns with those who have a better knowledge of the reality. If necessary, the information will be corroborated by people who are also related to the subject.

In each of these stages, the following concepts are analyzed in detail:

1. Strategy
   - Planning.
   - Communication.
   - Monitoring.
   - Control.

2. Structure.
   - Organization.
   - Personnel.
   - Information.

3. Design.
   - Customer needs.
   - Product design.
   - Process design.
   - Process control design.

4. Logistics
   - Suppliers.
   - Customers.
   - Inventory.
   - Production planning.

5. Operations.
   - Prevention.
   - Problem solving.
   - Continuous improvement.
   - Good housekeeping.
   - Visual control.
   - Process flow.
   - Product changeovers.
   - Maintenance.
   - Quality.

- Material control.
- Production control.
- Performance measurement.

6. Accounting and finance.
   - Financial accounting.
   - Management accounting.
   - Operational accounting.

Interpretation and use of the diagnosis

The diagnosis will allow us to establish a starting point in the implementation as well as the corresponding strategy. The interpretation will consist of simply observing, at each point in the diagnosis, where we are at a given moment and what the next step is. It is important to mention that it is not a matter of moving very quickly from the baseline to the top but to keep doing things gradually and think them through in order to reach the goal without setbacks or false starts. The outcome of the diagnosis will be used to formulate the plans and strategies to be addressed in the next chapter, which deals with the Hoshin kanri strategy.

Phases of the implementation of a Lean project

Phase 0. Traditional: preparation.
Phase 1. Application: create a continuous flow in pilot areas.
Phase 2. Value stream management.
Phase 3. Lean organizations: lean thinking.

The Lean way requires a clear understanding of the current situation and a good strategic plan and a committed and well-trained management team. The pilot stage serves to realize what the implementation involves, to acquire a first small-scale learning of the errors, to really know the personality of the organization and for everyone in the organization to see the power of transformation. In the value stream stage, the organizational structure becomes the basis for the implementation as it establishes a way of working managed by processes and not by functional departments; what is learned is applied to all areas of the organization, logistics are implemented, and Lean accounting supports the process by offering indicators and

The Lean maturity path

Figure 3.3

criteria for decision-making based on results and relevant information. The final stage is characterized by achieving the commitment of all, by holding knowledge as one of the main values and by establishing a knowledge management system that allows the organization to have documentary control of problems, improvements, means of prevention, and everything that is relevant to its correct operation. In addition, in a Lean company the working conditions at all levels reflect a firm commitment to adding value to the company. In the following explanation we will see a diagram in which dotted rectangles show the concept and implementation sequence and continuous rectangles the specific activities.

Phase 0. Traditional: preparation
Duration: 1-3 months.

Main activities:
- Performing Lean diagnosis.
- Training in Lean methodologies.
- Initial training in Lean Accounting.
- Establishment of people responsible and start-up teams.

- Establishment of process capacity.
- Making the value stream map.
- Establishment of the strategic plan (Hoshin kanri).
- Establishment of the implementation plan.
- Establishment of the basis and beginnings of 5S.
- Process mapping (value stream map).
- Communication of Lean strategy to all staff.

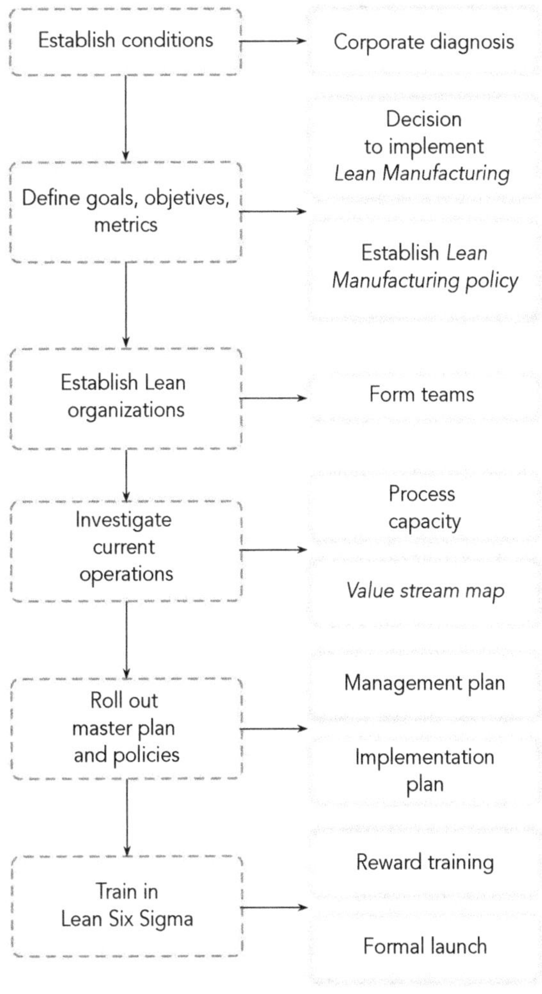

Figure 3.4

Participants:
- General management.
- Management of functional departments.
- Human resources managers.
- Implementation leaders.
- Personnel chosen for start-up teams.

Main obstacles:
- Resistance to change by some managers.
- Fear of the unknown.
- Postponement of plans and start-up.

Main advantages:
- Challenge to change.
- Need to learn something new.
- New business and change dynamics.

Phase 1. Application: create a continuous flow in pilot areas
Duration: 4-6 months.

Main activities:
- Establishment of pilot projects using Lean methodology.
- Application of 5S in the company.
- Preparation of the structure to receive Lean thinking.
- Implementation of standardized work.
- Pilot application of productive maintenance.
- Pilot application of cellular manufacturing.
- Work balance.
- Pilot application of quick changeovers.
- Pilot application of error-proofing system.
- Pilot application of Kanban.
- Application of Lean Accounting.
- Start of certification programs:
- Of suppliers.
- Of employees.
- Start of multi-disciplinary training for operators.
- Start of Lean logistics between suppliers and customers.

Participants:
- General management.
- Management of functional departments.
- Accountants and financial managers.
- Human resources managers.
- Implementation leaders.
- Sponsors.
- Operators.

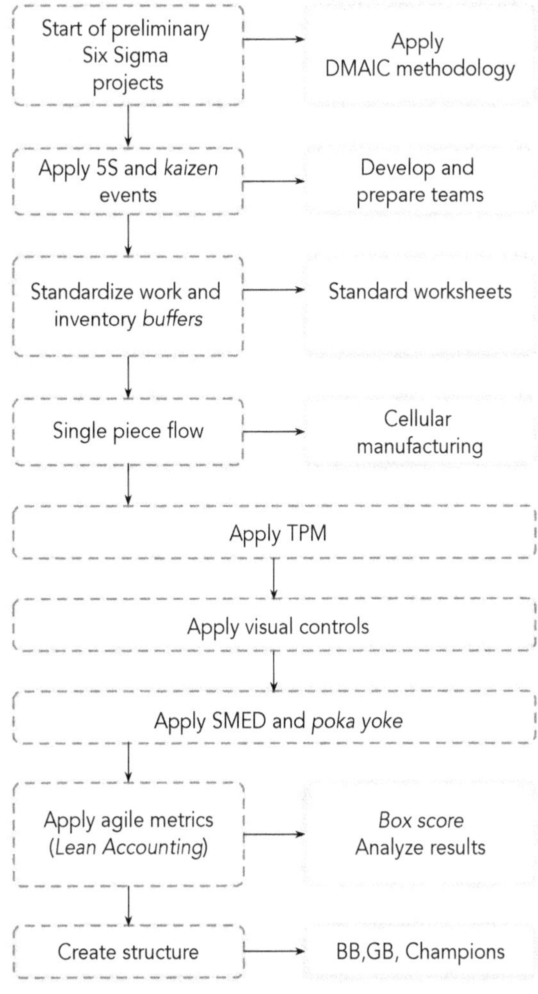

Figure 3.5

- Process and quality engineers.
- Maintenance personnel.
- Planning.

Main obstacles:
- Resistance to change by staff in general.
- Misapplication of knowledge.
- Necessary time not spent.

Main advantages:
- Some positive results start to be seen.
- Internal competitiveness to deliver the best results begins.
- Teamwork improves.
- There is a better understanding of techniques and structure.
- The results arouse greater interest on the part of management.

Phase 2. Value stream management: initial phase

Duration: 12 months.

Main activities:
- Analysis of the results achieved.
- Full use of pull production.
- Common development of Kaizen events.
- Start of Six Sigma projects for variation.
- Lean accounting:
  - Management accounting.
  - Financial accounting.
  - Operational accounting.
- Introduction of the value stream manager.
- Change from organization chart to value streams.
- Assignment of personnel to value streams.
- Common use of statistical control.
- DMAIC in all improvement projects.
- Introduction of Lean Office.
- Integration of cost accounting into the stream.
- Integration of financial planning into sales and streams.
- Certification.
- Integration of new incentive methods.

- Integration of logistics with suppliers and customers.
- Process improvements contributed by everyone.
- Introduction of the results table *(box score)*.
- Implementation of Lean in offices.

Participants:
- All.

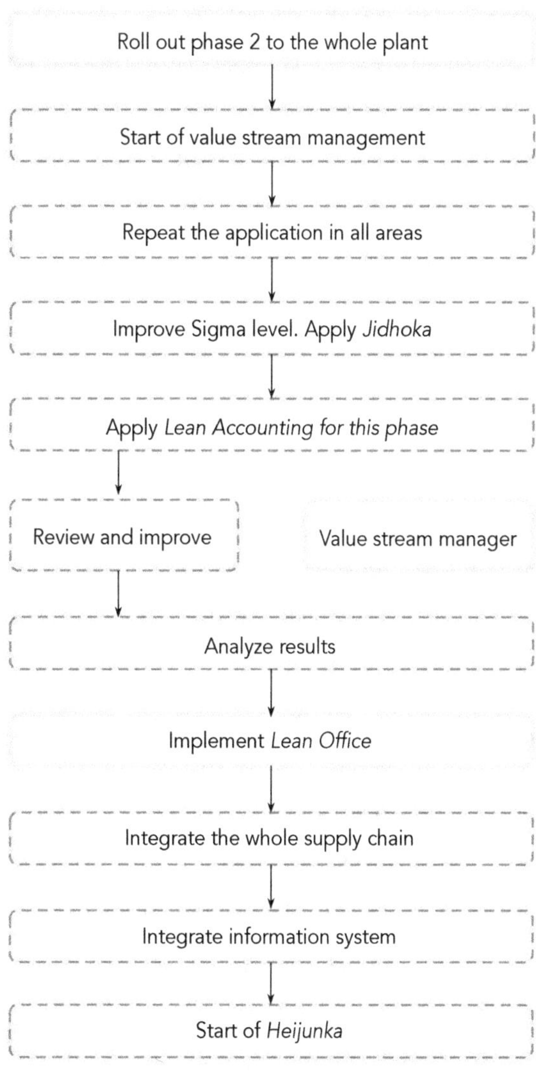

Figure 3.6

Main obstacles:
- Lack of integration between accounting and operations.
- The information factory is not connected to the operations.
- Possible use of previous control methods.
- Resistance due to possible loss of authority.
- Possible detection of lack of leadership capacity.
- Conflicts of interest between departments.
- Authority constraints in decision-making.

Main advantages:
- The results show a clear reduction in costs.
- Better communication and understanding between people.
- Teamwork improves interpersonal relationships.
- There is a better understanding of the way forward.
- Information is clearer and easier to use.
- The new business and operations language is communicated to all staff.

Phase 2. Value stream management: mature phase
Duration: 12-24 months.

Main activities:
- Start rethinking the entire *layout*.
- Redistribution of plant and equipment.
- The application extends to product design.
- Box score is used as a basis for making decisions.
- Use of Lean accounting in all processes.
- Start of the supplier development program.
- Production matches purchase speed.
- Customers and suppliers are integrated.
- Hoshin plans are restructured annually.
- The organizational structure is conducive to Lean.
- All staff are actively involved in improvements.
- Project information is shared.

Participants:
- All.

Main obstacles:

- Resistance to change by supplier companies.
- Resistance to change by customers.
- Inner fear of extending the application.
- Lack of concrete plans to integrate the entire stream.

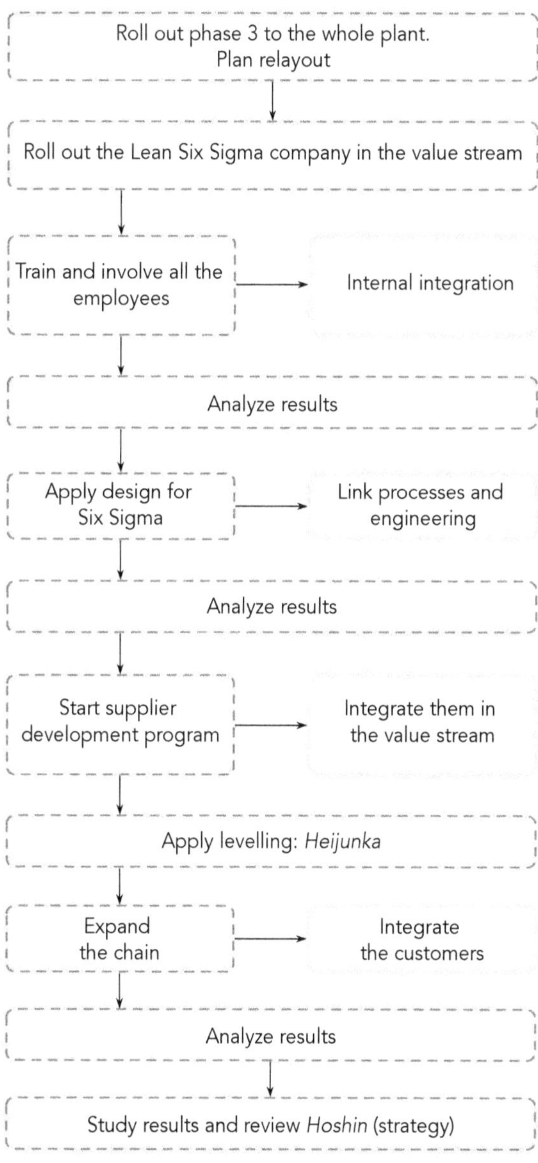

Figure 3.7

- Suppliers who lack the necessary knowledge.
- Customers who lack the necessary knowledge.
- Intention to copy models from other companies.

Main advantages:
- Need to improve faster.
- Clear and well integrated structure.
- People think and live with the tools.
- Lean becomes a way of thinking and a philosophy.
- Many commercial and competitive doors are opened.
- There are very good foundations for the continuity of the business.
- The focus is on projects and cost reduction.

Phase 3. Lean organizations: lean thinking

Duration: permanent.

Main activities:
- Continuous review of production flows.
- Continuous breaking of paradigms.
- Application of predictive technology.
- Use of new development and production technologies.
- Publication of operating and financial results.
- Be the best in class.
- Establishment of Lean projects as a basis for improvement.
- Immediate problem solving.
- Stable and continuously improving quality system.

Participants:
- All.

Main obstacles:
- Not striving for new improvement goals.
- Conforming with what has been achieved so far.
- Uncertainty in the global business environment.
- Not continuing to implement the accomplished strategies and being satisfied with the success achieved.
- Failure to renew product and operations strategies in time.

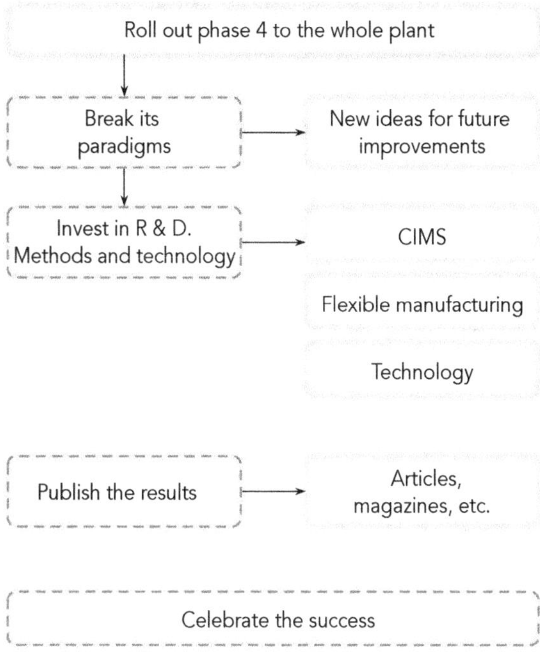

Figure 3.8

Main advantages:
- A renewed work culture that is always ready for change.
- Shared leadership.
- Everyone has the right tools and knowledge.
- Clear and constant understanding of goals and objectives.
- Lean manufacturing as a way of thinking.

Work model

The Lean manufacturing philosophy is based on a love of knowledge and work as a way to live and grow. Additionally, standardization, order, cleanliness, productive maintenance, and visual control are the pillars that make it possible to progress and fight off the main productivity constraints. As a pillar of the just-in-time system, cellular manufacturing is used to establish a continuous flow and eliminate batch work; the Kanban system to control material and production flow; quick changeovers as a basic flexibility resource, and integrated logistics as an operations strength. The *jidhoka* pillar shows the quality facet in the processes

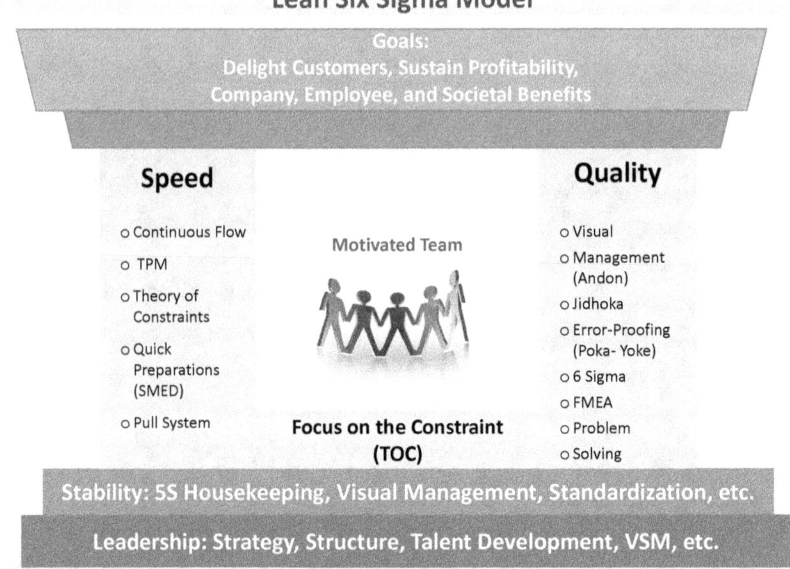

Figure 3.9

to produce quality products. This pillar uses visual cues to discover when defects occur and take immediate action to eliminate them, such as automatic stoppages and fail-safe mechanisms; it also establishes methods for problem solving and uses methodologies such as Six Sigma to reduce variations.

The element that makes this manufacturing machinery and these service processes function is teamwork, through planned improvement events with a clear purpose and achievable goals. Its main objective is the elimination of wasteful practices *(mudas)*.

All the above aims to achieve outstanding quality with minimal delivery times for customers, safety at work, and high motivation for the people that work in the companies who, by achieving their goals, contribute to building more prosperous nations and competitive economies worldwide.

Key factors for successful change

1. There must be a very clear purpose.
2. There must be a good plan.
3. Effective and committed leadership.
4. Make sure that everyone is committed to doing their best.

5. Commit to investing time and effort.
6. Deep knowledge of tools.
7. Create a business culture based on good habits.
8. Patience from beginning to end.
9. Make sure everyone understands the concepts.
10. Devote time and resources.
11. Establish cross-functions and eliminate departmentalism.
12. Do not think of it as just the program of the month.
13. Implement rules for teamwork and transformation.
14. Involve staff at all levels.
15. Try not to copy implementations from other companies or cultures.
16. Empower plant staff to contribute and make decisions.
17. Understand that there is a need to learn and teach.
18. Get everyone in the company to have deep self-confidence.
19. Establish well-founded plans.
20. Monitor plans in terms of activities and results.

Organizational structure

In an agile company, the structure of the organization is a key element for success. In a traditional scheme it is impossible to manage improvements throughout the organization because each manager seeks to achieve results and improvements for his area, something that does not necessarily entail a global improvement. Therefore, in a Lean company the organizational structure is managed as shown in figure 3.10.

Departments conceived as a functional administration disappear. Instead, value streams are managed (VSM). These focus on improvement from the beginning to the end of the stream and not on a departmental basis.

Value streams are business units that process a group of parts that we call a product family from start to finish. The nature of the streams are those operations by which a product or information is transformed, and which follow a process to convert a raw material into a finished product. Each value stream is assigned a value stream manager or coordinator who will focus on design and improvement from start to finish all the way to delivering clear and tangible results as a business unit.

Each value stream is made up of personnel from production, quality, machine maintenance who operate in each stream, from engineering, and in some cases,

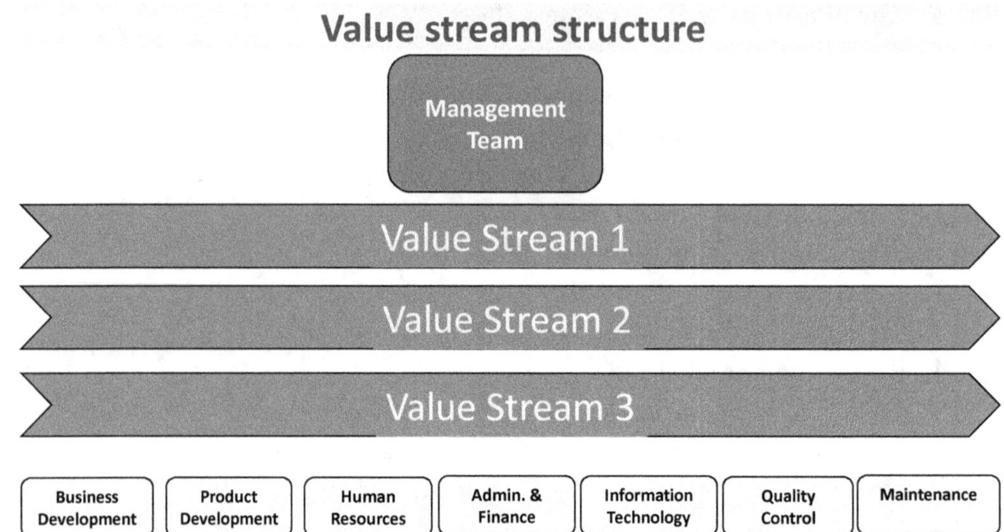

Figure 3.10

from the commercial area. The most important part of this concept is the approach that everyone forms part of a team and has a very specific mission: to make their value stream work and eliminate departmental barriers which will allow the sharing of information, knowledge, and experiences in the interests of teamwork and the common good.

The functional management represented in the diagram as commercial, quality, production, engineering, and accounting become areas of knowledge and strategy design within the specialty. They directly influence knowledge, elimination of problems, etc. in each value stream.

Finally, the departments shown at the bottom of figure 3.10 provide support to the value streams. Their objective is to provide the necessary support in their area of responsibility so that value streams are only dedicated to adding value and do not suffer interruptions or bureaucratic processes that distract their attention and are able to focus on meeting demand quickly and qualitatively.

It should be emphasized that the authority of value streams now rests with the managers or coordinators of the value streams, so the functional managers will participate by providing knowledge and direction in their areas of expertise.

It is advisable to apply this value stream-managed organizational chart after the pilot phase has been completed since by then, results will have been achieved.

Roles and responsibilities

Plant management

The leaders in creating change, setting the company's course. They work by eliminating the resistance to change, maintaining a constant focus on the timing of improvements and goals, and ensuring that every member of the organization knows their role and receives the necessary training.

Expectations:
- Ensure that the responsibility to lead the transformation of the plant's culture and structure is accepted at all levels.
- Establish and develop plant area and production area indicators.
- Prepare reports, set objectives, and assign staff for the implementation of specific programs.
- Strengthen the use of methodologies and tools to carry out improvement projects, solve problems, and prevent them.
- Establish a strong presence in the production plant to lead the change; analyze plant indicators in the very production area.
- Develop detailed plant plans to support company and business objectives.
- Establish Hoshin kanri plan guidelines together with shareholders or owners.

Functional direction/management

They are champions in transforming concrete programs with specific techniques and tools that require effective communication.

They monitor performance indicators in areas under their responsibility.

They resolve conflicts or restrictions on projects.

Expectations:
- Actively participate in the transformation of the culture and structure of their areas of responsibility.
- Establish programs and ensure that responsibility is accepted in their areas.

- Increase their skills and those of the staff and become experts in the transformation and handling of tools.
- Facilitate training in the use of the new tools.
- Develop goals for their areas of responsibility and participate in the hoshin plan, creating business strategies.
- Become masters and teach instead of supervising.
- Monitor project activities.
- Devote much of their time to directly supporting the plant.

Operators

They strongly support the successful accomplishment of the culture by daily improvement in working methods. They also support their colleagues in best practices and optimize all aspects of the work environment.

Expectations:
- Accept the transformation of work programs.
- Develop the application of initiatives with their work teams.
- Be an important part of improvement teams.
- Continuously contribute ideas for Lean Six Sigma initiatives.
- Use the tools at work and in everyday problems.
- Constantly eliminate waste and support controlled changes.

Value stream management / coordination

They are responsible for the value stream and their main goal is to improve it from start to finish. They have authority over the entire operation of their value stream and make decisions on any aspect that affects the operating, capacity, and financial results of the value stream.

Expectations:
- Actively participate in the transformation of the culture and structure of their value streams.
- To gain a thorough understanding of the processes and have the authority to design or redesign them.
- Facilitate training and the running of Kaizen events.
- Develop goals for their areas of responsibility and participate in the hoshin plan through the development of business strategies.

- Become masters and teach instead of supervising.
- Monitor project activities.
- Provide direct and constant support to the plant.

Support areas

This area is responsible for providing the necessary support to the value streams in accordance to their focus. They are providers of useful services and information so that the value streams are not distracted from creating value and may keep their resources focused on achieving the company objectives in their areas of expertise.

Expectations:
- Participate directly in the transformation of culture.
- Know the processes and contribute their knowledge and skills to the value streams.
- Increase their skills and those of the staff and become experts in the transformation and handling of the tools.
- Develop objectives for their areas of responsibility.
- Monitor activities of projects they are involved in.
- Provide direct and constant support to the plant.

Resistance to change

Resistance to change is the biggest obstacle to implementation and is driven by fear of the unknown and loss of authority.

It is very important to bear in mind that resistance to change exists and will always be present in such projects. Therefore, it is very important to:

- Present a clear view.
- Motivate staff to take on these new changes.
- Train staff to defeat the enemy of uncertainty.
- Have the necessary resources to make the changes.
- Have well-established plans.

The best way to overcome resistance to change is by demonstrating how beneficial it can be for the survival of companies.

Work ethics

In this process of transformation from traditional companies to world-class companies it is very important to consider the ethical aspect of directors, managers, and staff in general. No effort to achieve productivity improvements will bear fruit if there is no genuine interest as well as respect for honest work. For this reason, management must lead by example and demonstrate a sense of ethics in their daily actions, such as decision-making, respect for others' opinions, the language they use with colleagues and customers, comments about others and above all, the creation of a work environment where there is no mockery, distrust, laziness, waste of time, etc.

In this process of change through which progress is sought not only for companies but also for society, the personal care of health and daily activities will be very important in order to be able to face adverse situations and the commitments involved in a change of this nature.

The power of teamwork

Lean Manufacturing is based on the philosophy of the indispensable need for teamwork in order to deliver really outstanding results. We must learn that competition must never be internal, i.e. there must be no power or control struggles nor interdepartmental or personal competition on account of aspiring to better positions in the company. Globalization makes current organizations compete with companies around the world, which has helped to increase supply in our markets, and at times, restrict our share of them. The successful implementation of Lean Manufacturing will be reflected in achieving goals, customer satisfaction, and profitability, keeping in mind that competition must always take place outside the walls of the organization.

Summary

Keep in mind that the implementation process is a decisive factor in the success of this business strategy. The development of an initial diagnosis makes it possible to lay the foundations for a documented and realistic start with a knowledge of the general process of development of the implementation stages.

Chapter 4

Hoshin kanri strategy

Background

Chinese general Sun Tzu wrote *The Art of War* five centuries ago. It is the oldest book ever written on strategy and is still a valid read after such a long time. It is undoubtedly the best book on strategy development and has served as an inspiration to the great writers on the subject, both contemporary and ancient. It provides valuable teachings such as "The greatest victory is that which requires no battle" and many of the war terms it contains are easily adapted to strategic planning and execution nowadays.

The Hoshin kanri strategy design has its background in the teachings of a samurai warrior who never lost a single fight. In *The Book of the Five Rings,* Miyamoto Musashi explains that strategy is the basis of victory.

Dr. Yoji Akao, professor in the Department of Industrial Engineering at Tamagawa University, was one of the leading designers of quality control methodologies, quality function deployment, and Hoshin kanri.

The Japanese adopted and adapted the Deming and Juran techniques with management by objectives concepts, and so began the strategic planning for quality. Each company created its own strategic plan.

With the introduction of the Deming Quality Award in 1957, the dissemination of quality and planning practices began, from which Japanese companies evolved considerably.

In 1965, the Bridgestone Tire Company published an analysis of the Deming award winning companies, placing special emphasis on strategic planning called Hoshin kanri. By then, the concept was widely accepted in Japan.

The application of Hoshin kanri in the United States began in the 1980s in companies related to those who had won the Deming award, such as Yokogawa Hewlett-Packard Division (YHP), Fuji-Xerox, Texas Instruments and others.

Until the early 1990s, it was recognized that companies using Hoshin kanri had a broad competitive advantage over those that did not.

Definition

Hoshin kanri is a technique that helps companies focus their efforts and analyze their activities and results.

It is a systematic approach to identifying, ordering, and resolving activities that require drastic change or improvement.

The literal translation of *ho* is "direction" and *shin* means "needle", as in the direction in which a compass points.

The word *Kanri* can be divided into two parts: *Kan*, meaning control and *ri*, meaning reason or logic.

Hoshin Kanri therefore means "management and control of the organization directed towards an approach".

方針

Hoshin = direction of the needle.

管理

Kanri = management, control.

Figure 4.1

What is Hoshin kanri implemented for?

Hoshin kanri is a tool for effective strategic planning and it makes it easier to:

- Identify key objectives.
- Assess restrictions.
- Establish performance metrics.
- Develop implementation plans.
- Conduct periodic review meetings.

The concept of the strategic planning model is simple: it is a management system that aligns itself with the organization. It translates an institution's vision and mission into an understandable set of strategic objectives in which it defines performance indicators and transforms them into a project-based framework.

- Provides a clear focus to the entire organization.
- Involves coordination between the different departments and functions.
- Avoids duplication of efforts and actions that do not contribute to the achievement of organizational objectives.

Key elements of Hoshin kanri plans

All efforts should be focused on achieving the company's mission and vision.

- Phase 1. Definition of the strategic plan.
- Phase 2. Strategic management.

These two elements are living documents, i.e. they are constantly being modified.

Benefits of using Hoshin kanri

- Improves the organization's focus.
- Improves organizational liaison.
- Improves management accounting.
- Improves the selling of ideas.
- Improves communication.
- Improves staff engagement.

When is Hoshin kanri used?

Hoshin kanri is used when we want to carry out long-term strategic planning in the company and establish specific activities and projects at all levels of the organization to meet objectives.

The company plan should be reviewed and set annually, repeating the implementation procedure.

How long does it take to implement the Hoshin kanri plan?

The implementation of the basic plan takes two to three weeks. Results and activities are monitored every week.

Procedure for carrying out the Hoshin kanri plan

1. Set the company philosophy

- Who are we and what does the organization exist for? (Mission).
- Where is the organization headed? (Vision).
- How to get to where the company is headed? (Strategic objectives).
- How to achieve the stated objectives? (Strategies).
- What are customers looking for? (Key success factors).
- How to achieve the key success factors? (Key Result Areas).

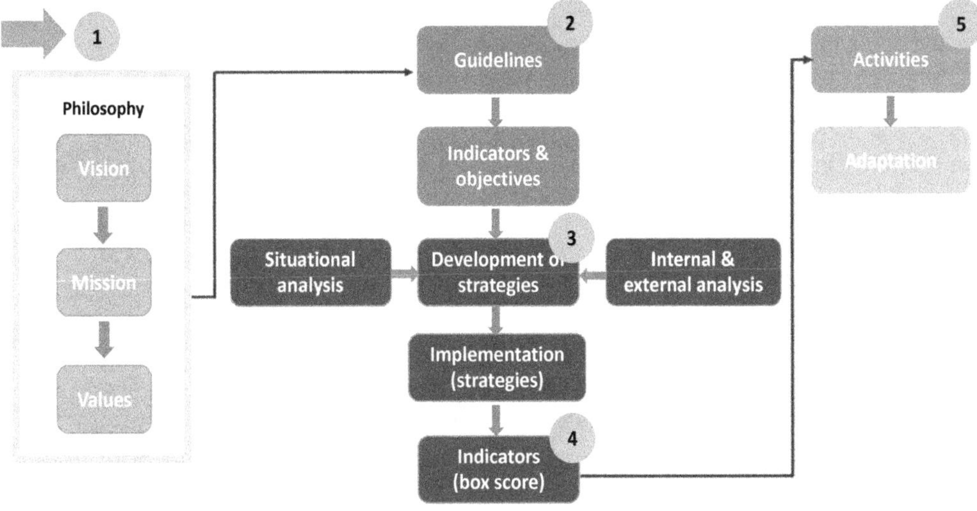

Figure 4.2

Mission

- The mission describes the raison d'être of the organization.
- Provides company members with a management unit that transcends individual, local, and transitory needs.
- Promotes a sense of shared expectations.
- Projects a sense of value and purpose towards different interest groups.
- Affirms the company's commitment to its existence, growth, and profitability.
- Requires answering the questions:
- What is our business?
- Why does the organization exist?

Vision

- The vision is a statement of the possible and desirable future state of the organization.
- The main strength of vision lies not in the anticipated description of the desired future but in a process by which a person's dream or indications become the feasible and shared desires of a collective.
- This conception strengthens leadership by sharing the consensus that expresses the collective motivations, desires, and interests.
- Requires answering the question: What do we want to become?

Values

- The values of a company are the set of beliefs that it considers most important or valuable. Values help to form the basic consensuses of social coexistence and provide the community with a sense of belonging and identity; this empathy is the basis of trust, which is an important factor for the progress and development of people.
- The consolidation and success of the company are closely related to its values as an institution since these govern its daily actions.

Values are principles that mark the path that humanity must follow so that all people may develop fully and live together in harmony. Therefore, they are ideals that must be reached, and they set challenges for daily life in every activity we perform and in every relationship we establish with others (see table 4.1).

2. Set guidelines (what)

- At this stage, those functional categories of the organization that are essential for better functioning are identified. It also provides a basis for identifying the key issues that need to be addressed before setting short-term goals within the framework of the future vision and long-term goals.
- Questions that need to be answered:
- What value proposition do our customers expect us to give them?
- What results does the corporation expect from us?
- What should we do to build the future state we want?

3. Set strategic objectives (how many "what's")

- At this stage, the objectives to be achieved for each of the defined indicators are set. The objectives represent the results expected when applying certain strategies and provide direction, enable synergy, assist in evaluation, set priorities, reduce uncertainty, reduce conflict, stimulate better performance, and assist in the distribution of resources.
- The target to be achieved for each indicator is set, considering the baseline that best represents current performance. Objectives must be specific, quantifiable, realistic, and achievable within a set time frame.

4. Create strategies (how)

To set strategies it is highly recommended they be based on Lean diagnosis.

- Strategies are the actions that will be carried out to achieve the long-term objectives. The strategy defines a conceptual structure or frame of reference to guide actions.

Strategic Plan: HOSHIN KANRI

Year: Company Name:

Philosophy

Vision:

Mission:

Values:

Strategic Priorities

2 -5 Years:

1 Year:

Date Prepared: Date Revised:

EXECUTIVE MANAGEMENT		PLANNING					EXECUTION					
Objectives (What's)	Indicators	Strategies	Indicators	Baseline	Objectives	Person Responsible	Key Activities/Improvement Projects	Observations	Leader	Start Date	End Date	Status
			Indicators (How much)									

1. Guidelines (What's)

2. Strategies (How's)

3. Projects (How's of Strategies)

4. Resources (Who)

Table 4.1

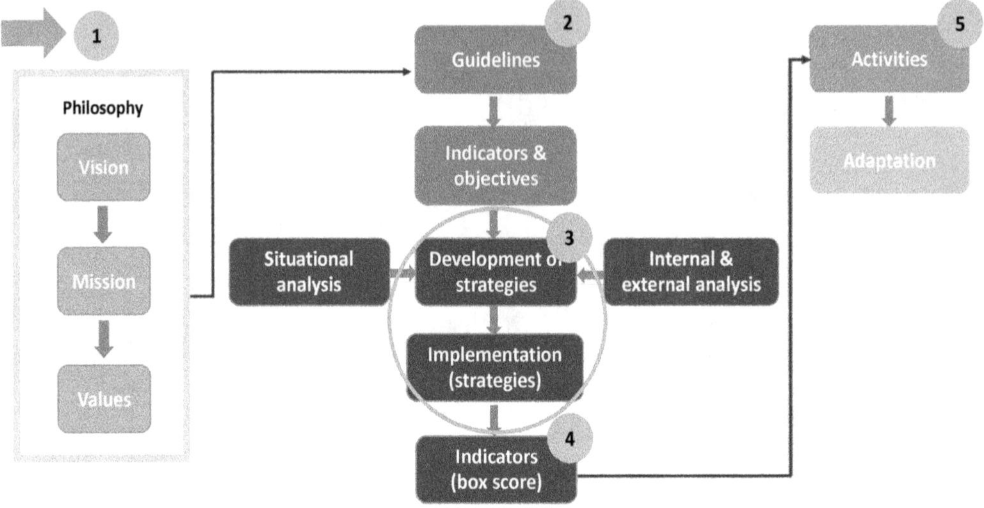

Figure 4.3

- A strategy reflects the extent to which the company understands the key relationships between actions, context, and organizational performance and directs the many decision makers to take actions that are consistent with its vision.
- The results of the situational analysis studies, both internal and external, are taken as the basis for generating strategies that turn the weaknesses of the company into strengths and those strengths into distinctive capabilities to mitigate threats facing the organization and take advantage of opportunities offered by the industry with the aim of strengthening the strategic competencies of the company in order to achieve its objectives.

5. Set indicators (how many "how's")

- Indicators help to understand the actual preperformance of the system as they serve as a translator of what is happening in the operation and tell us if the strategies are leading towards a set goal.
- It is advisable to check these indicators weekly or daily in order to know the short-term results and to have the possibility to react to a change or deviation from the objectives.
- To do this, a results table can be used to set the operating, capacity and financial "how's" and "how many's".

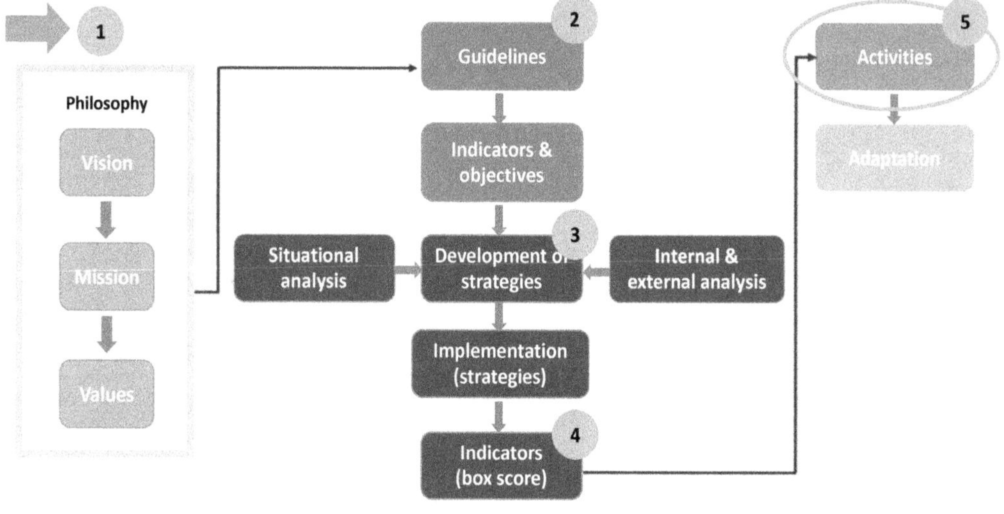

Figure 4.4

- Operating: these are indicators that help to understand the operation and monitor it and show whether the strategies have a well-defined course.
- Capacity: these indicators help to understand how the capacity of the system was used in a specific period.
- Financial: they are set out in the "how many's" of the guidelines in the Hoshin plan and help to understand the progress of the company in its financial objectives.

(See table 4.2. on the next page.)

6. Set activities

- In order to fully understand the strategies and meet the objectives set and measured in the indicators, it is very important to clearly describe the specific activities that must be carried out.
- It is also very important to clarify and describe who is responsible for implementing the activities and strategies, thereby giving a focus and responsibility to implement them.
- To set the activities, it is very important to ask ourselves whether we can carry out the strategies properly or if there are some missing or surplus activities.

Box Score – weekly indicators

BOX SCORE	Objective	Week 1	Week 2	Week 3	Week 4	Week 5	Week 6	Week 7	Week 8	Week 9	Week 10
Units per person	21	14,00	16,00	18,00	20,00	19,00	23,00				
On-time deliveries	100%	100%	100%	100%	100%	100%	100%				
Lead time (days)	4	3	4	1	3	4	5				
Days from door to door	3	6	12	23	14	9	7				
First pass quality	95%	80%	80%	80%	85%	85%	85%				
Sigma level	5	4,10	4,30	4,11	4,32	4,70	4,34				
Quality costs	$ 250	$ 1.125	$ 2.320	$ 645	$ 345	$ 1.245	$ 3.124				
Average product cost	$ 300	$ 343	$ 337	$ 362	$ 338	$ 337	$ 325				
Inventory value	$ 545.000	$ 3.004.234	$ 2.334.756	$ 2.945.893	$ 2.564.392	$ 1.945.678	$ 1.234.975				
Inventory turns	12	4,50	4,00	6,70	7,10	8,30	9,00				
Maintenance costs	$ 500	$ 2.820	$ 645	$ 2.323	$ 976	$ 1.733	$ 756				
5S Evaluation	100%	100%	100%	100%	100%	100%	100%				
OEE	85%	70%	73%	75%	79%	81%	81%				
Demand		500	600,00	550,00	495,00	620,00	545,00				
Production Capacity		650	650,00	650,00	650,00	650,00	650,00				
Available capacity		23%	8%	15%	24%	5%	16%				
Revenue		$ 432.050	$ 384.870	$ 422.456	$ 389.754	$ 389.455	$ 456.032				
Material Costs		$ 189.000	$ 125.679	$ 167.453	$ 133.456	$ 133.234	$ 197.034				
Conversion Costs		$ 131.200	$ 130.242	$ 132.000	$ 132.426	$ 128.034	$ 111.342				
Value Stream Profit		$ 111.850	$ 128.949	$ 123.003	$ 123.872	$ 128.187	$ 147.656				
Value Stream ROS		25,89%	33,50%	29,12%	31,78%	32,91%	32,38%				

Color codes

Prompt attention

Good

Alert

- The results of quality, delivery and costs are analyzed weekly to ensure that they are studied and decisions can be made weekly.
- Now there are 52 opportunities to make good decisions, contrary to only 12 when it is done monthly.

Table 4.2

Development of tactics

Key activities/improvement projects	PROJECTS												Progress	Leader
	1	2	3	4	5	6	7	8	9	10	11	12		
1.1 Reduce inventories														
1.2 Improve the use of our investments														
1.3 Reduce costs without sacrificing quality														
1.4 Achieve an agile costing to detect variations														
2.1 Design customer service packages														
2.2 Analyze purchase frequency and identify trends														
2.3 Implement SCRUM for product development														
2.4 Introduce concurrent engineering and DFSS														
3.1.1 Train personnel on Six Sigma														
3.1.2 YB, GB, BB certification														
3.1.3 Executive training														
3.1.4 Pilot implementation in area A														
3.1.5 Certify personnel as multiskilled operators														
3.1.6 Implement 5S in facility 1														
3.1.7 Implement TPM in the pilot area														
3.1.8 Implement continuous flow in the pilot														
3.1.9 Implement SMED in the pilot area														
3.2.1 Conduct internal audits														
3.2.2 Perform all corrective actions														
3.3.1 Implement kanban														
3.3.2 Implement heijunka														
3.3.3 Implement software														
4.1.1 Conduct a diagnosis of the organizational climate														
4.1.2 Train Coaches														
4.1.3 Develop training materials														
4.1.4 Perform pilot implementation														

Table 4.3

7. Monitoring and adaptation

Monitoring is done directly on the activities described in the previous step using a Gantt diagram to visually check the progress of the projects and the most important activities in the strategic plan. This monitoring of activities should be carried out every week to keep a strict control of them, their advances, obstacles, etc. and thus being able to anticipate or respond in the short term (see table 4.3).

8. Periodic review

To ensure the success of each mission, strategies should be monitored using table 4.4, "Periodic Review".

This periodic review should be carried out at weekly or fortnightly intervals so as not to lose sight of the relevant activities and results.

Presentation of results

Once the "how many's" of the "how" are defined, i.e. the indicators of compliance with strategies, and once these are set in the results table (box score), the results can be presented in the four quadrants table seen in figure 4.5.

It is recommended that the results obtained be presented in a documented and simple way so that everyone understands the achievements or setbacks.

In the first quadrant (top left) contains a trend chart of a specific indicator to observe its performance over a given period. The Pareto chart (top right) shows the main contributors to the result of the metrics to separate the vital few from the trivial many and keep a more precise focus. In the third quadrant (bottom left), the probable causes or hypotheses of the situation are placed in order to understand the root cause or the significant variables that influence the outcome of the indicator. Finally, the actions to follow are presented on the bottom right, indicating the week in which the actions were performed (first column), which is related to the trend graph to plot the time the action is carried out. The following column specifies a description of the action taken, which can be a:

- Corrective action: used when there is a problem.
- Preventive action: used to prevent problems.
- Improvement action: used to reach goals.
- Management action: used to sustain what is earned.

Periodic review

Location	Date
Description of objective	Process metrics
Estrategias	Process metrics
Expected results	
Actual results	
Deviation analysis	
Future implications	
Expected results in the next period	
Notes	

Table 4.4

Follow-up and documentation of meetings

Once the strategic plan has been drawn up, the most important step is the follow-up so it will be vital to hold frequent monitoring meetings (weekly or fortnightly) which must have a well-defined objective known to all. It is necessary to document the date, place, and time of the meetings, set an agenda and distribute it in advance to all the invitees, and to control the time allocated to

Key elements

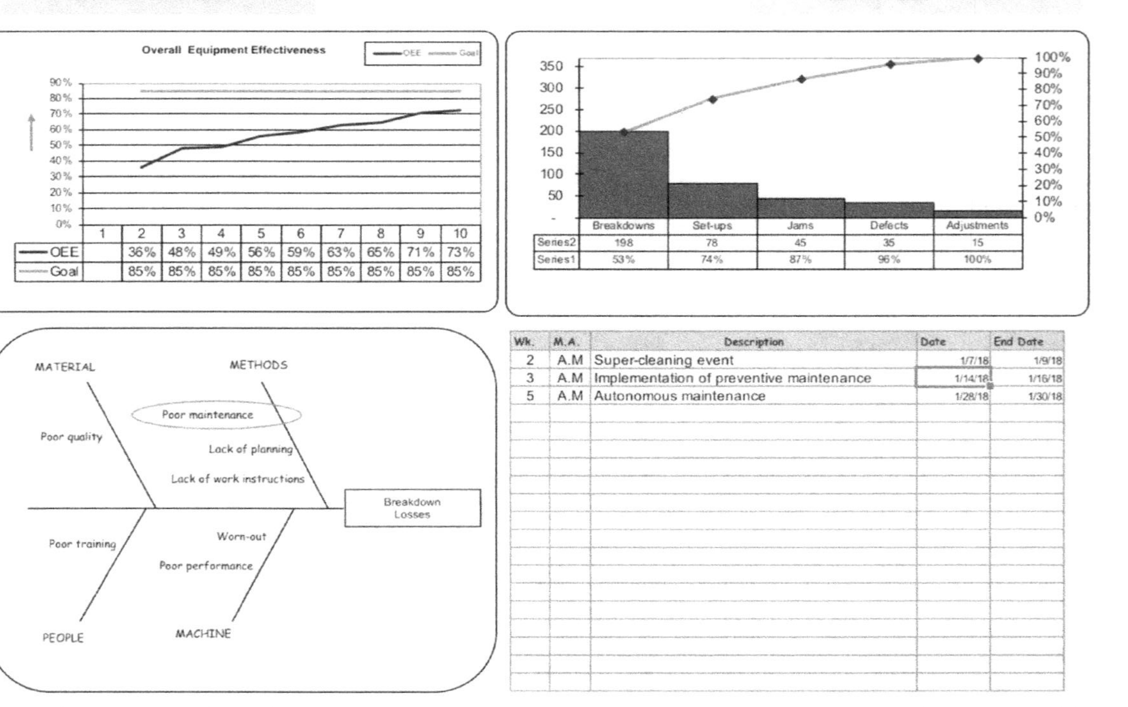

1. Trend Chart

Overall Equipment Effectiveness

	1	2	3	4	5	6	7	8	9	10
OEE		36%	48%	49%	56%	59%	63%	65%	71%	73%
Goal		85%	85%	85%	85%	85%	85%	85%	85%	85%

2. Pareto Chart

	Breakdowns	Set-ups	Jams	Defects	Adjustments
Series2	198	78	45	35	15
Series1	53%	74%	87%	96%	100%

3. Cause & Effect Analysis

4. Action List

Wk.	M.A.	Description	Date	End Date
2	A.M	Super-cleaning event	1/7/18	1/9/18
3	A.M	Implementation of preventive maintenance	1/14/18	1/16/18
5	A.M	Autonomous maintenance	1/28/18	1/30/18

Figure 4.5

Meeting minutes

Scheduled time		Meeting No.	
Start time		Date	
End time		Place	

Subject of meeting

Objective

| Invitees | | Agenda | | |
Name	**Attended**	**No**	**Item**	**Time**
	09.00	1		
	09.00	2		
	09.00	3		
	09.00			
	09.00			
	09.02			
	09.02			
	09.02			
	09.04			
	09.04			
	No.			
	09.00			

Agreements

Item number	Date	Estatus	Agreement	Responsible
I				
I				
I				
I				
I				

| Next meeting | | | |
| Date | Place: | | Time: |

Comments and observations

Table 4.5

each topic to comply with the specified schedule. Write down all the agreements on the topics covered in each meeting, assigning corresponding personnel and due dates. Table 4.5 can be useful if one is disciplined in following up strategy meetings or any other meetings.

This table documents all the actions to follow as well as the agreements reached at the meetings.

Organization during meetings is a key element in making good use of time. One of the big wastes in management and leadership tasks is the time that meetings take, especially when there are no well-defined and well-known objectives.

Waste also occurs when invitees arrive late, when there is no agenda or clear focus, and when members have to leave to attend to other matters. Waste also comes in the form of missing information and when only opinions are discussed and no substantial information is presented

For these reasons, and because meetings are an everyday matter in all the areas, there must be a methodology for conducting meetings. A secretary must be appointed to read the objectives, take roll, make note of participants' arrival time, start the meeting, indicate the time allocated to each topic, and write down the agreements reached. It is estimated that a good meeting with well-informed people who are prepared in advance and really committed to their work on the stated objective should last at most one hour.

Important considerations

Each stage should be carried out as a team. It all starts with the management team, and from there the management and department level plans are carried out until the entire array of guidelines, strategies and activities contained in the *hoshin* are completed.

The success of strategic planning depends primarily on the establishment of good plans as well as the follow-up of activities and results.

Part II

Detailed knowledge of the processes

Chapter 5

Value mapping

Value maps are used to gain an in-depth understanding of the process, both within the plant and in the supply chain.

This tool has made it possible to fully understand the flow and to detect activities that do not add value to the process; in addition, it has been one of the pillars for establishing improvement plans with a very precise objective and focus.

As a starting point, let us establish some aspects of the operations that we must answer when making a value map.

1. What is the capacity of the production system?
2. What is the bottleneck?
3. At what speed does the customer buy?
4. What is the percentage of available capacity?
5. Are our restrictions internal or external?
6. What are the constraints on our company's objectives?
7. How can we design our system to meet commitments?

Value analysis can provide valuable information to answer these questions and above all, to design a system that adapts to fluctuations in demand given the changing needs of the customer.

In this age of international competitiveness, only companies whose primary objectives are speed of delivery and quality will prevail. The direction is no longer determined by large corporations but by companies who are the most innovative and fastest in customer response.

Definition

A value map is a graphical representation of production elements and information that allows us to understand and document the current and future state of a process; it is the basis for the analysis of the value that is added to the product or service and is the source of knowledge of a company's real restrictions since it allows us to visualize where the value is and where the waste is.

In the value map we may observe and understand the information flow and the materials flow since a manufacturing company not only manufactures goods but also produces information.

What is a value stream?

They are all the operations that transform products in the same family, and which are necessary to offer the customer a product from concept or design through to production and shipping. In a value stream there are tangible and intangible elements such as equipment, people, materials, methods, knowledge, diverse skills, energy, etc.

Mapping the value stream consists of seeing all these elements expressed in a drawing in order to understand and improve them and not just acknowledging that they exist.

Types of maps

- Current state map.
- Future state map.

The current state map will be a reference document for determining excesses in the process and documenting the current situation of the value stream.

In this map we can see the inventories in process and information for each operation relating to its capacity, availability, and efficiency. It also provides information on customer demand, how customer information is processed to the plant and from the plant to the supplier companies, how it is distributed to the customer and the distribution by those companies and finally, how the information is supplied to the processes. A value map is a valuable tool for analyzing information because, on a single sheet of paper or on one screen we can see:

- Demand from customers and the way to confirm orders.
- Demand for suppliers and a way to confirm orders.
- A way to plan production and purchases.
- The delivery process from suppliers to the customer.
- The sequence of production operations.
- The relevant information for each operation.
- Inventories of raw material, processes, and finished product.
- Actions that add value and actions that don't add value.
- Delivery times from raw material to finished product.

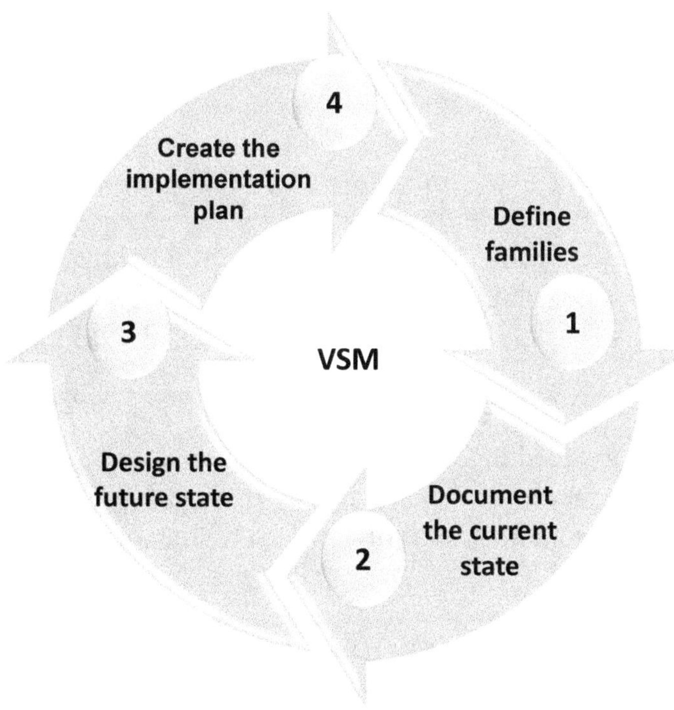

Figure 5.1. Implementation of the value stream map.

A value stream map is a very useful tool that allows us to visualize the activities that add value to the processes and those that do not. This helps to detect bottlenecks and key points in the process. Additionally, it serves as a basic tool for knowing where to focus improvement efforts and it identifies the areas where improvement efforts are not needed.

The future state map presents the best short-term solution for the operation considering the improvements to be incorporated into the production system. It is important to note that future state maps present pull systems unlike current state maps which show push systems.

The future state map represents part of the action plan that implements Lean tools given a previously analyzed situation. The Lean tools shown on this map as a burst represent the series of Kaizen events that the team must perform.

It is important to clarify that not all improvements are implemented at the same time but rather prioritization of activities is presented. The future state map is the starting plan for the construction of a new work scheme, and it should be clear so that the whole team speaks a common language and is aware of the changes and improvements that will be introduced in the process. Additionally, the future state map forms the basis for Lean implementation.

Important metrics

Cycle time

a) **Individual cycle time:** is the time that each individual operation lasts, such as painting a part, grinding, or packing.

   The time of each individual operation can be divided into specific elements, such as gathering materials, moving parts, doing assembly work, etc. This level of detail will be documented in the standardized operations combo box provided in Chapter 18, "Standard work".

b) **Total cycle time:** is the time it takes all operations to be performed and is calculated by adding the individual cycle time of each operation in a given process.

Takt time

Takt time is the speed at which the customer buys. It's the time the production system must adapt to in order to meet the customer's expectations.

Formula: time available / demand.

Ejemplo

Time available per day
= 8 hours – 30 minutes for food and rest = 450 minutes.

450 min./ shift × 1 shift × 60 sec./minute. = 27,000 sec.

Monthly demand = 7,510 pieces.
Daily demand = 7,510 pieces = 22 working days = 341 pieces daily.

Takt time = 27,000 sec. ÷ 341 pieces = 79 sec./piece.

This means that the customer is willing to purchase one piece every 79 seconds (see worksheet in table 5.1).

In the image we can observe the demand trend and see the *takt* time calculation for a monthly demand of 7,510 units and daily time available of 27,000 seconds, resulting in a *takt* time of 79 seconds per piece.

What is a value map for?

The following are benefits of a value map:

- Establish a graphical method to understand the entire supply chain in a single document.
- Display all the operations and information of a product family.
- Detect areas of opportunity.
- Know the direct value contribution to the products.
- Recognize forms of waste.
- Know the process in detail.
- Detect bottlenecks.

When is a value map used?

We make a value map when we are going to start an improvement process in a specific product family. What we need to do is focus on the tools that will help

Product   various
Description   Dashboards

January	February	March	April	May	June	July	August	September	October	November	December
7920	6340	5255	7344	9210	8714	9456	6940	5679	6710	8710	7840

						Monthly Demand	7510
Working days	22	Available Time	27000	seg.			
hrs. X shift	8	Daily demand	341		7920		
Shifts	1					0	
Breaks per shift (min)	30	**TAKT TIME**	**79**	sec/unit			

Customer is willing to buy one piece each   79   seconds

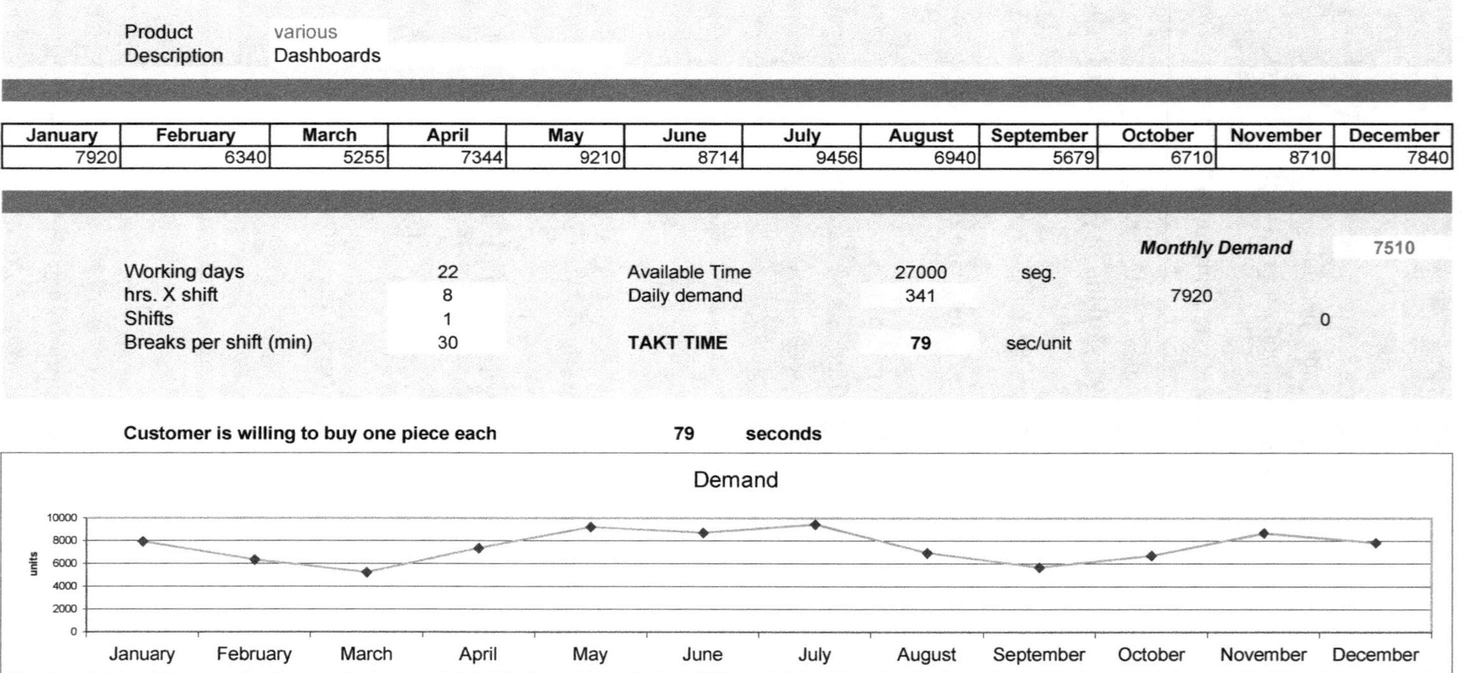

Table 5.1

us find the points of greatest impact and focus our efforts on them. These points can be bottlenecks, key points, areas with potential, etc.

How long does it take to make a value map?

The making of a value map takes between four and seven days.

Symbols used in a value map

External sources: represent customers and suppliers.

Transfer arrow from supplier to plant or from plant to customer.

Transport by cargo truck.

Transport by train.

Transportation by plane.

Process operation.

Data box placed underneath the operations. It includes information such as cycle time, changeover time between products, machine reliability, time available per shift, *yield*, etc.

Push arrow used to connect operations in which the material is moved using a push system.

PEPS Operations link based on "first in, first out" sequence.

Kaizen burst. Used to imply that at this point in the value stream an improvement event aimed at implementing the Lean tool containing the burst should be performed.

Procedure for making a value map

- Establish product families.
- Create the current state value map.
- Create the future state value map.
- Make improvements by applying Kaizen events.

To illustrate the concept, we will draft a sample value map and the steps for carrying it out.

Example

The Lean Shop company makes production and indicator control boards. The board models it manufactures are the following:

AX - 1	Basic board
AZ - 2	Remote control board
WB - 3	WEB board
XR - 4	Color board
MN - 5	Standard manual
MN - 6	Financial manual
MN - 7	Global manual

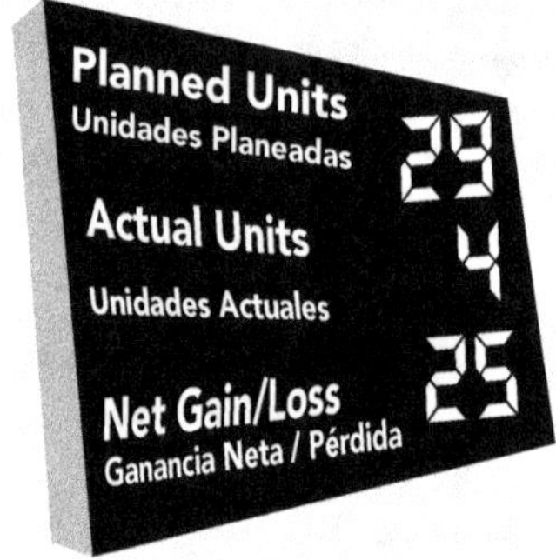

Establish product families.

To establish product families, we must list all part numbers and indicate the operations that a product goes through as well as record the cycle time for each operation.

Cycle time = time that elapses from when an operation starts until it ends.

In the table in figure 5.2 the first four products go through the same number of operations whereas the manual boards do not go through three of the operations. Thus, at this time there are two families identified.

Products / Operations		Cutting	Painting	Drilling	Electrical Assembly	Upload Software	Control Module Assembly	Final Assembly & Testing	Packaging & Shipping	Total
Model	**Description**									
AX - 1	Basic dashboard	18	45	12	45	22	30	114	35	**321**
AZ - 2	Remote control dashboard	20	45	14	63	22	24	134	42	**364**
WB -3	WEB dashboard	18	45	19	56	22	31	121	33	**345**
XR - 4	Colors dashboard	22	45	11	50	22	32	119	44	**345**
MN - 5	Standard dashboard	15	45	15	x	x	x	123	47	**243**
MN - 6	Financial dashboard	10	45	15	x	x	x	123	49	**242**
MN - 7	Overview dashboard	6	45	15	x	x	x	123	43	**232**

Figure 5.2

A family is a group of part numbers that go through the same number of operations and whose total aggregate time does not exceed 30% of the range.

Create the current state value map.

For this example, we will map the family of electronic boards.

To make the map we need the following:

- Obtain cycle time data for each process operation.
- Obtain availability data for each machine in the process (see Chapter 9).
- Obtain the product changeover time for each process in the operation (see Chapter 11).
- Determine the inventories observed at each stage in the process, starting with the raw material, then the inventories in process, and finally the finished product.
- Know customer demand, the way they order and the quantities they order.
- Determine how purchase forecasts are prepared, how to order and the quantities ordered from suppliers.
- Understand both the process and information flow.
- Draw the corresponding symbol for the client and connect it to the process control symbol using the information arrows.

- Write MRP, if the company uses MRP for material planning.
- Draw the information arrows towards the supplier company.
- Connect the supplier to the material warehouse.
- Draw the process sequence and consider intermediate inventories.
- Draw the information control process symbol.
- Using the process boxes, make the following segment of the map: basic production processes.
- Add up the lead times for each process and each inventory triangle in the material flow to obtain a fairly accurate estimate of the delivery time for the total production.
- Add up the times for each value-added process or transformation of the value stream and compare it to what was obtained in the previous point.

The following data is obtained:
Raw material inventory: 4 days.

Operation 1: cut pieces.
Machines: semi-automatic cutting machines with manual material feeding.
Cycle time: 22 seconds.
Changeover time between products: 25 minutes.
Machine reliability: 80 %.
Operators per machine: 1.
Inventory in process: 712 pieces.

Operation 2: paint.
Individual paint booths with automatic baking mechanism.
Cycle time: 45 seconds.
Changeover time between products: 5 minutes.
Machine reliability: 95 %.
Operators per machine: 1.
Inventory in process: 450 pieces.

Operation 3: drill.
Pedestal drills with capacity for one bit.
Cycle time: 19 seconds.
Changeover time between products: 0 minutes (all drilling is standard).
Machine reliability: 95 %.

Operators per machine: 1.
Inventory in process: 632 pieces.

Operation 4: electronic assembly.
Assembly table with capacity to store components.
Cycle time: 63 seconds.
Changeover time between products: 0 minutes (manual activities only).
Machine reliability: 100 %.
Operators per station: 1.
Inventory in process: 310 pieces.

Operation 5: load software.
Personal computer with software-to-chip loading device.
Cycle time: 22 seconds.
Changeover time between products: 0 minutes (just select the file).
Machine reliability: 98 %.
Operators per station: 1.
Inventory in process: 110 pieces.

Operation 6: control module assembly.
Assembly table with capacity to store components.
Cycle time: 32 seconds.
Changeover time between products: 0 minutes (manual activities only).
Machine availability: 100 %.
Operators per station: 1.

Operation 7: final assembly and testing.
Assembly table with capacity to store components.
Cycle time: 134 seconds.
Changeover time between products: 0 minutes (manual activities only).
Machine reliability: 100 %.
Operators per station: 1.
Inventory in process: 217 pieces.

Operation 8: packing.
Packing table.
Cycle time: 49 seconds.

Changeover time between products: 0 minutes (manual activities only).
Machine reliability: 100 %.
Operators per station: 1.
Inventory in process: 1456 pieces.

Draw the current state map

1. To draw the current state map, we start by placing the customer symbol in the top corner of the double letter paper and connect the information flow to the production control, which in turn sends the requirements to the supplier with the material forecasts.

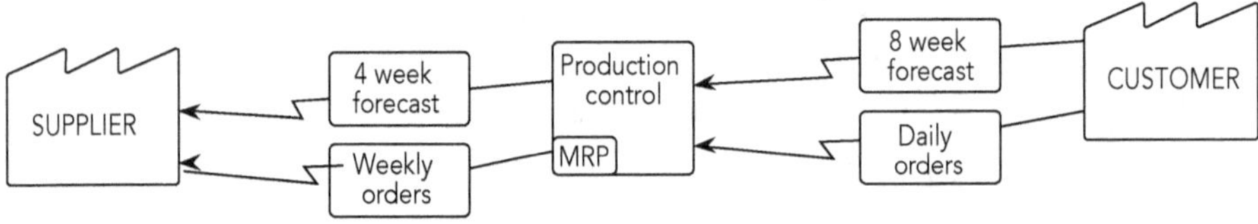

2. We draw the deliveries of the supplier companies.

3. We draw the sequence of operations by setting the time for each operation, the product changeover time, the availability of equipment, the time available, and the inventories in process.
4. We connect the information factory with the products factory by means of the arrows that indicate the production program that is being carried out for each operation (see figure 5.4).
5. We integrate the entire map and evaluate the time that adds value (see figure 5.5).

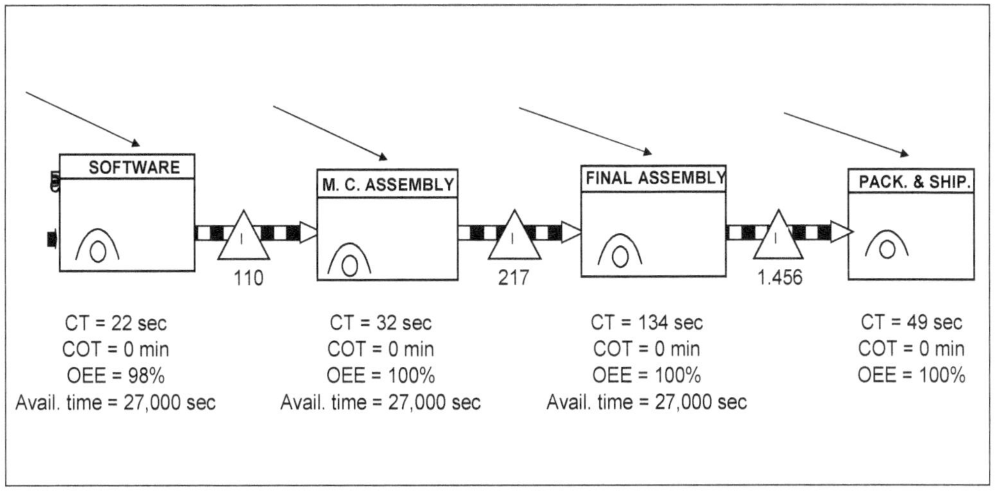

Figure 5.4

At the bottom we draw a ladder; on the lower steps we put the time that adds value and on the upper steps the time that does not add value. In this case we convert the inventories into days, dividing each inventory by daily demand (341).

6. We calculate the takt time.

Time available = 27,000 seconds per day.

Demand = 341 boards daily.

$$\textit{Takt} \text{ time} = 27{,}000 \text{ sec.} \div 341 \text{ pieces} = 79 \text{ sec./piece.}$$

That means the customer is willing to buy a board every 79 seconds so that will be our production target.

Calculations in detail:

Total time = 8 hours = 480 minutes.

Lunch time = 30 minutes.

Time available = 450 min. ÷ 60 sec./min. = 27,000 sec.

Monthly demand = 7,510 units.

Working days = 22.

Daily demand = 7,510 units ÷ 22 = 341 units.

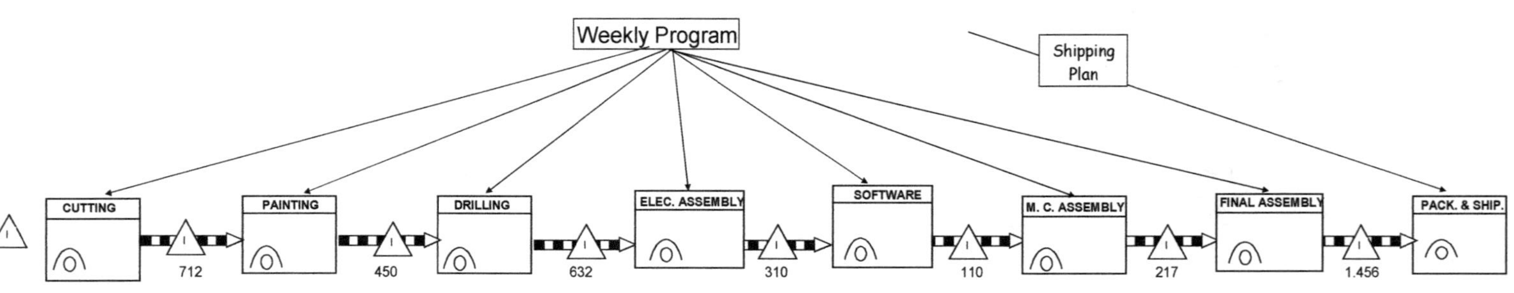

Figure 5.5

VALUE STREAM MAP
SUPPLIER
4-week forecast
Weekly Orders
Production Control
MRP
8-week forecast
Daily Orders
CUSTOMER
Demand
Weekly Program
Shipping Plan
CUTTING
PAINTING
DRILLING
ELEC. ASSEMBLY
SOFTWARE
M. C. ASSEMBLY
FINAL ASSEMBLY
PACK. & SHIP.
712
450
632
310
110
217
1.456
CT = 22 sec
COT = 25 min
OEE = 80%
Avail. time = 27,000 sec
CT = 45 sec
COT = 5 min
OEE = 95%
Avail. time = 27,000 sec
CT = 19 sec
COT = 0 min
OEE = 95%
Avail. time = 27,000 sec
CT = 63 sec
COT = 0 min
OEE = 100%
Avail. time = 27,000 sec
CT = 22 sec
COT = 0 min
OEE = 98%
Avail. time = 27,000 sec
CT = 32 sec
COT = 0 min
OEE = 100%
Avail. time = 27,000 sec
CT = 134 sec
COT = 0 min
OEE = 100%
Avail. time = 27,000 sec
CT = 49 sec
COT = 0 min
OEE = 100%
3
2,1
1,3
1,9
0,9
0,3
0,6
4,3
14,4 DAYS
22
45
19
63
22
32
134
49
386 SEC

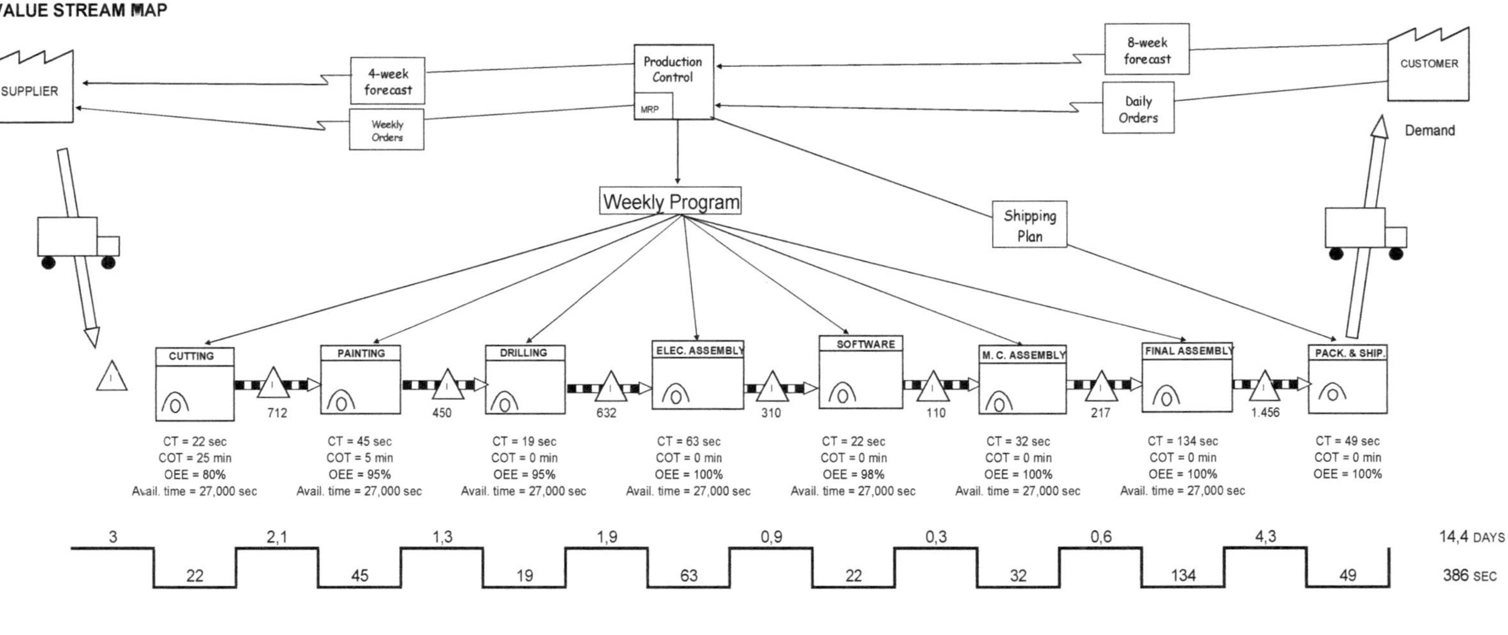

Figure 5.6

Creating the future state

To draw the future state map, the following factors should be considered:

a) Develop a continuous flow provided that operations can be one immediately after the other.
b) Where operations cannot be merged for some reason, introduce supermarkets to merge discontinuous flows.
c) Propose Kaizen events to apply Lean tools as needed.
d) Draw the future state map.
e) Draw the plan of the plant in the future state.

a) Develop a continuous flow (see Chapter 10, "Cellular manufacturing")

To illustrate the example, we will first merge all the operations that enable a continuous flow to be set up to create a production cell and represent it on the future state map. In this case, all operations will be merged into a single flow, getting materials to move from one station to another.

b) Create supermarkets

Since it was possible to group all the operations without any restrictions, we then proceed to set up the supermarkets. We place one in the materials warehouse and the other in the finished product warehouse.

In this diagram we can observe that, when withdrawing a product from the finished product supermarket, a Kanban card is removed from that product and sent to the cell to indicate that it has to produce the product or set of

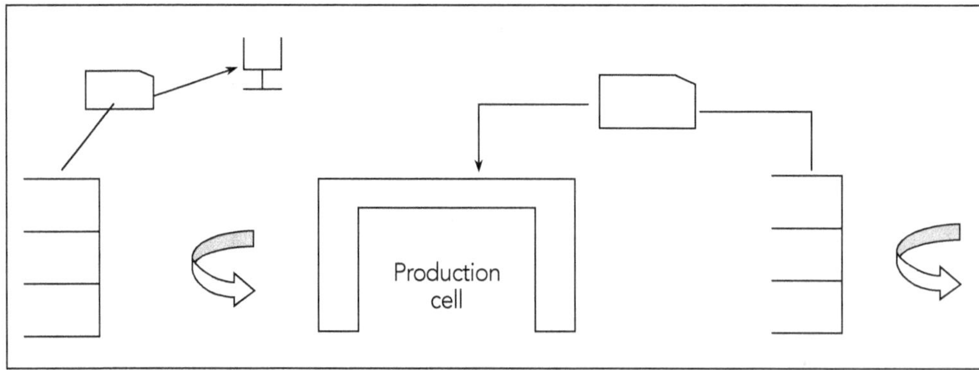

Figure 5.7

products in order to replace what the customer withdrew; as the cell requires materials, it withdraws them from the supermarket and simply sends a card to purchasing to indicate to the supplier that the relevant materials need to be replenished.

c) Make improvements by applying Kaizen events

The bursts on the future state map indicate that improvement events will be held to implement all the modifications in the process. Chapter 6 explains in detail the process of conducting a Kaizen event.

The first Kaizen event sets the stage by establishing activities and times for the operators who make up the work cell team (see Chapter 10).

The second Kaizen event could be to implement total productive maintenance to improve the availability of machines and in this case, we would like to start with the cutting machine. However, we don't want to dismiss the other machines as they too should have their daily maintenance plan (this topic will be discussed in more detail in Chapter 9 "Total productive maintenance").

The third Kaizen event would consist of implementing quick changeovers to make multiple models on the same day in order to have greater flexibility in the face of any change in demand (this topic will be discussed in more detail in Chapter 11, "Quick product changeovers"). Chapter 6 will explain how to prepare, conduct, and monitor improvement events.

What events should be held first?

The sequence of Kaizen events is determined by the priorities observed in the analysis of the future state map. It usually starts with continuous flow or cellular manufacturing. If the process has machinery it is followed with total productive maintenance, quick changeovers, and Poka-yoke. This sequence depends on each company's priorities.

To carry out the future state map, we must first ask ourselves whether the plant will implement a Kanban in finished product or send the product directly to the customer without storing it. In the case of Lean Shop, it was decided to implement a four-day finished product supermarket and afterwards calculate the correct Kanban size. This will result in a continuous flow between cell operations.

On the future state map, although customer information is still being used for work, the flow has become a pull system rather than a push system as it was in the previous concept. Now, when the customer buys, a Kanban card imme-

8 week forecast
Weekly orders
Production control
4 week forecast
Weekly orders
Cellular manufacturing and reduction of cycle times
1
2
3
TPM in all equipment
SMED
4
2
337
TOTAL TIME: 6.0039 DAYS
TVA= 337 SECONDS

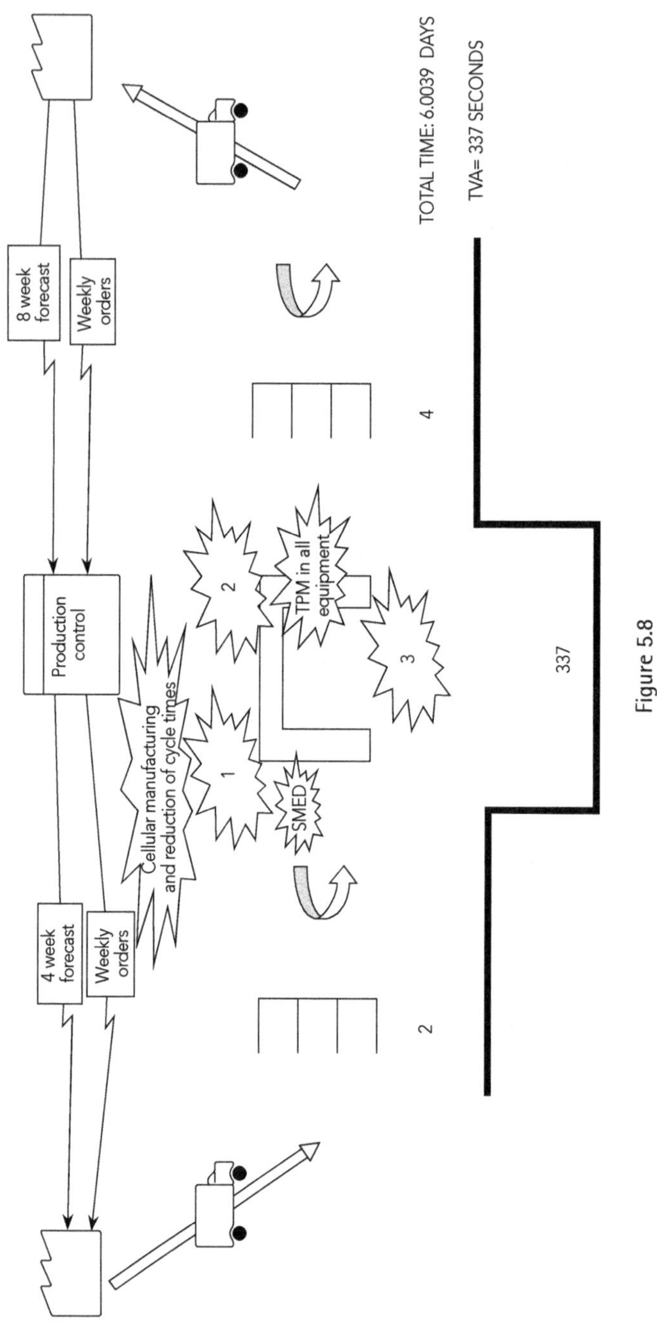

Figure 5.8

diately notifies the previous process, i.e. the cell, that it must replenish what the customer has withdrawn; the supplier must resupply the material that the cell used in order to keep the supermarket stocked with the necessary materials so as to not halt production.

Production planning and material control are now completely dependent on the Kanban system and production is automatically replenished (a detailed explanation of this system will be found in Chapter 16, "Kanban for material and production control").

d) Draw the future state of the plant

When we draw the distribution of the new work scheme, the flow has become continuous and space has been freed up. In addition, three cells are now available, each of which can make three different models at the same time. The total travel distance is 185 meters for each board produced in this plant.

Achievements to date

With the changes that have been made, mainly in policies such as the production sequence, the production planning, the material control method, the combination of jobs between operators and the proposed Kaizen improvements, the following results were achieved:

	BEFORE	AFTER	% IMPROVEMENT
Space required (sq. ft)	1259	640	619
Number of employees	10	5	5
Distance traveled	185	92	93
Lead time (days)	14,4	6,004	8,396
Raw materials inventory (days)	3	2	1
WIP inventory (days)	7,1	0	7,1
Finished goods inventory	4,3	4	0,3
Inventory Turnover	16,7	40,0	23,3

Figure 5.9

These results show major achievements in a very short period of time and above all, it proves that the company is becoming more flexible in the face of constantly changing markets with ever increasing demands.

It is very important not to make the improvements without having previously done the current and future state mapping because if the improvements are made directly without doing a deep and detailed analysis, there will be no definite approach and the Lean implementation will be a probable cause of failure. When formulating your map make sure to draw it out. When we draw using pencil and paper, we entertain deep thought and we gain a deeper understanding of the process and that should not be replaced by computers. Once the map has been made manually and we have understood where the value is and where the waste is, we can use specialized software or spreadsheets with symbols to make a computerized map.

Useful tools and concepts for the application

- Know the rate of demand (takt time).
- Determine in which elements of continuous flow can be introduced.
- Set up supermarkets using Kanban cards.
- Detect the points of restriction within the system.
- Introduce production leveling.
- Introduce improvements to the process by improvement events.

Part III

Basic tools

Chapter 6

Kaizen events to apply process improvements

Background

Kaizen the Japanese word for "improvement". However, the term "continuous" was added after its principles began to be adopted by Western organizations. In the Japanese culture it is clear (by tradition) that when talking about improvement we are talking about constant changes while in the West it is customary to specify what is needed. So, today we all relate the concept of Kaizen to "continuous improvement".

"Wise is not he who knows a lot but he who applies what little he knows."

Kaizen is a powerful way to make improvements at all levels of the organization and today it is practiced by leading corporations around the world. Its main utility lies in a gradual and orderly application which involves the joint efforts of everybody in the company to make changes without large capital investments.

To understand the power of continuous improvement we must ask ourselves how many improvements each of us provides to the organization in which we work. For example, if each worker made only ten proposals a year, that would be 10,000 improvements a year in a company of 1,000 employees. As a result, we would have endless changes and new opportunities to be more productive. Dramatic changes are not needed, just ones over 1%, but we have to do them every day.

"On one occasion a hen was asked to lay 30 eggs in a month, which upset her very much and made her think that they were abusing her capacity. However, she was later asked to lay just one egg a day and she replied happily 'That being the case, I'll lay up to two eggs a day without any problem'.".

Definition

A Kaizen event is a chain of actions carried out by work teams whose aim is to improve the results of existing processes. Through these actions, process owners and operators can make significant improvements in their workplace that will translate into productivity gains and, consequently, profitability for the company.

What are Kaizen events for?

Kaizen events are extremely effective in quickly improving a process by implementing tools that help to:

- Reduce waste (fewer *mudas).*
- Improve quality and reduce variability (fewer *muras).*
- Improve working conditions (fewer *muris).*

In the implementation of these Kaizen events, the need to use some of the Lean tools mentioned in this book will arise, depending on the goals that each organization wants to achieve.

Implementation of Kaizen events.

When are Kaizen events used?

Typically, the application of improvement events takes place when:

- There is a quality problem.
- We wish is to improve the distribution of the areas.
- It is necessary to reduce the setup time of the machines.
- We need to reduce the delivery time to customers (internal or external).
- We want to reduce operating costs.
- We need to improve housekeeping.
- We want to reduce the variability of a quality characteristic.
- We want to make more efficient use of the machines.

What can be achieved with Kaizen events?

- Rapid improvements in the performance of specific production processes or manufacturing cells.
- Very short product changeover times.
- Better plant distributions.
- Better machinery performance.
- Improvement in housekeeping.
- Better quality at the first attempt.
- Better communication between operators.
- Increased production capacity.
- Safer and more ergonomic working conditions.

As can be seen in figure 6.1, in a company with a traditional approach, activities that do not add value far exceed those that do, and they are the main cause of competitiveness problems.

Expected results after a Kaizen event

The goal of a Kaizen event is that, at the end of each improvement project, the company will appreciate changes in the results of the processes because it is eliminating their sources of loss *(muri, mura, muda)*. The waste in the total work of a process should be less and less, thereby making better use of the company's resources and increasing its profitability and customer response.

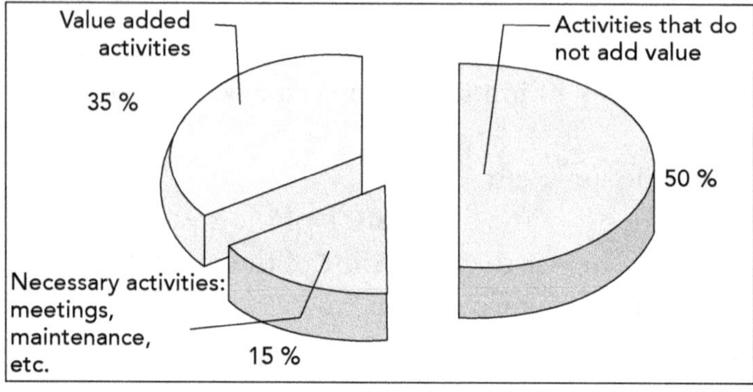

Figure 6.1

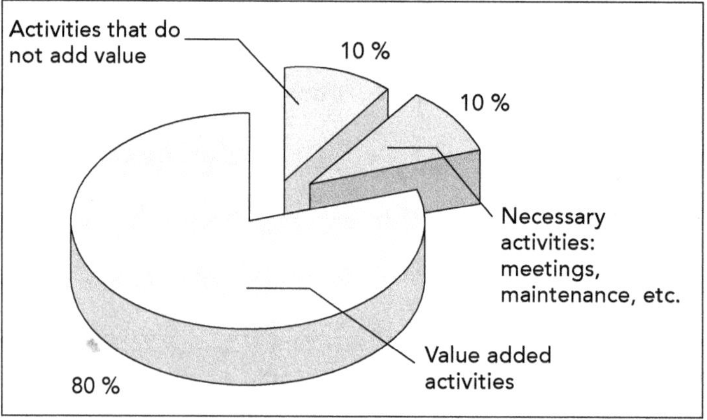

Figure 6.2

How long does it take to carry out a Kaizen event?

It depends on the impact it will have on the process as well as the difficulty of performing the event. However, it usually takes between one and five days to conduct each Kaizen event. It is important to be clear that this range is not random; this means that each team must have a well-defined work agenda before starting the event. Therefore, it is necessary to know in advance whether one, two, or five days will be dedicated. This is because all team members must schedule their work agenda ahead of time so they can devote themselves uninterruptedly to the event, without daily tasks distracting them from it.

If we quantify the actual time we spend on a job that has taken months to complete and has produced significant changes, we will realize that it takes us no more than 40 or 48 actual hours. The problem is that we are always busy solving short-term problems and as a result, we do not spend actual time on improvement.

> "The wise one does not teach with words but with deeds."
>
> LAO TSE

Procedure for carrying out a Kaizen event

Before conducting a Kaizen event

Kaizen events are planned up to two months in advance, during the planning stage, the following is done:

1. Opportunities for carrying out an event are proposed and discovered. These opportunities are presented by managers, clients, or anyone else who can visualize them.
2. The team leader is chosen (person with leadership skills and knowledge of the subject).
3. The event sponsor is chosen (person with authority and able to make decisions to support the team's proposals).
4. The team is chosen. It is recommended that there be between 7 and 10 participants in total, including operators, engineers, administrative, and quality staff, sometimes even customers or suppliers.
5. The logistics of the event (boardroom, area, production, etc.) are prepared.
6. It is communicated to the participants.
7. Table 6.1, "Definition of the Kaizen event", is filled in.
8. The necessary documentation is prepared according to each type of event. This documentation is included in each of the application topics in Chapters 7 to 17.

Kaizen event leader

Each Kaizen event must be led by a facilitator. This must be a member of the company who knows both the tools and the methodology very well so that they can direct the activities of the team members towards the achievement of the objectives within the set time.

Definition of *kaizen* event

Project	
Objetive	

Project	
Scope	

	Name	Telephone
Sponsor		
Leader		
Co-leader		

Members	

	Dates
Start date	
End date	

PROGRESS

20%	40%	60%	80%	100%

Metric	Current	Goal	Reached	Saving

Resource	Quantity

Summary of savings

Concept	Saving	Validator

Investments made

Concept	Date	Cost

	Total	

Summary of actions carried out

Action	Date	Result

Comments

Table 6.1

The facilitator is an indispensable channel to connect the results of the Kaizen event to the company's objectives set by senior management (see Chapter 4, "Hoshin Kanri strategy"). Successful team facilitators have the following characteristics:

- They are skilled as trainers and in personnel management.
- They are recognized and respected by group members; people trust them.
- They are clear that they are not responsible for the Kaizen event nor its outcome. They only function as a support for the team members.
- They do not necessarily belong to the area or department that is carrying out the Kaizen event as they are experts in the methodology and tools of the event, but team members are experts in the process to be improved.
- Their role is essential to maintaining the focus of the team on the subject of the event, as a source of information and as support for the enthusiasm of the members.

During the Kaizen event

First day

The first day is an inauguration meeting with the entire team, managers, and management. The following agenda proposal is made:

Proposed agenda

1. The director shares a few words (5 minutes) to the group explaining the reason for the improvement event and stresses the need for the changes.
2. The team leader introduces the entire team (their workplaces, skills, and strengths) and provides the objectives, scope, agenda, rules and deliverables of the event (15 minutes).
3. An introduction about the event is made; depending on the purpose of the event and the Lean tool to be applied, a simple presentation is made on the subject, where the following elements are explained:

   - Background.
   - The definition of the tool; e.g. TPM, Kanban, SMED, etc.
   - Important metrics.
   - The benefits of implementation.
   - Implementation time.
   - The procedure for carrying it out.

- The activities the team will perform during the event.
- Important implementation considerations.

4. The current situation is established. The value stream map is analyzed, and process inputs and outputs are highlighted. The situation can also be determined by reviewing the trend charts of the situation that motivated the event, such as machine reliability, changeover times, quality defects, problems due to large inventories, etc.
5. A visit to the area is made to detect opportunities. It is very important for the entire team to visit the area where the improvement event will be carried out as the "crime scene" is the starting point for solving a problem, improving any situation, or performing any analysis. When visiting the areas, it's important to ask staff how they perceive the situation, how they are currently doing the work or if they have suggestions for improvement. Likewise, observation will be a decisive element in identifying opportunities.
6. Opportunities are identified. The team initiates the identification of opportunities, which may be in any of the productivity constraints presented in Chapter 2 and should be documented on the opportunity cards (see table 6.2).

Oportunity cards

During the days of the event, ideas are proposed and the ones that can be executed in the same event are carried out. The ideas are normally classified as A, B and C. The A ideas are immediately applicable (1 to 4 days). B's can be carried out during the event or a little later (one to two weeks) and the C's require more time (not more than two months), as they may need special authorizations, investments, etc.

The upper part of the card is stuck in the place where the opportunity was found while the lower stub, which contains the same information, is taken by the team to be transcribed in table 6.3, "activities to be performed in the Kaizen event".

Progress in the following days

Each event has a particular theme and objective but the aim is always to provide ideas for improving and applying them.

For the development and implementation of each application, see the following chapters:

<table>
<tr><td colspan="2" align="center">OPPORTUNITY CARD</td></tr>
<tr><td>Date:</td><td>Number:</td></tr>
<tr><td colspan="2">Area:</td></tr>
<tr><td colspan="2">Opportunity detected: (muda, muri, mura)</td></tr>
<tr><td>Activity to be performed:</td><td>Classification</td></tr>
<tr><td colspan="2">Equipment:</td></tr>
<tr><td colspan="2">Observations:</td></tr>
<tr><td>Date:</td><td>Folio:</td></tr>
<tr><td colspan="2">Area:</td></tr>
<tr><td colspan="2">Opportunity detected: (muda, muri, mura)</td></tr>
<tr><td>Activity to be performed:</td><td>Calssification:</td></tr>
<tr><td colspan="2">Equipment:</td></tr>
</table>

Table 6.2

- Chapter 7, "The 5S of good housekeeping".
- Chapter 8, "Visual control".
- Chapter 9, "Total productive maintenance".
- Chapter 10, "Cellular manufacturing".
- Chapter 11, "Quick product changeovers".
- Chapter 12, "Prevention with FMEA".
- Chapter 13, "Poka-yoke error proofing".
- Chapter 14, "8 D problem solving".

Activities to be done in *kaizen event*

No._______ Sheet_______ of _______   Date _______________

Reply/ card no.	Description	Progress 25% 50% 75% 100%	Person responsible	Classification	Observations

Table 6.3

- Chapter 15, "Six Sigma for variation reduction".
- Chapter 16, "Kanban for material and production control".
- Chapter 17, "Heijunka for production sequencing".

In each of the chapters you will find forms or files for the application of the Kaizen event.

Also, table 6.3 must be filled in, "Activities to be performed in the Kaizen event".

This table details the number of the proposals or cards, describes the activities, the progress in the implementation of the improvement, the person responsible for carrying out the activity, the classification of the activities, and the necessary observations in each proposal.

This document must be in a visible place where the event is being applied so that everyone can track the improvements.

Last day of the event

On the last day of the event the details of the implementation are finalized, and a presentation is made to the managers in which all team members participate. This presentation should contain the following points:

1. The situation they found.
2. The actions they carried out.
3. The results they obtained.

This presentation shows photos and the list of opportunities that the team found as well as the actions that could be carried out during the event, those that were started and those that remained pending. The quantitative and qualitative results are then presented and compared with the objectives set out in table 6.1.

After the Kaizen event

Finally, over the following four weeks, improvements are monitored so that the process owners may carry them out daily.

Applicable concepts for Kaizen events

Suggestion system

It is recommended that the company have a suggestion system so that regardless of the execution of Kaizen events, improvements can be made in all areas with the enthusiastic participation of all staff.

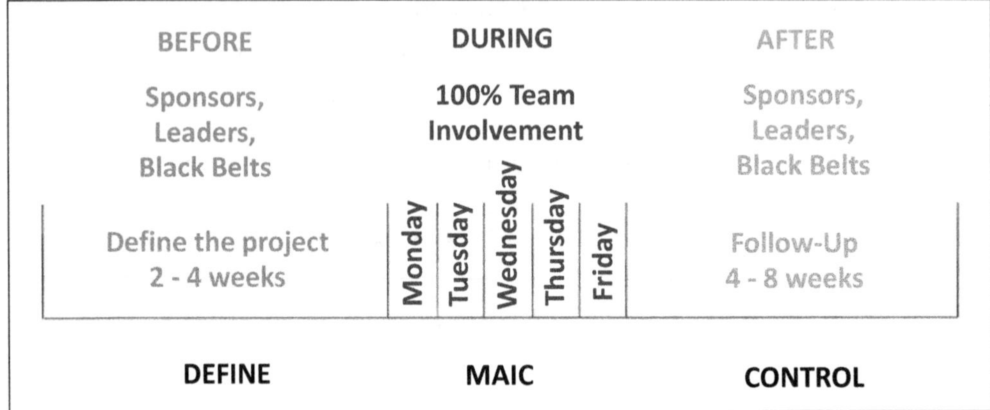

Figure 6.3

The continuous improvement concept can be used whenever someone finds an opportunity for improvement in any part or area of the company. It is therefore suggested as a method to motivate the generation of practical ideas that can be carried out and produce tangible results at short notice. This simple concept can replace suggestion boxes which do not necessarily capture opportunities but rather complaints.

Guide for the suggestion system

- First, remember that a suggestion system is a necessary component for a continuous improvement program. Future Kaizen events can originate from it at the same time helping to improve staff motivation by allowing them to contribute their ideas.
- Fully integrate the suggestion system into the management system, including the performance system.
- Choose a program development champion who should be clear that suggestion programs cannot be dictatorial or imposed but rather a labor of love and commitment.
- Recognize only the ideas implemented. It is not enough to have ideas; they have to be implemented.
- Be efficient and effective in awarding prizes for implementation. Do it immediately and hold recognition celebrations for those who have implemented the most ideas or achieved the biggest savings.
- Keep suggestion formats simple and easy to understand for any employee.

Kaizen event rules

Whenever you participate in a Kaizen event, remember the following:

- Keep an open mind on making changes.
- Maintain a positive attitude even to negative things.
- Never keep disagreements to yourself.
- Help create a cooperative environment.
- Make sure there is mutual respect.
- Treat others as you would like them to treat you.
- All votes have the same importance, regardless of the hierarchical position of who votes.
- Silent questions are not allowed, i.e., if you have a doubt, ask!

Important considerations

- Events are just the structure for the application of any Lean tool.
- It is advisable to have a project database that contains all event details. This database will be a great support for a person who has the same needs as someone who has developed a successful Kaizen event.

Suggestion system

Continuous improvement programs do not depend solely on Kaizen or improvement events that are performed in a planned manner. A continuous system of suggestions should also be implemented so that all employees, when they find an improvement in productivity, costs, material procurement, safety, quality, etc. may document it immediately for evaluation and implementation. If this becomes a habit, the staff will take responsibility for its results.

For this program a documentation system of ideas for improvement should be established so that any employee can, at any time, contribute an idea. Opportunity cards serve this purpose. These cards are stuck in a pigeonhole where any employee can grab them. When the idea has been generated, one part of the card is stuck in the place where the idea was suggested so that it is visible.

An improvement program will only be successful if all employees provide suggestions and management takes them seriously. This idea can create a universe of possibilities for the creation of value proposals since it combines creativity, ability, passion for work well-done and above all, encourages people's initiative. I firmly believe that companies where all the people, in addition to fulfilling a defined responsibility contribute something to the common good, improve

<table>
<tr><td colspan="2" align="center">OPPORTUNITY CARD</td></tr>
<tr><td>Date:
13-may-21</td><td>Number:
001</td></tr>
<tr><td colspan="2">Area:
Assembly line 4</td></tr>
<tr><td colspan="2">Opportunity detected: (muda, muri, mura)

A compressed air leak can be heard
in the pressure gauge air filter</td></tr>
<tr><td>Activity to be performed:

Tighten coupling</td><td>Classification

A</td></tr>
<tr><td colspan="2">Equipment:
Press 4</td></tr>
</table>

Table 6.4

a hundred times faster than companies where the initiative comes only from management.

Priority signal

The priority signal is a way to fight off mudas at any time. It consists of placing a button connected to a light bulb and a horn. When a problem arises, the person who detects it presses the button and immediately the horn sounds and the bulb lights up. A team, either directive or managerial, must address the request with extreme priority. It should be clarified that the system will be used for problems related to quality, service, safety, etc. the signal only stops when the problem has been fixed. This system will ensure that preventive measures are always taken to prevent problems and give a sign of leadership in prioritizing rapid action requests.

Chapter 7

The 5S of good housekeeping

Background

Lean tools represent a great advance for the implementation of process improvements that generate value in a company. However, one of the most important elements for this has to do with culture and habits developed over time. Therefore, keep in mind that throughout this subject we are considering not just the application of a basic tool but rather the development of good housekeeping habits that establish more consistent and noticeable basis for the building and application of many of the tools that will be seen later.

The 5S method was developed by Hiroyuki Hirano and represents one of the cornerstones that frame the beginning of any improvement tool or system. Therefore, it is said that a good improvement event is one that starts with 5S.

This system is known as 5S because each of the original words (in Japanese) of the methodology begins with the letter "S":

Seiri	Sort
Seiton	Set in order
Seiso	Shine
Seiketsu	Standardize
Shitsuke	Sustain

Definition

5S is a discipline for achieving improvements in workplace productivity by standardizing housekeeping habits. This is achieved by implementing process changes in five stages, each of which will serve as the foundation for the next, in order to maintain its long-term benefits.

It is said that if the implementation of 5S has not worked in a company, all other process improvement systems are destined to fail. This is because it does not require special technology or knowledge to implement them, just discipline and self-control on the part of each of the members of the organization.

This self-sufficient organizational method acquired through these five stages will be the foundation for more complex and more technological systems with higher investment.

A 5S program is built by developing the following stages:

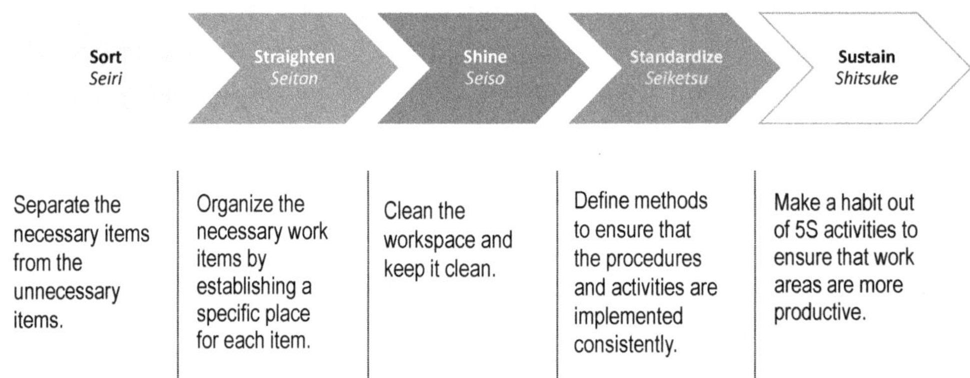

"One of the benefits we experienced when implementing 5's was that our factory was always impeccable, it looked like an exhibition, we were able to show the people who visited us where and how we made our products.

We know found that people who understand how we carry out our operations trust us more; thanks to this trust, it strengthened our relationships and, consequently, our business opportunities."

LORENZO GONZALEZ. OPERATIONS MANAGER OF MEXICAN TECHNICOLOR

- ***Seiri* (sort)**
  Consists of removing all unnecessary items from our workplace.

- ***Seiton* (set in order)**
  Consists of organizing the articles that we need for our work, establishing a specific place for each thing so that it is easy to identify, locate, arrange, and return to the same place after use.

- ***Seiso* (shine)**
  Consists basically of removing dirt and avoiding dirt, always with the idea in mind that, when cleaning, we are also inspecting what we clean.

- ***Seiketsu* (standardize)**
  Consists of ensuring that the procedures, practices, and activities achieved in the first three stages are consistently and regularly implemented to ensure that *sort, set in order,* and *shine* are maintained in the work areas.

- ***Shitsuke* (sustain)**
  Consists of making a habit of 5S activities by properly maintaining the processes generated by everybody's commitment as well as participating

in Kaizen events resulting from the needs for improvement arising in the workplace.

What is 5S implemented for?

A 5S program helps improve the cleanliness, organization, and use of our work areas. With this we manage to:

- Make better use of our resources, especially our time.
- Make anomalies and problems visible and obvious.
- Enjoy a safer and more pleasant working environment.
- Increase our capacity to produce more better-quality items.
- Have a presentable place for our customers.

When is 5S used?

When we need to reduce cycle times by making the most of the time available for production and reducing the time for tool changeovers. They are also useful when we want to implement new systems in value stream management (such as ISO 9000, statistical process control, Six Sigma or, Lean Manufacturing) since all these depend to a large extent on the quality (discipline) of the people involved in them. This tool is very powerful and can be applied in areas such as:

- Warehouses.
- Production areas.
- Areas of common use.
- Offices.
- Workshops.
- Vehicles.
- Portfolios.
- In our own home.

How long does it take to implement 5S?

Initial implementation, with the first three stages at an acceptable level, takes one to six months. It should be borne in mind that the fourth and fifth stages consist of standardization and sustain, this process has a beginning but never an end.

When we talk about implementation time, we recommend following this sequence:

Stage 0. Planning and preparation: 1 month.
Stage 1. Sort: 1 month, "the sort month" for everything.
Stage 2. Set in order: 1 month.
Stage 3. Shine: 1 month.
Stage 4. Standardize: 1 month.
Stage 5. Sustain: never ends.

Procedure for implementing 5S

Stage 0. Planning and preparation

1. Provide a training course for all staff, explaining what 5S is, what it will be used for and how its implementation will take place.
2. Prepare a communication campaign in the company about 5S, explaining the usefulness and benefits that its implementation will represent for everyone.
3. Make visits to other plants where 5S has been implemented.
4. Apply 5S to one or two sample areas so everybody understands the process.
5. Establish the areas for which everyone will be responsible at each stage.
6. Make a dashboard that shows all the areas where the implementation took place and its gradual progress.
7. Set a day to formally start implementation. The highest-ranking person in the company must give the starting signal along with a message to all company members which makes them see that this project is a strategic effort to achieve a clean, safe, and productive company. This start can be complemented with dynamics, games, videos, or other activities that give it due relevance.
8. Photograph the areas before starting to establish the starting point.

Stage 1. Implementation of the first S (sort)

1. Assign a lead group or guide group for this phase. This group will be responsible, among other things, for photographing the designated areas and generating an initial assessment of all areas.
2. Sort means removing all unneeded items from the workplace, so at this stage we must remove everything that we do not need or do not know if we really need.

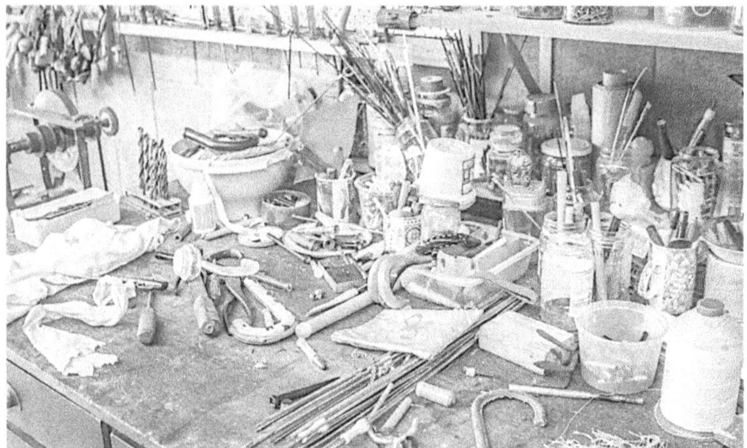

Sorting of unnecessary items.

When sorting, consider all objects that have not been used and will not be used in the future and remove them to free up space.

3. Set sorting criteria as in figure 7.1.

You can set sorting criteria based on frequency of use, time, or the quantity to be used.

Select as:	Frequency
Necessary	What is used more than once a month
Not necessary	What is used less than once a month

Examples

Sort as necessary everything that will be used during a month of production.

Sort as unnecessary whatever is surplus to use in the workspace.

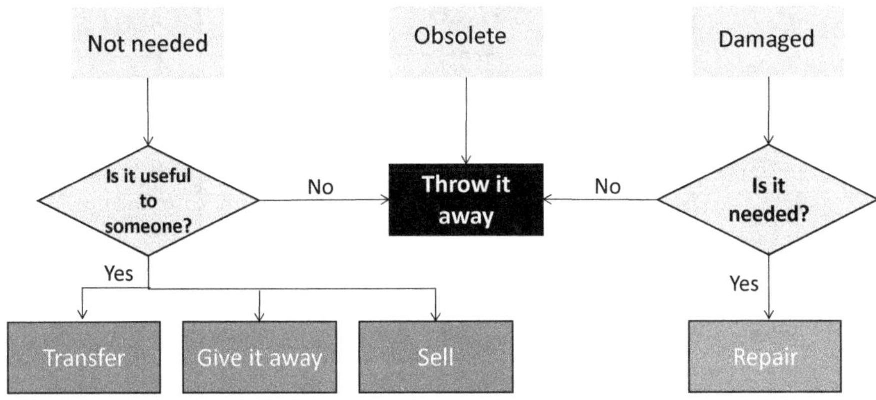

Figure 7.1

4. Objects sorted as unnecessary are identified and confined to a previously defined quarantine area. The red card in table 7.1 can be used as a control tool.

   Once the time to decide is up, the items labeled with red cards can be displayed in an internal company bazaar for everyone to see and decide if they can be useful to someone else, sold, or donated.

   The key to a place without useless elements is to not allow any unnecessary objects that can accumulate in the areas.
5. A deliverable for this stage is a list of necessary objects in each area where 5S is applied (see table 7.2).

The principle that should govern at this stage is: *only what is needed, only the amount needed, and only when it is needed.*

Stage 2. Implementation of the second S (set in order)

At this stage we must set in order the items that we sorted as necessary for our work, establishing a specific place for each thing so that it is easier to identify, locate, arrange, and return to the same place after using it. For this we need to:

1. Divide our work area into manageable and easily identifiable parts.
2. Create a location guide.
3. Set places for each object.
4. Draw outlines or color the positions of objects in the designated areas.

5S RED TAG	
Date:	**Tag #:**
Item Description:	
Quantity:	
Location:	
Tagged By:	

Date:	Tag #:
Item Description:	
Quantity:	
Location:	
CATEGORY	
Equipment	
Tools and Jigs	
Finished Goods	
Instruments	
Consumable Materials	
Machine Parts	
Raw Materials	
Work-in-Process	
Stationery, etc.	
Misc.	
Other (specify):	
REASON FOR RED TAG	
Not Required	
Defect	
Scrap	
Aged/Obsolete	
Use is Unknown	
Other (specify):	
Tagged By:	
Date of Decision:	
Final Destination:	

Table 7.1

List of necessary items		
		Area
No.	**Item**	**Location**

Table 7.2

Basically we should arrange the items and furniture that we put on the list of necessary objects and establish a proper place to have these items at hand for our work.

It is convenient to establish specific, marked, or designated areas to place each object. This way, we will not put them in places they do not belong in. When carrying out this step, consider designating specific places in shelves, desks, drawers, electronic files, warehouses, etc.

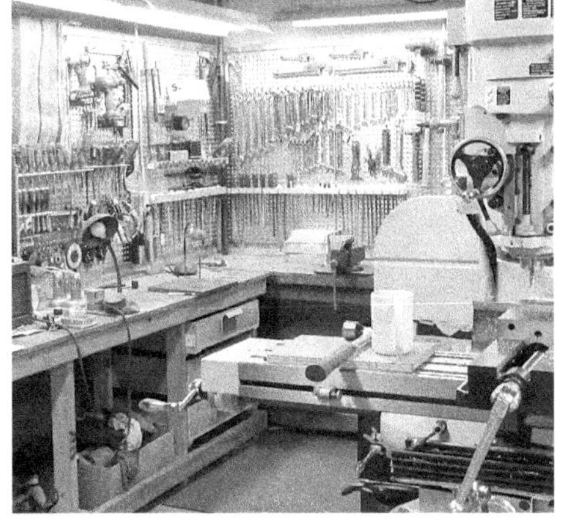
Workplace in perfect order.

In addition to designating a place and marking it to visually locate it, a deliverable for this stage can be a guide specifying the coordinates or location of all items so they can be located quickly (less than 30 seconds). If it succeeds, its work will have been satisfactory.

After a period of 30 or 40 days, we should decide what to do with the objects located in the quarantine areas, for which it is advisable to conduct an internal bazaar so that staff in all areas can see what objects could be useful for other areas.

Stage 3 Implementation of the third S (shine)

Shine basically means removing dirt, bearing in mind that while cleaning we are also inspecting. This allows for potential problems to be discovered before they become crititcal.

Cleaning process

- Design the cleaning program.
- Define cleaning methods.
- Establish discipline.
- Make staff responsible for cleaning activities.
- Define their frequency and when they should be carried out.
- List each of the cleaning activities to be performed.
- List the items and cleaning equipment that are needed.
- Document cleaning activities in a procedure.

Implementation of the cleaning process.

At this stage, assignments are made so that each employee is responsible for taking care of the cleaning, even if it is an activity performed by the cleaning department. Furthermore, it is important to consider that this is not only about cleaning but also about finding ways to avoid dirtying and making sure that the activities that generate trash can contain that trash as it is being generated.

"The cleanest place is not the one that is cleaned the most but rather the one that is dirtied the least."

Stage 4. Implementation of the fourth S (standardize)

Standardizing is ensuring that procedures, practices, and activities are executed consistently and regularly to ensure that sorting, *setting in order,* and *shining* are sustained in work areas.

Process

- Integrate 5S activities into regular work.
- Evaluate the results.

At this stage it is also advisable to develop a standardization manual so that 5S is sustained and there is continuity in aspects such as:

- Standardization of colors.
- Colors and types of lines.
- Coding of articles, spaces, shelves, etc.
- Location guides.
- Labels.
- Standards for organizing.
- Standards for cleaning.
- Regulation.

Evaluations should be objective and carried out by personnel designated exclusively for that purpose. Once the implementation has matured, anybody will be able to evaluate an area other than their own.

Below is a model assessment that can be used to create our own. These assessments are usually designed to be applied in warehouses, offices, and production areas.

When conducting an evaluation, it is very important to compare the evidence found in the previous evaluation with the results obtained in the current evaluation.

In the presentation of results, we can see the previous situation and the current result (see table 7.3).

The most important thing about evaluations is that they influence the culture of the organization and above all, create a competitive environment that enables the continuity of what has been achieved. Evaluations are not grounds for punishment or pressure, this makes the project an obligation rather than a shared achievement that provides many benefits.

A deliverable for this stage is a standardization guide by areas where we can consult the location of objects, the distribution drawing, the standardization guide for colors and labeling as well as the follow-up rules.

"Say what you do, do what you say and prove it."

Stage 5. Implementation of the fifth S (sustain)
Sustain means to turn the 5S activities into a habit, properly maintaining the processes generated through everybody's commitment.

At this stage it is advisable to:

- Run promotional campaigns about what we have earned.
- Organize visits to the facilities.
- Provide ongoing training.

<table>
<tr><td colspan="4" align="center">5S Audit</td></tr>
<tr><td colspan="2">AREA AUDITED</td><td>AUDITING TEAM</td><td>SIGNATURES</td></tr>
<tr><td colspan="2"></td><td></td><td></td></tr>
<tr><td colspan="2"></td><td></td><td></td></tr>
<tr><td colspan="2">DATE</td><td>AUDITED TEAM</td><td>SIGNATURES</td></tr>
<tr><td colspan="2"></td><td></td><td></td></tr>
<tr><td colspan="2"></td><td></td><td></td></tr>
<tr><td colspan="3" align="center">Audit items</td><td>SCORE</td></tr>
<tr><td rowspan="6">SORT</td><td>1.1</td><td>There is a list of required items in the work area</td><td></td></tr>
<tr><td>1.2</td><td>The quantity of required items in the work area has been established</td><td></td></tr>
<tr><td>1.3</td><td>The required items are in good condition for use</td><td></td></tr>
<tr><td>1.4</td><td>The list of required items matches what is actually in the work area</td><td></td></tr>
<tr><td>1.5</td><td>The aisles and work areas are free of obstacles and unnecesary items</td><td></td></tr>
<tr><td>1.6</td><td>Unnecesary items were either sent to the quarantine area, thrown away, relocated or sold</td><td></td></tr>
<tr><td></td><td></td><td align="right">Total</td><td></td></tr>
<tr><td rowspan="9">STRAIGHTEN</td><td>2,1</td><td>Location codes have been established for each item in the list of required items</td><td></td></tr>
<tr><td>2,2</td><td>Locations have been established for each item (equipment, tools, materials, etc.)</td><td></td></tr>
<tr><td>2,3</td><td>Identification methods have been established and standardized (color coding, location codes, organization and labeling of racks and tools)</td><td></td></tr>
<tr><td>2,4</td><td>Areas have been taped off according to color codes</td><td></td></tr>
<tr><td>2,5</td><td>The locations and codes are respected for each item (the required items are properly identified and in their place)</td><td></td></tr>
<tr><td>2,6</td><td>There is visual information that communicates the organization of areas, objects and required items</td><td></td></tr>
<tr><td>2,7</td><td>The information which is posted is up to date</td><td></td></tr>
<tr><td>2,8</td><td>It is possible to identify when something is out of place</td><td></td></tr>
<tr><td>2,9</td><td>It is possible to find any item in 30 seconds or less</td><td></td></tr>
<tr><td></td><td></td><td align="right">Total</td><td></td></tr>
<tr><td rowspan="6">SHINE</td><td>3,1</td><td>Work areas are clean</td><td></td></tr>
<tr><td>3,2</td><td>Tools and required items are clean</td><td></td></tr>
<tr><td>3,3</td><td>Methods have been established to prevent areas/items from getting dirty</td><td></td></tr>
<tr><td>3,4</td><td>Cleaning schedules have been established and cleaning activities are documented</td><td></td></tr>
<tr><td>3,5</td><td>The required cleaning supplies and equipment is available and in good conditions</td><td></td></tr>
<tr><td>3,6</td><td>The team members' appearance looks clean (Uniform, shoes, face, etc.)</td><td></td></tr>
<tr><td></td><td></td><td align="right">Total</td><td></td></tr>
<tr><td rowspan="5">STANDARDIZE</td><td>4,1</td><td>Color coding, labels and written signs have been standardized</td><td></td></tr>
<tr><td>4,2</td><td>Furniture, tooling, work items, work materials, etc have been standardized</td><td></td></tr>
<tr><td>4,3</td><td>The use of safety equipment has been standardized (for those operations that require it)</td><td></td></tr>
<tr><td>4,4</td><td>A standardization manual has been established (5S rules, item locations, area layout, racks, etc.)</td><td></td></tr>
<tr><td>4,5</td><td>Completed last weeks' audit of the corresponding area in a timely manner</td><td></td></tr>
<tr><td></td><td></td><td align="right">Total</td><td></td></tr>
<tr><td colspan="2">OBSERVATIONS</td><td colspan="2">Scoring Guide</td></tr>
<tr><td colspan="2" rowspan="6"></td><td colspan="2">0 = Implementation between 0 and 20%</td></tr>
<tr><td colspan="2">1 = limplementation between 20 and 40 %</td></tr>
<tr><td colspan="2">2 = Implementation between 40 and 60 %</td></tr>
<tr><td colspan="2">3 = Implementation between 60 and 80 %</td></tr>
<tr><td colspan="2">4 = Implementation between 80 and 90 %</td></tr>
<tr><td colspan="2">5 = Implementation between 90 and 100 %</td></tr>
</table>

Table 7.3

- Run communication campaigns.
- Conduct follow-up meetings.
- Make project presentations.

> *"The hardest part is not getting there, but staying there."*

Important considerations

The best tool to implement 5S is the company management's leadership and support so that everyone is infected with enthusiasm for the project. This will make everyone strive to make companies not only look better by being tidier and cleaner but also increase productivity significantly by eliminating search times. Usually, a lot of our time is spent searching for something. We search for objects, documents, files on the computer, tools, orders, etc. Besides improving the aesthetic aspect, we must also focus on the productivity that can be achieved.

It is advisable to take pictures at the end of each implementation stage, preferably from the same place and with the same lighting, so that it is noticeable that the changes are in the same place.

When the 5S process has reached maturity, perhaps after a continuous period of six months to a year, and when it has become a habit, people from other companies will be able to visit your company, just like those visits you made. It will be a source of great pride for your entire company to show the progress and achievements made.

Chapter 8

Visual control

Background

In ancient times, armies began to be distinguished by their flags and uniforms, tribes painted signs on the walls as a legacy as well as a way to depict the customs of hunting and warfare.

Andon was known in ancient times by the Japanese as "lamp". An Andon was made of paper sections placed around a base with a candle inside and the lid off. Andon functioned as a visual cue that from a distance gave a message to communicate something.

Visual cues are all around us in the streets, companies, hospitals, etc. to help us quickly understand a specific situation and make decisions without having to ask.

We human beings capture information through our senses. Our sense of sight is the one we capture the most information with, 80%, followed by hearing with 10%, smell with 5%, taste with 3%, and touch with 1% (Slater, 2002).

> "People perform just as they are measured."
>
> ELI GOLDRATT

Definition

Andon is related to simple visual and audio cues that are easily identified and understood. These cues are efficient, self-regulated, and managed by operators.

This information may be used to identify, instruct, or indicate that a normal or abnormal condition exists and that some action may be required.

In this photograph we see a team of operators working in a manufacturing cell who have an Andon board to compare the degree of progress they have with what they should have. Such a board allows them to make the decision at any time to work faster or slower as necessary.

Andon is an element of the *jidhoka* principle that, through ingenious mechanisms, detects when an error occurs and then, generally by way of a visual cue, warns the operator that a problem has occurred.

Andon is a cue that incorporates visual, auditory, and text elements which are used to report quality problems or stoppages. It also provides real-time information and feedback on the status of a process.

Figure 8.1

The concept of *Andon* is to measure processes and not people. Visual communication generates attitudes towards responsibilities, not against individuals.

What is Andon implemented for?

Andon cue elements are used to:

- Improve quality.
- Reduce cost.
- Improve response time.
- Increase safety.
- Improve communication.
- Understand problems immediately.

When we use visual control, we must ask ourselves:

- What needs to be monitored?
- Where are the key monitoring points?
- How are anomalies indicated?
- How easily can they be checked?
- What action should be taken?

When is Andon used?

When we want to give a cue to take some action or make a decision in areas like:

- Warehouses.
- Operations.
- Equipment.
- Quality.
- Safety.

Types of visual control

1. Alarms

They provide a warning signal in emergency situations and can be used with different sounds depending on their application.

2. Lights and towers

To know the status of machines, cells, or areas, color cues are used on towers or flags. Each of the colors indicate the following concepts:

- **Blue:** material-related problems (supply or lack of material).
- **Green:** Line or cell working satisfactorily.
- **Yellow:** line or cell stopped due to lack of maintenance or about to make some change if it is intermittent.
- **Red:** line or cell stopped due to quality problems or accident.

Lights or towers are used when you want to visually highlight some operating condition to draw the attention of the person responsible for making a decision.

3. Kanban

Kanban is a visual information system that tells operators when to start a production activity. It also indicates that it is necessary to replenish material in supermarkets, thus preventing shortage.

4. Information boards

These boards are useful for continuous and automatic monitoring of the production plan. On an information board, we program the production rate, which is the rate the customer buys at (takt time), and it automatically starts the count and compares it to data sent from the line in order to record in real time the production that is being obtained.

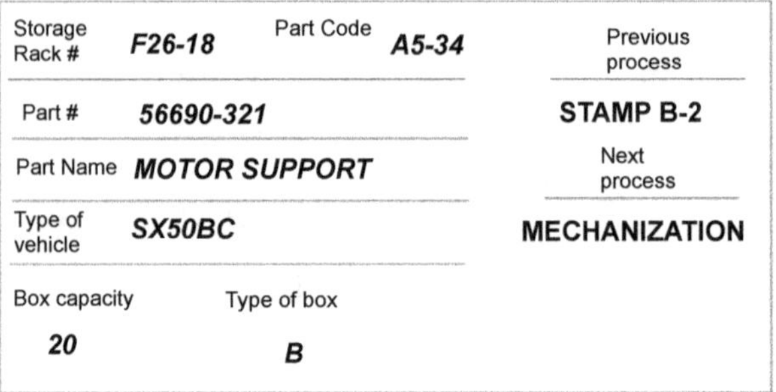

Figure 8.2

5. Checklists

Checklist
Loading and start-up of 3CX mill

1. Feeding guides have been checked ☐

2. Previously mixed material has been fed in ☐

3. Mix specifications are ready ☐

4. Temperature has risen to 450 degrees centigrade ☐

5. Equipment pressure reads 120 psi ☐

6. Oil level is optimal ☐

7. Metal support is ready ☐

Notes: Make sure to wear face shield and safety mask ☐

Figure 8.3

6. Floor markings

- **Green:** indicates good product.
- **Yellow:** delimits corridors.
- **Blue:** indicates raw material and product in process.
- **Red:** indicates non-compliant product.
- **Red and white:** delimit safety areas.
- **Black and white:** delimit maintenance areas.
- **Black and yellow:** delimit caution zones.

Visual control of floor markings.

How long does it take to implement Andon?

It depends on the type of cue and its complexity. It usually takes one to four weeks to implement it in each area.

Procedure for implementing Andon

- Decide what information is to be given and to whom it is addressed.
- Create the type of Andon or cue required.
- Train staff to use cues.
- Create discipline with good leadership to enforce cues.

Decide what information is to be given and to whom it is addressed

In deciding on the type of information to be provided in the visual control, the need to provide information relating to 6M (machinery, manpower, method, measurement, Mother Nature, and materials) must be considered. What we are looking for when considering 6M is to make problems visible without having to find them directly but rather that the indicators attract the attention of those who must solve the problems or carry out improvement or preventative actions.

Visual management exchanges real-time information about the state of the plant, so the following questions need to be answered:

- What are the necessary metrics and their objectives?

- What do we need in order to know the status of these metrics?
- What are the indicators like currently and what should they be like?
- What should I do to achieve the goal?

Create the type of Andon or cue required.

If a dashboard is required for in-plant monitoring or any other of the cues mentioned above, the necessary information is described, and the type of cue is designed.

Work cell boards

Quality, cost, delivery, and personnel indicators can be included in the boards in figures 8.4 and 8.5 and the following reports can be placed in each topic from top to bottom:

- Trend chart.
- Pareto chart that explains the most common causes.
- List of actions to improve, prevent, or correct.

Boards should also have a space to place opportunity cards.

Safety indicators

Figure 8.6 shows the days elapsed in the month and the types of incidents or accidents with the following references:

Green: nothing to indicate, the day passed without accidents.
Yellow: first aid.
Red: accident.

A key letter is assigned for each type of accident.

Train staff to use cues

The most important step is for everyone in the plant or company to know and understand the message about the goal and the result. Training will therefore be key to understanding, usage, and decision-making.

Create discipline with good leadership to enforce the cues

Andon will give good results only with the commitment of management in the use of cues. The importance all employees place on these indicators will depend on the importance managers and leaders place on them.

Results Board
Space for calculator
Area
Shift
5S
Prod. schedule
Background
Operational control
Totals
Part no.
Time
Availability
Efficiency
Quality
OEE
X
X
=
Product
Defects D
Units U
Opportunities OP
Total opportunities TOP = U X OP
Defects per opportunity DPO = D/TOP
DPMO
Sigma level
Defect
Cause
Solutuion

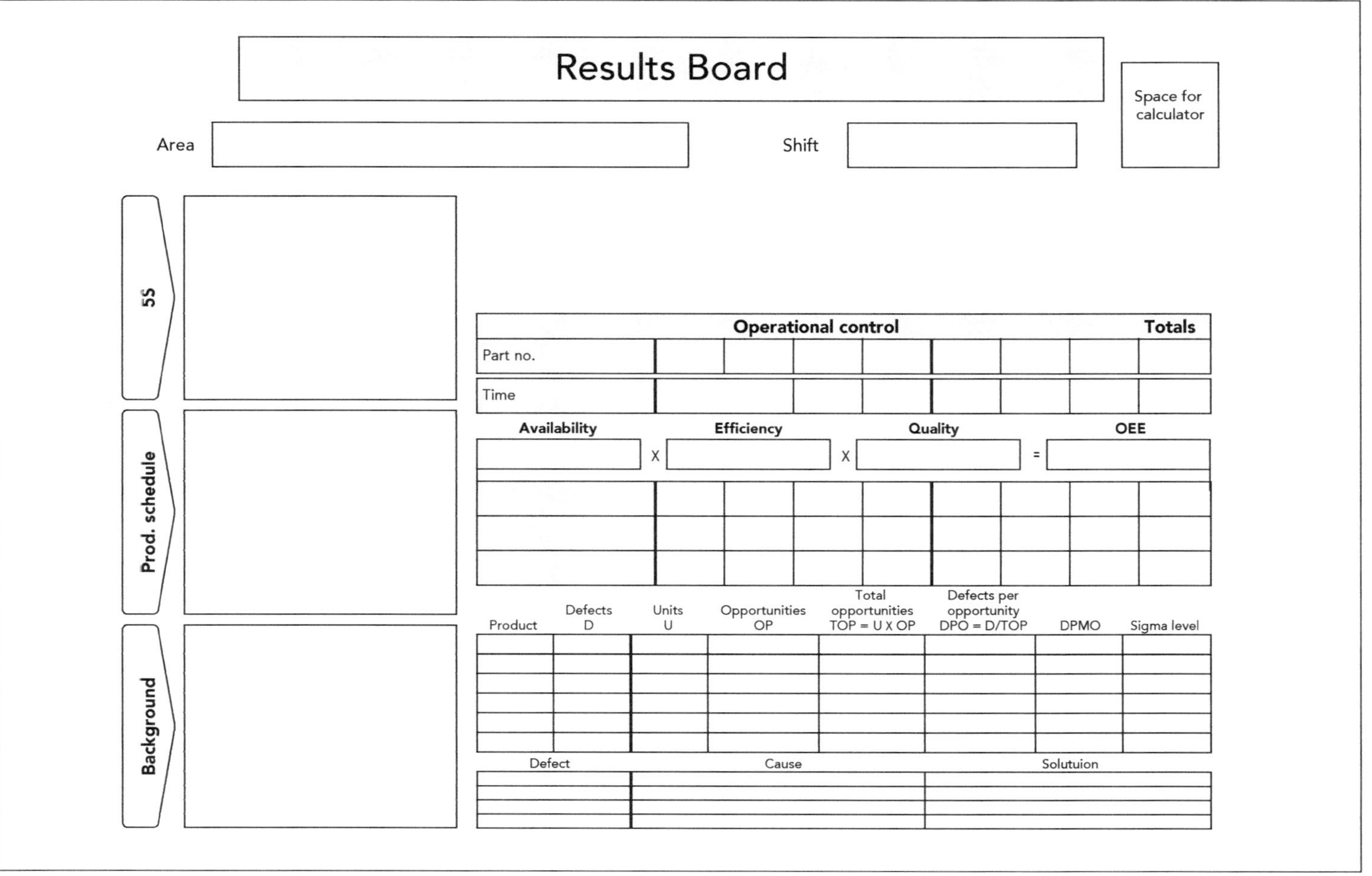

Figure 8.4

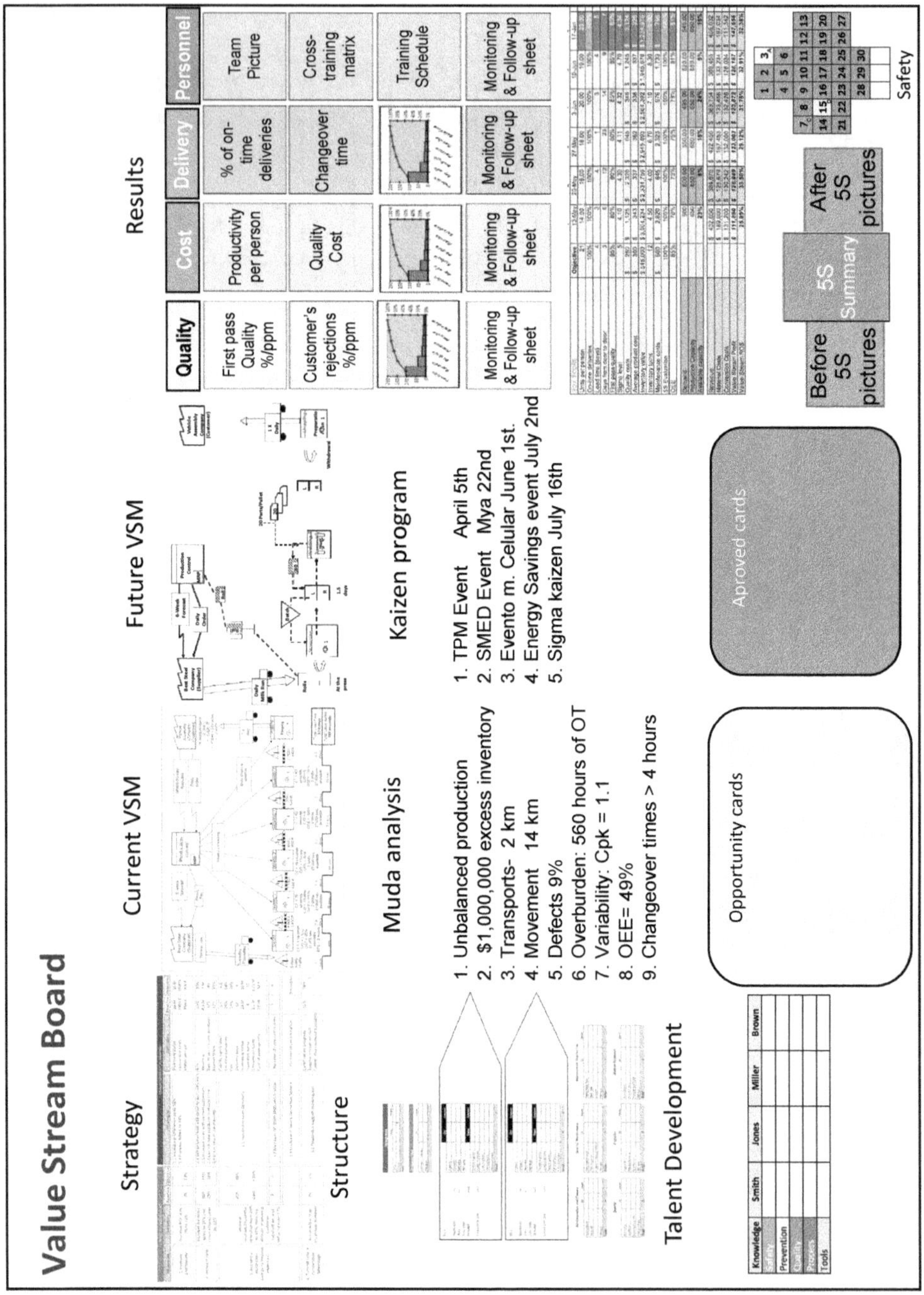
Value Stream Board
Strategy
Current VSM
Future VSM
Results
Quality
Cost
Delivery
Personnel
First pass Quality %/ppm
Productivity per person
% of on-time deliveries
Team Picture
Customer's rejections %/ppm
Quality Cost
Changeover time
Cross-training matrix
Training Schedule
Monitoring & Follow-up sheet
Monitorng & Follow-up sheet
Monitorng & Follow-up sheet
Monitong & Follow-up sheet
Structure
Muda analysis
1. Unbalanced production
2. $1,000,000 excess inventory
3. Transports- 2 km
4. Movement 14 km
5. Defects 9%
6. Overburden: 560 hours of OT
7. Variability: Cpk = 1.1
8. OEE= 49%
9. Changeover times > 4 hours
Kaizen program
1. TPM Event April 5th
2. SMED Event Mya 22nd
3. Evento m. Celular June 1st.
4. Energy Savings event July 2nd
5. Sigma kaizen July 16th
Talent Development
Knowledge
Smith
Jones
Miller
Brown
Safety
Prevention
Quality
Process
Tools
Opportunity cards
Aproved cards
Before 5S pictures
5S Summary
After 5S pictures
Safety

Figure 8.5

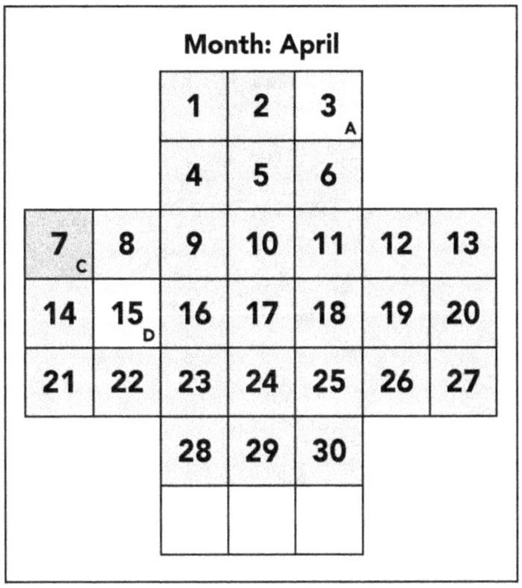

Month: April

		1	2	3 A		
		4	5	6		
7 C	8	9	10	11	12	13
14	15 D	16	17	18	19	20
21	22	23	24	25	26	27
		28	29	30		

Figure 8.6

Tools to improve team effectiveness

Total Production Maintenance

Background

Total productive maintenance (TPM) has its origins in the United States where many manufacturing companies used certain practices to prevent errors and thereby prevent untimely stoppages and emergency repairs. In the post-war period, while Japan was rebuilding its economy, several Japanese managers and engineers visited these plants to assimilate ideas and put them into practice in Japan.

It was in Nippondenso, a factory supplying auto parts for Toyota, where maintenance concepts were first applied, involving all the organization's employees (not just maintenance specialists). Emphasis was placed on the implementation of practices in which operators were responsible for the maintenance and care of their machines. Thanks to this, in 1971, the company won for the first time the award for the most distinguished plant, awarded by the Japanese Plant Maintenance Institute. That same year, Seiichi Nakajima published the implementation process for this system as well as the elements that compose it. Not many years later, in 1987, the historical circle was closed when the TPM (Total Productive Maintenance) system returned to its homeland, with Kodak being the first company to implement it.

Definition

Total productive maintenance is an improvement methodology that allows the continuity of the operation in machines and plants by introducing the concepts of:

- Prevention.
- Zero defects caused by machines.
- Zero accidents.
- Zero defects.
- Full participation of the people.

In manufacturing companies, machine maintenance is a problem if it is not adequate as it prevents continuity in production. In addition, it is one of the largest waste producers in products and operating expenses due to repairs. This is key if processes are heavily dependent on automation or if they are continuous processes.

What is TPM implemented for?

The following are some of the benefits of TPM:

- Quality improves as more precise machines produce parts with less variation and therefore of better quality.
- Productivity improves as machine availability increases. In this way, time will mainly be used in activities that generate value.
- It improves customer service and therefore their confidence since machines will be more reliable and available when needed.
- It gives continuity to plant operations.
- The use and maximization of machines is improved.
- It involves operators in the care and maintenance of their machines.
- It significantly reduces corrective maintenance costs (unscheduled breakdowns).
- It reduces the number of defects and rejected products that are generated by machines in poor condition.
- It reduces operating costs by up to 30%.

It is also known that, in general, the maintenance cost in a plant can represent between 10 and 40% of the operating cost, hence the importance of its correct implementation.

Total productive maintenance.

Moreover, it is very common that 50% of total maintenance expenditure is due to the bad operation of equipment and between 10 and 15% to bad lubrication. Then the importance is even greater since ignorance about the correct operation of the machines and the little care that is taken with them increases the probability of risks and expenses.

In summary, TPM will be a key instrument for implementing other tools since machines are a basic input in the processes.

The machines suffer natural wear due to normal use and forced wear due to carelessness. TPM eliminates forced wear and gives the operator the perpetual responsibility of taking care of their machine to keep it in optimal condition.

When is TPM used?

TPM is used when it is desired that plants, machines, and equipment of all types are in optimal condition, including facilities, materials transport, and handling equipment.

One of the situations in which TPM is most useful is when it is known that the personnel operating the machines and the personnel servicing them are not fully trained for doing so. Ignorance is one of the main causes of poor maintenance and bad operation which ultimately results in unreliability of operations and, consequently, of companies.

How long does it take to implement TPM?

The implementation of TPM in a manufacturing plant is perhaps one of the most complex projects and it takes considerable time, sometimes years, if all the machines are taken into account. This is because it is a plant-wide project and requires all personnel to have comprehensive knowledge of their equipment. Besides a company's operating staff is not used to accepting responsibility for maintenance and maintenance personnel are afraid of leaving them certain responsibilities for equipment, sometimes because they consider them incapable and other times for fear of being replaced in the future.

TPM must first be applied on one machine, which takes four to five days, and then it is implemented successively in well-organized events, following the procedure explained below.

An improvement event focused on implementing TPM on a specific machine or area is prepared one or two months in advance. Once this implementation event is completed, there should be follow-up by managers to ensure that the remaining activities are carried out.

The six pillars of total productive maintenance

For TPM to be implemented in a truly comprehensive manner, it must include the following pillars:

1. Focused improvements.
2. Autonomous maintenance.
3. Planned maintenance.
4. Quality maintenance.
5. Training.
6. Safety.

The six big equipment losses

The six constraints on equipment that will ultimately affect the company's results are:

1. Downtime from unexpected stoppages.
2. Downtime due to product changeovers.
3. Minor stoppages.
4. Speed reductions.
5. Defects in the process.
6. Defects due to start-up and product changeover.

How to combat the six big equipment losses

Figure 9.1 shows how to combat equipment losses.

Figure 9.1

Some important metrics
Overall equipment effectiveness

Overall equipment effectiveness (OEE) is an essential measurement for discovering the real ability to produce without defects. To measure OEE, you need to obtain the necessary information every day, process it, and make the following calculations.

Formulas

Total time = available time + scheduled time (lunch, meetings, etc.).
Available time = total time - scheduled time.
Operating time = total time -scheduled time - downtime.
Downtime = breakdown time + product changeover time.
Availability = (available time − downtime) ÷ available time.
Efficiency = total production ÷ (operating time × capacity).
Quality = (total production − defects and repetition of tasks) ÷ total production.
OEE = availability × efficiency × quality.

Other metrics

Mean time between failures

Mean time between failures (MTBF) is an indicator obtained by adding up all the failure times and dividing the result by the number of failures observed. This number indicates the approximate time a machine runs without errors.

Mean time through repair

Mean time through repair (MTTR) is an indicator obtained by adding up all the repair times and dividing the result by the number of repairs observed. This number indicates the estimated time a machine will be idle while it is being repaired.

Procedure for carrying out total productive maintenance

Before conducting the Kaizen event

- Define the machine or equipment on which the TPM Kaizen event will be carried out.
- Create the implementation team.
- Train staff on TPM matters.

Overall Equipment Effectiveness

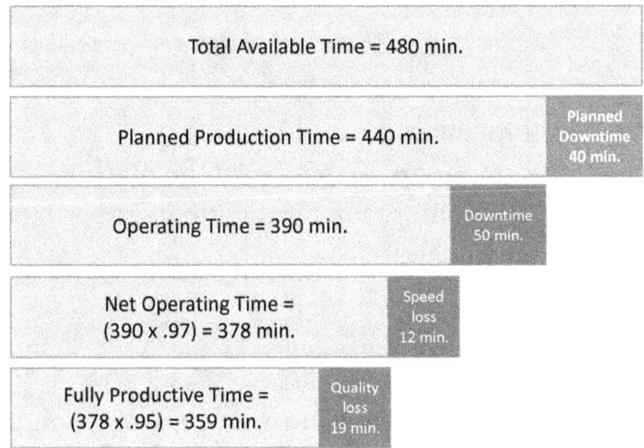

Goal	73 units				Date: 01/01/20	
Capacity	10 units per hour					
Hours	**Goal**	**Actual**	**Accumulated**	**Downtime (minutes)**	**Type**	**Defects**
8 to 9	10	10	10			
9 to 10	8	7	17	10	Break	
10 to 11	10	10	27			
11 to 12	10	5	32	20	Setups	
12 to 1	5	4	36	30	Lunch	
1 to 2	10	11	47			
2 to 3	10	2	49	30	Breakdown	3
3 to 4	10	11	60			
Total	73	60		90		3

$$\text{Availability} = \frac{\text{Operating Time}}{\text{Planned Prod. Time}} = 390 \text{ min} / 440 \text{ min} = 89\%$$

$$\text{Efficiency} = \frac{\text{Units Produced}}{\text{Operating time x Capacity}} = \frac{63 \text{ units}}{(390 \text{ min}/60 \text{ min}) \text{ x } 10 \text{ units}} = 97\%$$

$$\text{Quality} = \frac{\text{Good units on the first pass}}{\text{Total units produced}} = \frac{60 \text{ units}}{63 \text{ units}} = 95\%$$

$$\text{OEE} = \text{Availability X Efficiency X Quality}$$

$$\text{OEE} = .89 \text{ x } .97 \text{ x } .95 = 82\%$$

Figure 9.2

- Create plans and policies for implementation.
- Prepare documents (opportunity cards, records, instructions, manuals, etc.).

During the Kaizen event (four to eight days)
- Thoroughly clean the machine and its area.
- Implement autonomous maintenance on the machine.
- Establish a preventive and predictive maintenance program.
- Establish a reliability analysis.
- Make a presentation of the achievements made.

Thoroughly clean the machine and its area

In this initial step, we first explain to all team members the general procedure for applying TPM and its benefits. After that, the equipment and the selected area are thoroughly cleaned, using cloths or rags with degreasing agent.

While the thorough cleaning is carried out, the team leader explains to the members that everyone should participate by not just cleaning but by using the cleaning to detect opportunities, such as unsafe conditions, lack of lubricant in the machines, damaged components, loose or broken parts, etc.

When cleaning, team members will likely encounter weak or loose components, misaligned engines, lack of lubricants, air leaks, missing components,

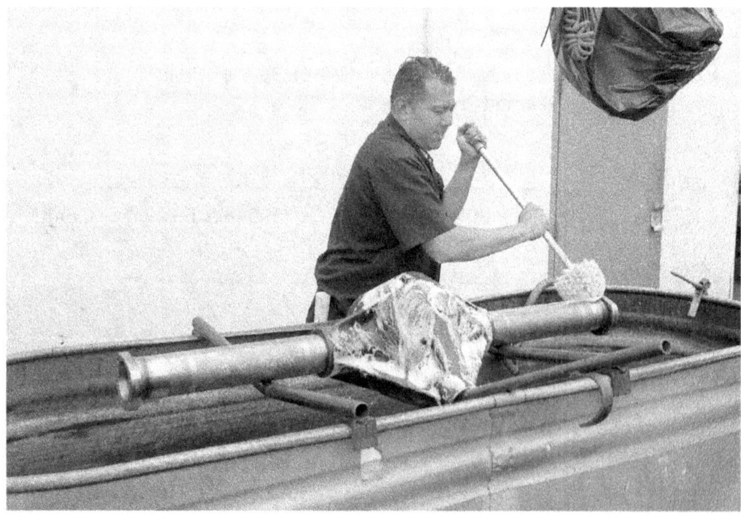

Super-cleaning event.

safety risks, etc. Whenever an improvement opportunity is found, it should be recorded on an opportunity card and the stub should be put in the place of the opportunity so that it is in plain sight.

Each opportunity should be classified as A, B, or C. A opportunities should be done while the event is being held, i.e., no more than one week; B opportunities should be done within two weeks maximum and C opportunities should be done within two months maximum. This classification is assigned to give a formality to the execution times.

Implement autonomous maintenance on the machine

For this step it is important to have the 5S implemented in the area since good housekeeping is the basis of autonomous maintenance (see Chapter 7).

During the afternoon of the first day and the second day, the autonomous maintenance program begins, which represents the heart of total productive maintenance as the operators will now have permanent responsibility for knowing their equipment, taking care of it, and detecting errors before they occur.

To implement autonomous maintenance, the team must gather relevant information from both machine manuals and the experience and knowledge of operators, engineers, technicians, etc. in order to set a daily schedule that considers the following activities:

- Lubrication.
- Equipment cleaning.
- Check levels, parameters, etc.
- Minor adjustments.

Then a record is prepared which should be filled in and signed daily by the operator when he carries out these activities.

This record must be on the machines or nearby so that the operator can see it and record the activities, writing his payroll number for each activity in the corresponding table and the day of the month in which they are executed. This way we will know who carried out the activity and the supervisor or leader can evaluate it and confirm that each day the corresponding activity has been carried out.

Furthermore, it is very important to create instructions so that the activities are carried out without any doubt and always following the right steps.

These instructions will be of great help for the operator to understand the detail of the autonomous maintenance record.

Autonomous Maintenance Daily Log

Month

Machine

		1	2	3	4	5	6	7	8	9	10	11	12	13	14	15	16	17	18	19	20	21	22	23	24	25	26	27	28	29	30	31
Before the shift starts																																
1	Check lubricant level on work table guides																																
2	Check oil level for cutting																																
3	Check hydraulic oil level																																
4	Check hydraulic pump pressure																																
During the shift																																	
5	Verify that burrs don't get stuck to the fan																																
6	Identify unusual sounds																																
7	Check safety switches																																
8	Clean the floor and coolant lines																																
9	Keep the work area clean																																
At the end of the shift																																	
10	Lubricate daily points																																
11	Clean the machine and work area																																
12	Clean accumulation of burrs																																

Supervised by:

Comments:

Table 9.1

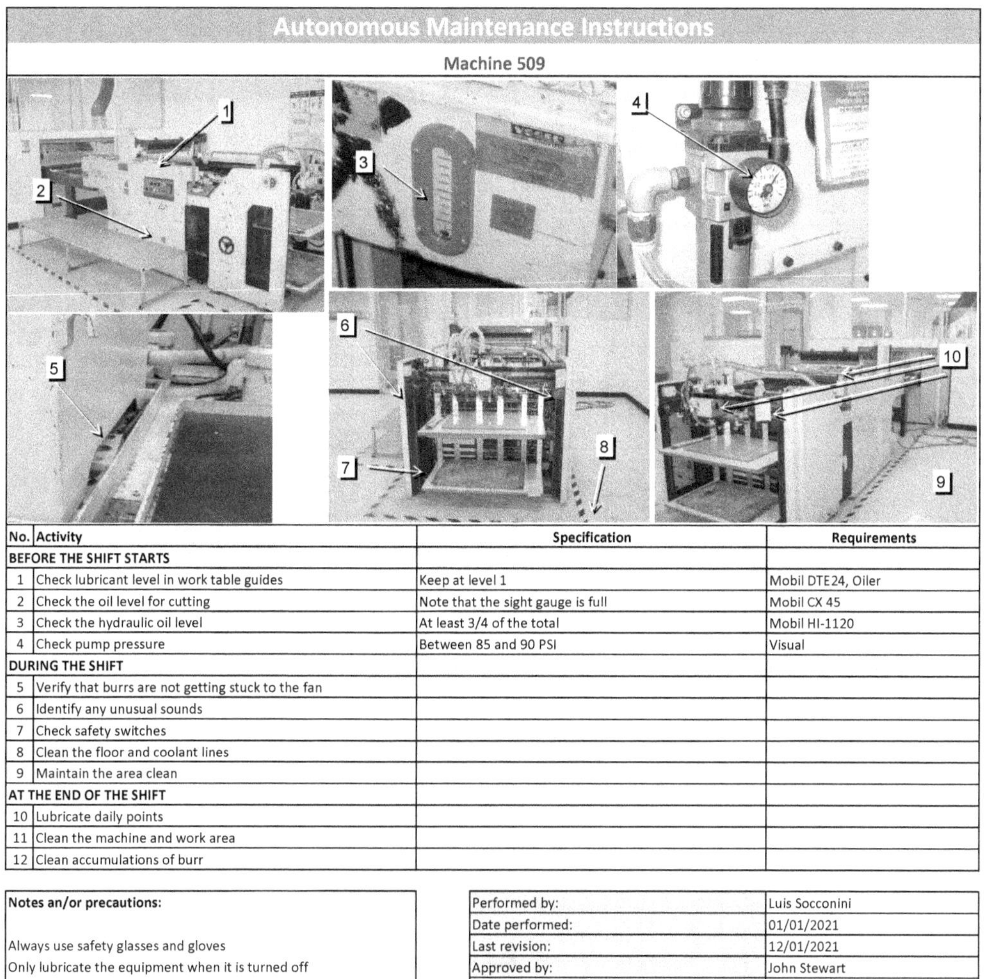

No.	Activity	Specification	Requirements
	BEFORE THE SHIFT STARTS		
1	Check lubricant level in work table guides	Keep at level 1	Mobil DTE 24, Oiler
2	Check the oil level for cutting	Note that the sight gauge is full	Mobil CX 45
3	Check the hydraulic oil level	At least 3/4 of the total	Mobil HI-1120
4	Check pump pressure	Between 85 and 90 PSI	Visual
	DURING THE SHIFT		
5	Verify that burrs are not getting stuck to the fan		
6	Identify any unusual sounds		
7	Check safety switches		
8	Clean the floor and coolant lines		
9	Maintain the area clean		
	AT THE END OF THE SHIFT		
10	Lubricate daily points		
11	Clean the machine and work area		
12	Clean accumulations of burr		

Notes an/or precautions:		
Always use safety glasses and gloves		
Only lubricate the equipment when it is turned off		

Performed by:	Luis Socconini
Date performed:	01/01/2021
Last revision:	12/01/2021
Approved by:	John Stewart
Version:	2

Table 9.2

Set a schedule for preventive and predictive maintenance

To ensure the elimination of forced wear, the schedule for preventive and predictive activities will be key in the application of total productive maintenance.

During the third day of the event the team must carry out a plan of periodic activities based on the documentation of manuals, manufacturer's recommendations, the experience of mechanics and experts as well as the operators' inputs. Once the maintenance frequency has been established, the team should also consider which spare parts should be available in the storeroom.

Preventive and Predictive Maintenance Plan Month

Machine:		1	2	3	4	5	6	7	8	9	10	11	12	13	14	15	16	17	18	19	20	21	22	23	24	25	26	27	28	29	30	31
WEEKLY																																
1	Lubricate maintenance unit filters					X							X							X							X					
2	Grease cylinder vacuum					X							X							X							X					
3	Grease sliding base frame					X							X							X							X					
MONTHLY																																
4	Verify that burrs don't get stuck to the fan													X																		
5	Identify unusual sounds													X																		
6	Check safety switches														X																	
7	Clean the floor and coolant lines														X																	
8	Keep the work area clean														X																	
BI-ANNUALLY																																
9	Check bearings		X																													
10	Change oil																															
ANNUALLY																																
11	Check connections									X																						
12	Retightening of bolts																															
13	Change filters																															
14	Deep cleaning of the machine																															

Supervised by:

Comments:

Table 9.3

To carry out the maintenance plan it is necessary to have sufficient and trained staff to perform these preventive routines (preferably, they should have knowledge of mechanics, electricity, and electronics). This pillar will be applied with the coordination of production planning to carry it out in a disciplined manner and devote the time necessary for its execution.

Establish a reliability analysis

To establish a reliability analysis of the equipment, a Failure Mode and Effects Analysis (FMEA) must be performed, which is explained in detail in chapter 12.

The reliability analysis is a document that identifies all the key components in the equipment and establishes the errors that can occur and cause breakdowns, quality problems, and accidents that affect the operators and users of the process.

This document must be started during the event and is a living document, its development never ends. Errors, their causes, and how to detect them are continually being added. The reliability analysis helps improve the quality with which equipment works, thus giving companies greater confidence to deliver on time, reduce costs, and anticipate any errors or problems.

Make a presentation of the achievements made

When progress is being made during the event, opportunities are recorded along with photographs of the findings and the activities performed as well as the documentation that is being generated. On the last day of the event, a presentation is prepared so that management or plant management may observe the results of the event. This presentation is divided into three parts:

1. Current situation: how the area was, conditions, opportunities, etc.
2. What was done: the actions performed during the event are described.
3. What was achieved: achievements (activities, plans, training, etc.) are displayed.

This presentation should involve all team members and management should devote a few minutes to give the event the importance it deserves.

Follow-up activities after the Kaizen event

1. Follow up on activities 2 and 3 (medium and long term).
2. Ensure correct application with operators and supervisors.

3. Make follow-up visits.
4. Make one-point lessons of no more than 10 minutes to explain the actions imple-mented.

Considerations on the implementation of total productive maintenance

- 5S is an essential tool to facilitate productive maintenance activities.
- It is very important to document work instructions.
- Training for operators and maintenance personnel is essential for the success of TPM.
- Management commitment to implementation and follow-up is a key element for the success of TPM.
- TPM is applicable to all equipment, including computers, vehicles, real estate, etc.

Part V

Tools to improve delivery time and capacity

Chapter 10

Cellular manufacturing

Background

In 1776, Scottish economist and philosopher Adam Smith demonstrated that the division of labor into specific tasks resulted in an increase in productivity and that if each person did their job well, the result would be a common good. This concept was supported by Frederick Taylor, father of the scientific management. He discovered that the work of specialists dedicated to repetitive tasks would result in a more productive flow.

With the application of Henry Ford's concept of production lines, the idea of specializing the work and carrying it out by means of huge assembly lines was given greater impetus.

Currently the demand and volume conditions have changed from large batches of the same product to small batches with great variety, making it impossible to continue working in the same way. Therefore, since its first applications in Toyota by Shigeo Shingo, Lean Manufacturing proposes continuous flow work.

The cellular concept proposes the elimination of large batches that must be manufactured in each department in order to prevent production from stopping in any of these areas. Now we will seek to introduce a continuous flow from the first to the last operation.

In a new perspective, we will not only seek our own good but also the common good, thereby achieving amazing results.

Cellular manufacturing.

Definition

Cellular manufacturing is a manufacturing concept in which plant distribution is significantly improved making production flow uninterrupted between each operation, drastically reducing response time, maximizing staff skills, and making each employee perform multiple operations.

Cellular manufacturing consists of grouping machines and sequential operations in which a complete product can be manufactured from start to finish, avoiding the use of transport as much as possible. Cellular manufacturing eliminates inventories in process and makes production flow continuous. In traditional companies, processes are separated or departmentalized which means that materials must be stored, moved, transferred, and handled in many areas before they are finished.

What is cellular manufacturing implemented for?

The following are some of the benefits of applying manufacturing cells:

- It gives continuity to plant operations.
- It eliminates inventories in process that have an economic cost and generate defects by manipulation.

- It creates flexible processes by producing multiple products in a single area.
- Companies' flexibility and efficiency increases.
- Operators can be more efficient since the same can be produced with fewer people.
- Operators engage in more tasks related to the product, sometimes a single worker makes a complete article, thus increasing their sense of belonging to that product.
- It directly connects operations to avoid transport, delays, material movements, inventories in process and overproduction.

When is cellular manufacturing used?

Cellular manufacturing is used when we need to shorten the response times of a process or delivery to the customer through greater variety and low volumes. Additionally, it is used when market demand becomes very volatile, and the range of products demanded is larger than before.

How long does it take to implement cellular manufacturing?

The design of new processes takes one to two months since not all the necessary information (such as the work standards already explained) is always available to support the project.

If it is a question of redesigning existing processes, it can take one to two weeks, as it is easy to collect the necessary information and the elements are there to do it in a short time. However, in some companies, this time may be longer because changing the location of workstations may require special foundations or installations.

Procedure for implementing cellular manufacturing

Before carrying out the Kaizen event (one to two months per team)

- Determine the objective, scope, and documentation of the project (project format).
- Draw the current plan of the production system.
- Form the team (including operators).
- Provide training on Lean Manufacturing and specifically on cellular manufacturing.

During the Kaizen event (four to eight days)
- Create a spaghetti diagram.
- Draw the current state value map.
- Perform a *mudas* analysis and detect opportunities.
- Determine the takt time and number of operators.
- Draw the future state value map.
- Draw the design of the new cell.
- Implement the cell in the process.

Create a spaghetti diagram

The spaghetti diagram (see figure 10.1) marks the path of materials through all stages of production and is used to understand the flow of production from the material warehouse to the finished product warehouse, including the process.

Draw the current state value map.

The value map is a graph in which we represent all the activities in the process, both those that add value and those that only add cost and time. It also allows us to see the flow of information from the order entry to delivery.

In this value map we observe that given the conditions of the current system, the delivery time is 14.4 days, and the value-added time is only 337 seconds, indicating that the material spends a lot of the time waiting and in inventory in process (see figure 10.2).

The current state value map will help us understand the current flow and detect opportunities to create a continuous flow.

Perform a mudas analysis and detect opportunities

This analysis uses the waste identification sheets contained in the "2 Analysis Mudas.xls" file.

To perform the opportunity analysis, it is advisable for the team implementing the continuous flow cell to analyze all the opportunities for improvement that exist in the area, where *mudas, muras,* and *muris* may be discovered.

Determine the takt time and number of operators

Takt time

As we saw in Chapter 5, takt time is the speed at which the customer buys and is the time the production system must adapt to meet the customer's expectations.

Formula: takt time = available time ÷ demand.

Spaghetti Diagram
Spot Welding II
Storage
Assembly I
Spot Welding I
Storage
Storage
Assembly II
Shipping
Stamping Storage
Finished Product Storage
Stamping
Steel Coils Warehouse
Receiving
movement of People
movement of Materials

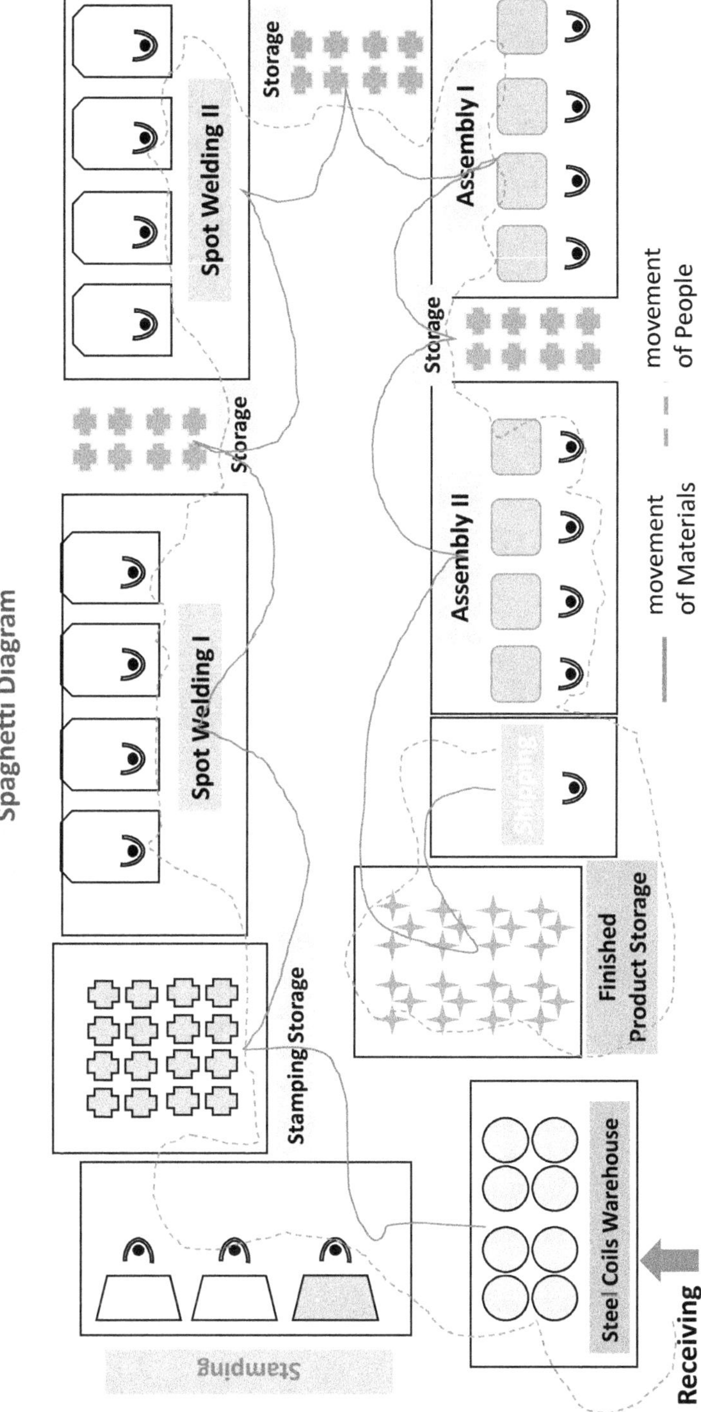

Figure 10.1

CUSTOMER
Demand
8-week forecast
Daily Orders
Production Control
MRP
Shipping Plan
Weekly Program
4-week forecast
Weekly Orders
SUPPLIER
CUTTING
CT = 22 sec
COT = 25 min
OEE = 80%
Avail. time = 27,000 sec
PAINTING
CT = 45 sec
COT = 5 min
OEE = 95%
Avail. time = 27,000 sec
DRILLING
CT = 19 sec
COT = 0 min
OEE = 95%
Avail. time = 27,000 sec
ELEC. ASSEMBLY
CT = 63 sec
COT = 0 min
OEE = 100%
Avail. time = 27,000 sec
SOFTWARE
CT = 22 sec
COT = 0 min
OEE = 98%
Avail. time = 27,030 sec
M. C. ASSEMBLY
CT = 32 sec
COT = 0 min
OEE = 100%
Avail. time = 27,000 sec
FINAL ASSEMBLY
CT = 134 sec
COT = 0 min
OEE = 100%
Avail. time = 27,000 sec
PACK. & SHIP.
CT = 49 sec
COT = 0 min
OEE = 100%
712
450
632
310
110
217
1.456
3
2,1
22
1,3
45
1,9
19
0,9
63
0,3
22
0,6
32
4,3
134
49
14,4 DAYS
386 SEC

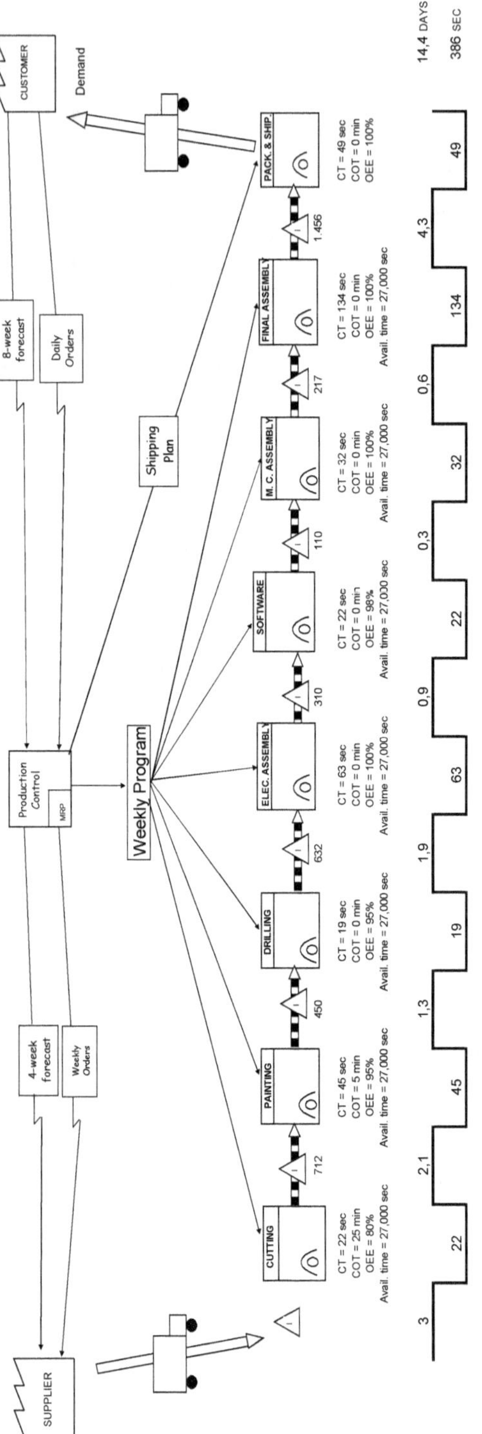

Figure 10.2

Document Waste

Form of Waste	Notes	Opportunity	Proposed Actions
Overproduction			
Excess inventory			
Defects or rework			
Unnecessary movement			
Overprocessing			
Waiting and Searching			
Transport			
Talent without action			
Waste of energy			
Pollution / Contamination			

Table 10.1

Example

$$\text{Time available per day} = 8 \text{ hours} - 30 \text{ minutes for food}$$
$$\text{and rest} = 450 \text{ minutes}$$

$$450 \ \frac{\text{min.}}{\text{shift}} \times 1 \ \frac{\text{shift}}{\text{day}} \times 60 \ \frac{\text{seconds}}{\text{min.}} = 27{,}000 \text{ seconds.}$$

Monthly demand = 7,510 pieces.
Daily demand = 7,510 pieces ÷ 22 working days =
341 pieces per day.

Takt time = 27,000 sec. ÷ 341 pieces = 79 sec./piece.

This means that the customer is willing to buy one piece every 79 seconds.

Number of operators required

To determine the number of operators required, we divide the total cycle time, which in this case is 386 seconds, by the *takt* time, which is 79 seconds, giving a total of 4.88 operators. This means that by occupying all the time of each person and combining the work of various operations, five people could, without any delay or interference, meet the time required to produce each piece in 79 seconds.

It can be seen in figure 10.3 that each operator has a value-added time of 77.2 seconds, i.e., a time very close to the *takt* time. For this to be possible, we must get rid of any waste that distracts operators from performing activities that only add value. This may seem idealistic, but it should be the starting point for a detailed analysis of operations to achieve higher productivity.

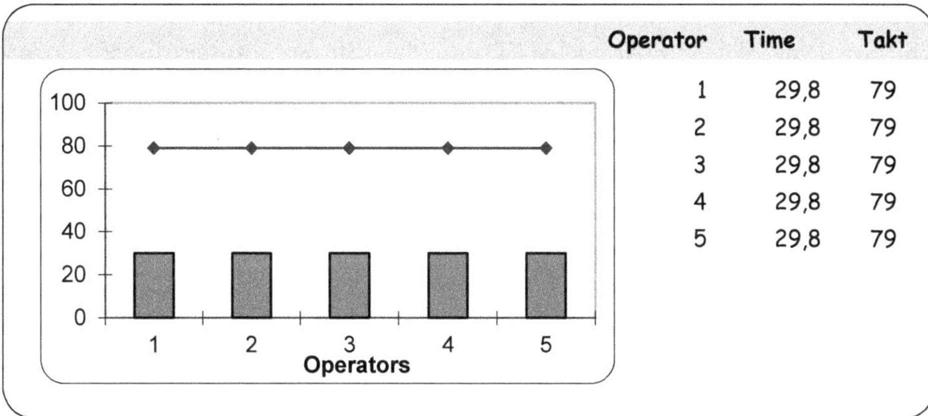

Operator	Time	Takt
1	29,8	79
2	29,8	79
3	29,8	79
4	29,8	79
5	29,8	79

Figure 10.3

Balance in operations

As can be seen, each worker was assigned more than one operation to compensate for the times. However, in order to work under the *takt* time, process improvements must be made to reduce the times of operators B and E. It should be mentioned that this first design is somewhat ideal so the nature of the operations must be considered in deciding on the feasibility of combining them.

Operator	Time	Operations
1	22	A + B
2	45	C + D
3	42	E + F + Part of G
4	77	Part of G
5	0	Part of G + H

Draw the future state value map
In this case we will take the future map that was made in Chapter 5 (see figure 5.4).

Develop continuous flow
Continuous flow can be created by joining the following operations: cutting + paint booth + drilling + electronic assembly + software loading + control module assembly + final assembly + packaging. This represents a total paradigm shift because process elements will no longer be managed, instead it becomes a production system. We should simply ask ourselves if something prevents us from placing one operation immediately after the next.

This is represented by the symbol corresponding to a work cell.

In this cell, the continuous flow is established by bringing together all operations consecutively.

Draw the design of the new cell.
Now we must draw the installations with the proposed alternatives (it is advisable to work with paper and draw the machines at the same scale to move them freely on the paper and see the flow scheme, distances, conveniences, and inconveniences of the new layout).

To accommodate the equipment and tables in the cell it's advisable to first draw the internal corridor and place the first and last operations at the beginning to begin to form the horseshoe; immediately afterwards place the second and the second to last operations, and so on until closing the U.

In this case, by accommodating one machine or station immediately after another continuous flow is achieved but, above all, we get better communication between operators, as everyone is close and can receive immediate feedback.

At this point the following should be done:

- Plan how the materials will be moved.
- Establish the quantities of material needed in the process.
- Analyze the ergonomics and safety conditions in the area.

Ergonomics is a key element for the optimal development of a work cell since a site that is poorly lit, uncomfortable, inflexible, etc. has negative effect on the

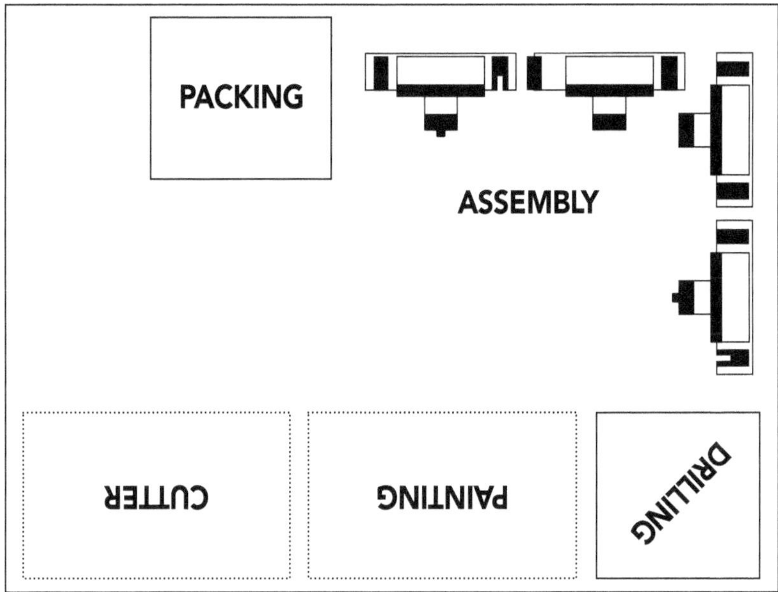

Figure 10.5

productivity of the entire system. Therefore, we must consider the following aspects for each workstation:

- Height.
- Space layout.
- Positioning of materials.
- Work above the heart.
- Fields of vision.
- Lighting.
- Position Settings.

Follow-up activities after the Kaizen event

a. Follow up on activities b and c (medium and long term).
b. Prepare service installations before moving equipment.
c. Make the team aware of the new work rules.
d. Train staff continuously in Lean tools.
e. Hold a meeting at the start of each shift to see the previous day's goals and achievements.

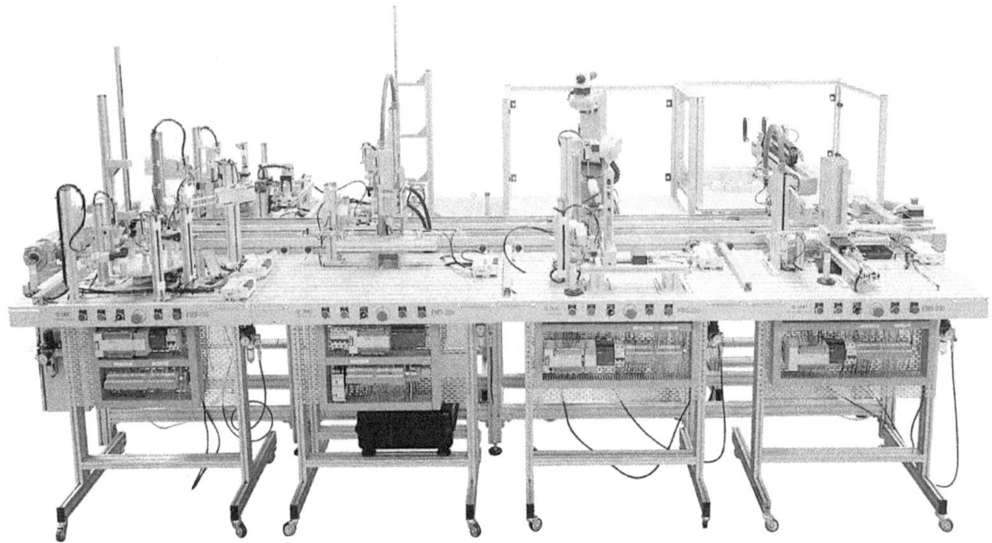

f. Create production tracking boards (see Chapter 8).

g. Choose a cell leader who not only operates but also keeps his workmates alert and supportive.

h. Evaluate opportunities constantly, especially at the beginning.

i. Establish an incentive system that rewards teamwork and individual work.

Useful tools and concepts for the application

1. 5S is an essential tool for facilitating manufacturing cell implementation activities.

2. Consider implementing TPM before implementing manufacturing cells. This will make the calculations more realistic and the equipment more reliable for working in a cellular environment.

3. Certify operators in multiple operations and perform a training matrix in which operators can operate, maintain, and analyze quality in each workplace.

4. Ensure the supply of materials at all stations by using the Kanban system (which will be explained later) or other methods so that production is never stopped for lack of materials.

5. Develop visual controls so workers understand their operations thoroughly using visible boards and instructions in their workplace.

6. Apply Andon or visual control (lights, sounds, or other means) to communicate that material, maintenance, assistance, etc., is needed. This way, the support team will learn about the anomalies without the operator leaving the workplace and the cell will remain productive.
7. Establish hourly job progress measurements where operators record the production they have done so far and compare it to the production they should have done.
8. If possible, set up single piece work (batch size one). This is achieved by balancing the production cell and having operators move materials directly from operation to operation as the process progresses.
9. Consider applying SMED (quick changeovers) to ensure that the cell works to its maximum potential and support "batch size" one production explained in point 8.

Chapter 11

Quick product changeovers

Brief History

Engineer Taiichi Ohno, Toyota's head of production, looked to the U.S. auto industry to understand how they were able to use many presses to make different models without having to change molds, because in some cases the changeover took more than 24 hours. In Toyota they had a limited number of presses, and the challenge was to manufacture a wide range of vehicles with a much smaller number of machines. For this they hired engineer Shigeo Shingo as a consultant and by 1970 he was already making changeovers in 1,000-ton presses in just three minutes.

Definition

Single minute exchange of die (SMED) means changing tools in single digit minutes, i.e., in less than ten minutes.

Changeover time is the time that elapses from the last good piece of a previous batch to the first good piece of the next batch after the changeover. Imagine a racing car at a *pit stop,* the changes must be done quickly to get the car back on track as fast as possible. The same goes for companies that are looking to make their processes faster by maximizing activities that add value and by minimizing changeover times that do not add value.

When is SMED used?

SMED is used when we need to reduce cycle times by making the most of the time available for production and using less time for tool changeovers.

The following are some of the benefits of SMED:

- It makes it possible to manufacture a wide variety of products.
- Production capacity increases.
- It enables the production of a wider variety of products.
- Material losses are reduced.
- The number of changeovers increases.
- Batch size is reduced.
- It decreases inventory levels.
- Delivery time is reduced.
- It increases flexibility to respond to customer demands.
- Customer response time improves.
- It minimizes the time lost during changeovers.

How long does it take to implement SMED?

When performed at a Kaizen event it may take between three and five days, plus one or two months to follow up the activities.

Procedure for implementing SMED

Before the Kaizen event (one to two months)

- Make a value stream map and use it to determine if the machine is a bottleneck. Determine the impact of running a Kaizen event, as machines that have long changeover times are not always the ones that have the best opportunities to improve, especially if they are not bottlenecks.
- Determine the equipment or machine to focus on, given the opportunity found to improve changeover time. This is important as it will allow us to get big improvements on that machine or equipment.
- Establish a multidisciplinary team of people from various areas, such as production operators, quality, maintenance, etc.
- Review the production schedule to set a start date for the Kaizen event.
- Set an agenda for the event and distribute it among all team members.
- Get a video camera.
- Make an introduction to the subject of quick changeovers for the staff who make up the Kaizen team.

During the Kaizen event

During the Kaizen event, the following steps are taken to improve changeover times:

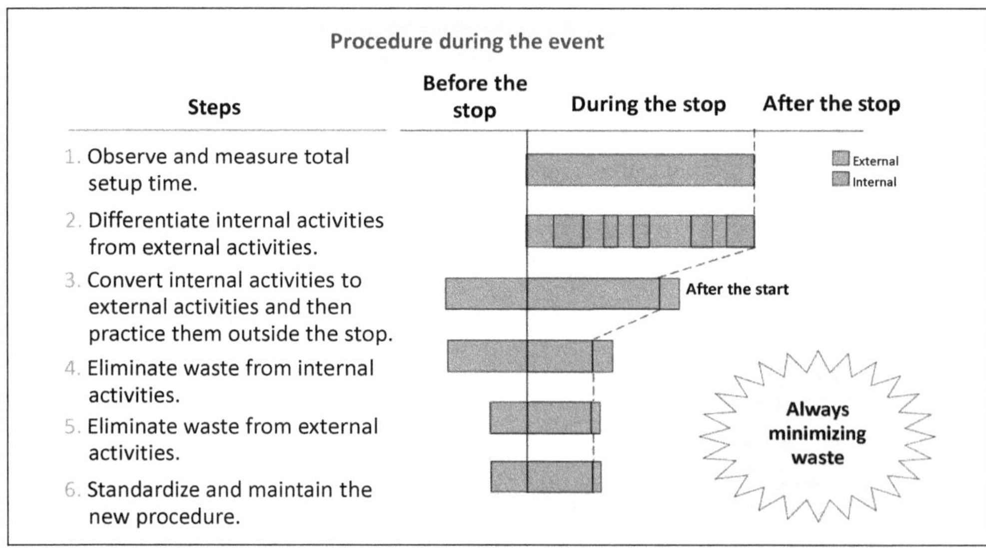

Figure 11.1

1. Observe and measure the total changeover time.
2. Separate internal and external activities.
3. Convert internal activities into external ones and move external activities away from the stoppage.
4. Eliminate waste from internal activities.
5. Eliminate waste from external activities.
6. Standardize and maintain the new procedure.

1. Observe and measure the total changeover time.

In this stage the Kaizen team will observe a change in detail. One of the team members will videotape the entire sequence, including movements of people and hand movements of the staff doing the product changeover. The rest of the team will look for opportunities for improvement.

It is very important that the changeover time be recorded by starting the stopwatch when the last good product from the previous batch comes out and stopping it when the first good product from the next batch comes out.

Guide for the video

- Clearly identify all those involved in the changeover.
- Respect the wishes of those who do not want to be filmed.
- Record a panoramic view of the entire process.
- Film hand movements, gathering of tools, and interactions with other processes.
- Get close enough to capture manual activities.
- If possible, apply the function "see date and time".
- Use voice recorder to get details.
- Edit the video with those involved as soon as possible.
- Schedule meetings to go through the video.

2. Separate internal and external activities.

When the team meets to analyze the video, the meeting will start by going through each activity and writing it down in table 11.1, "SMED analysis for reduction of changeover times".

External activities are classified as any activity that can be performed before or after stoppage. When the machine needs to be stopped to carry out activities, these are classified as internal.

SMED Analysis for Changeover Time Reduction
The change is started once the machine is stopped

Area:

Date:
Kaizen:

No.	Changeover activity	Operators					Accumulated time	Time	Potential	Classification activity		Waste	Comments
		1	2	3	4	5				Internal	External		
1													
2													
3													
4													
5													
6													
7													
8													
9													
10													
11													
12													
13													
14													
15													
16													
17													
18													
19													
20													
21													
22													

Total time:	
Total Waste:	

Comments:

Team:

Leader:

Table 11.1

3. Convert internal activities into external ones and move external activities away from the stoppage

This step will analyze which of the activities carried out during the stoppage can be simplified or improved. For this, the following guide is presented.

Common activities in a changeover

- Have at hand the tools necessary for the changeover.
- Communicate the need for change.
- The operator must communicate with the supervisor.
- Do inspections and paperwork for change.
- Contact the changeover staff when production stops and wait for them to arrive.

Suggested activities for this step

- Keep tools close or in a die cart.
- Implement an *Andon* system to communicate that a change will be made.
- Standardize roles in operations for each team member.
- Wait until the activity is running to start the paperwork.
- Carry out a changeover plan, contact the changeover staff before production stops and train operators to make their own changeovers.

4. Eliminate waste from internal activities

- Use quick-action tools to reduce the changeover of parts.
- Reduce the need to go to each end of the machine by working as a team.
- Design standard parts to eliminate part changeovers.
- Relocate parts and materials to reduce activities such as walking or searching.

Traditional methods in this step

- Use of pulley wheels and nuts.
- Use of hand tools (wrenches, screwdriver, etc.).
- Use of long screws.
- Manual centering.
- Manual setting of front-back positioning.
- Manual settings.
- Manual temperature and speed settings (using trial and error).
- Manual button reset on automated equipment.

Proposed methods for this step

- Use fewer nuts and bolts.
- Use pneumatic tools.
- Use one-touch fasteners.
- Use pins and guides for centering.
- Use stops to secure position.
- Use measuring strips to measure positioning.
- Set temperature and speed to a default standard.
- Move controls close to operators for instant resetting.

It's very important to document the path during the changeover to determine the effect of the proposals. For this, it's recommended to create a spaghetti diagram (see figure 11.2).

5. Eliminate waste from external activities

- Reduce paperwork to eliminate waste from outside activities.
- Relocate storage to reduce transfer time and movements.
- Use checklists to improve efficiency and accuracy.

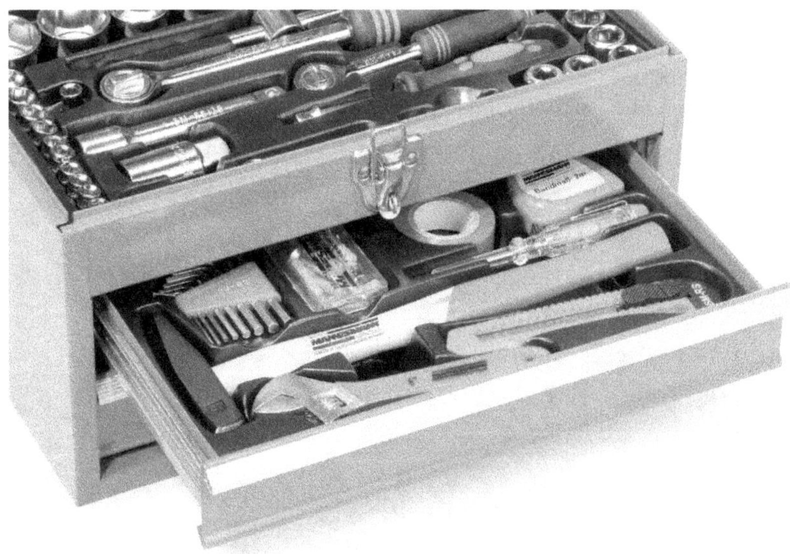

Eliminate waste from external activities.

ENTRY (blocked)
Cloth without shelf
Shelf
Shelf
Shelf
PASILLO
Shelf
Shelf
Cloth
Raw material warehouse
ENTRY
Loading and unloading area
Ramp
DRILLING
PAINTING
CUTTER
ASSEMBLY
PACKING
DRILLING
PAINTING
CUTTER
ASSEMBLY
PACKING
DRILLING
PAINTING
CUTTER
ASSEMBLY
PACKING
Shelf
Shelf
ENTRY
ASSEMBLY
LEAN SHOP
FUTURE LAYOUT

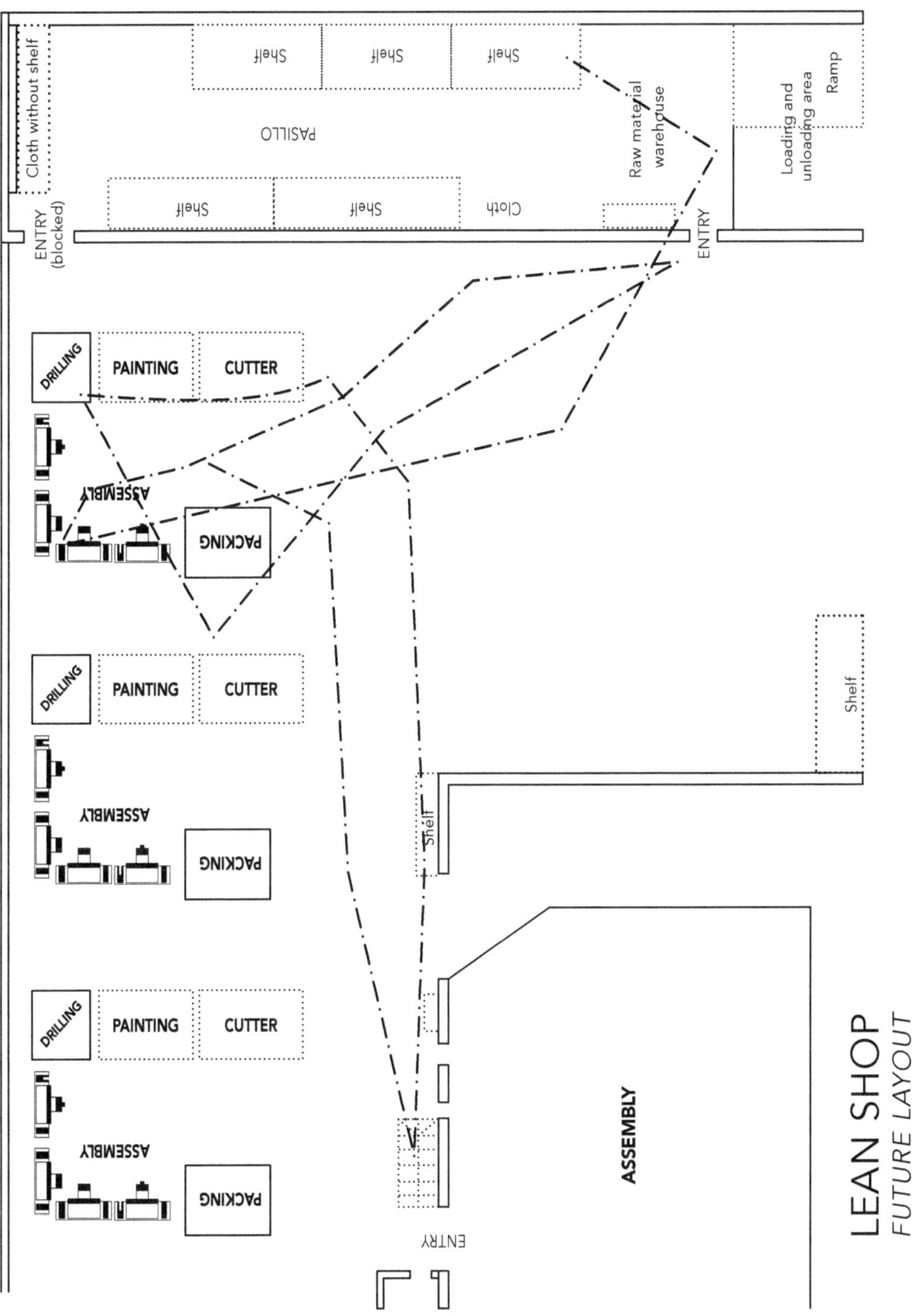

Figure 11.2

Current situation

- Tools are stored in a central storage area.
- Materials needed to make a changeover are fetched.
- Activities are done without coordination before the changeover takes place.

Suggested situation

- Store tools in a local area near the equipment on which they are to be used, placed in the order they will be used.
- Ensure adequate materials are provided in all areas of the plant.
- Use a checklist for standardized preparation.

6. Standardize and maintain the new procedure

In the last stage of improvement, a very clear and simple procedure or instructions should be established for making the changeover, as well as a checklist to ensure that achievements in the application of the methodology are consistently maintained.

- Document improved changeover procedures.
- Maintain communication with all involved.
- Train people involved in a changeover.
- Place standardized work instructions in workplaces.
- Set a goal for changeovers.
- Measure, publish, and track changeover times.

Useful tools and concepts for the application

1. 5S is an essential tool to facilitate improvement activities in a product changeover.
2. Thoroughly analyze the fasteners and try to standardize screws, nuts, and pulley wheels.
3. Study the use of the tools and standardize them.
4. Remember that the number of turns is not the most important aspect of screw fastening as tightening occurs only in the last turn of the screw. Therefore, be sure to have screws of strictly the necessary length.
5. Replace nuts with clamps to allow immediate fastening.
6. Use guides and accessories *(mixtures)* whenever possible.

7. Standardize all the activities and document them on checklists.
8. Use quick and easy connectors whenever possible.
9. Use color codes to distinguish changeover items and achieve quick matches or searches.
10. Organize the tools in the order they will be used and keep them nearby.

Tools to improve quality

Chapter 12

Prevention with FMEA

Background

Failure Mode and Effects Analysis (FMEA) was developed by the U.S. Army in conjunction with engineers from the National Aeronautics and Space Administration (NASA); it was known as the MIL-P-1629 military procedure, entitled "procedure for the execution of a failure mode, effects, and criticality analysis", developed on November 9, 1949.

Failure Mode and Effects Analysis was used to assess reliability and to determine the effects of equipment and system errors on mission success and the safety of personnel or equipment.

It was first used in the aerospace industry in the mid-1960s with the Apollo program.

FMEA in the launch
of a space rocket.

Definition

The FMEA (Failure Mode and Effect Analysis) is a very powerful tool that makes it possible to identify errors in products and processes and objectively evaluate their effects, causes, and detection elements in order to prevent their occurrence and have a documented method of prevention.

In addition, the FMEA is a living document in which a large amount of data about our processes and products can be stored, making it an invaluable source of information.

Types of FMEA

- Product: used to detect possible errors in the design of products and anticipate the effect they may have on the user or manufacturing process.
- Process: an analysis of errors that may occur at each stage of the process and is used to prevent such failures from having negative effects on the user of the product or service or at later stages in the process.
- Systems: used in the design of software to anticipate errors in its operation.
- Miscellaneous: FMEA exists for many other types of errors that generate negative effects and whose causes need to be documented to anticipate problems.

What is FMEA implemented for?

This structured prevention method is used to:

- Know a process in depth.
- Include information as a basis for operations training.
- Identify possible errors in a process or product.
- Determine the effects of each error that may occur.
- Assess the severity of the effects.
- Identify possible causes of errors.
- Determine the level of reliability of our error detection mechanisms.
- Objectively evaluate the relationship between severity, occurrence, and detectability.
- Document actions to reduce risks.
- Understand the mechanics that create defects and errors.
- Collect the knowledge generated in a company.
- Identify opportunities to initiate improvement projects.

When is FMEA used?

- When designing products or services.
- When designing processes.
- When we want to avoid problems or errors.
- When processes and products must be documented.
- When it is necessary to train operators in a process.
- When required by the customer.

In Chapter 3, "Diagnosis and implementation", it was mentioned that the preventive action mechanism is used to prevent the generation of problems. Therefore, in the following figure we observe that by using key indicators, errors can be prevented by a preventive action mechanism such as FMEA.

It is important to note that when the cycle is completed, the implementation, documentation, and training are also contributing to the generation of knowledge in the company. Thus, it's very valuable for all this information to be available in databases that may be consulted subsequently when a similar problem occurs again. It will also be useful to look again at the indicators to analyze the degree of contribution to the company's results.

How long does it take to implement FMEA?

From one to four days in an initial phase. Being a living document, it never ends because learning never ceases, and it can be fed continually.

Procedure for carrying out the FMEA process

The procedure is as follows:

- Develop the process map.
- Form a work team and document the process, product, etc.
- Determine the key steps in the process.
- Determine the potential errors in each step, define the effects of the failures and assess their severity level.
- Identify the causes of each error and evaluate the occurrence of failures.
- Indicate which controls are in place to detect and evaluate errors.
- Obtain the priority number for each mistake and make decisions.
- Take preventive, corrective, or improvement actions.

Develop the process map

This step describes each step in the process and sets the sequence to enter that information into the FMEA format.

Form a work team and document the process, product, etc.

- A team of four or five people is formed.
- The team must have knowledge of the product and process involved.
- Members must have teamwork skills.
- Operators are included.

Roles of team members

Leader

- Is the team representative.
- Directs the use of the methodology.
- Coordinates meetings.
- Guides the work of the team.
- Summarizes agreed decisions and actions.
- Documents results.

Members

- Provide knowledge and skills.

Figure 12.1 documents the part number that is manufactured in the process, the description of the item or part, the company name, and the department (optional). We also specify whether it belongs to a project, write down the name of the process to be analyzed and specify the dates and those responsible for carrying it out.

Determine the key steps in the process

In this step it is advisable to start the FMEA from the analysis of errors that may occur in key elements of the process, i.e., of possible failures that seriously affect the health of customers or employees that put product quality at risk or that may stall the operation. This is generally done by drawing on the experience of those who know the process and risks of making mistakes.

For this example, cutting and painting operations were chosen (see figure 12.2).

Determine the potential errors in each step, define the effects of the failures, and assess their severity level

For each stage in the process, all errors that may occur or may have occurred previously should be identified as well as their effect on safety described.

When searching for the causes of errors we must go to the root of the problems. It is very common to write only symptoms, so it is necessary to ask ourselves "Why?" several times to understand the mechanics that create failures. The occurrence table is used to evaluate occurrence.

Occurrence is a numerical value of how often the error can occur as a result of the specific cause. Each cause has an occurrence value from 1 to 10, as shown in the table.

When a process is in statistical control, the capacity of the process can be used as an indication if the index is representative of the cause.

Qualification	Occurrence (ppm)
1	$\times < 1$ ppm
2	$1 < \times < 250$
3	
4	$250 < \times < 12.500$
5	
6	
7	$12.500 < \times < 50.000$
8	
9	$50.000 < \times$
10	

Indicate which controls are in place to detect and evaluate errors

The "Current process control" box in the table in figure 12.3 describes the type of control used to detect the error and the following box describes its effectiveness.

Detection is a numeric value that indicates the possibility of detecting the error. This factor is rated on a scale of 1 to 10. The greater the probability of not detecting the error with the controls, the greater the detection value.

Obtain the priority number for each mistake and make decisions

The risk priority number is the product of the multiplication of severity × occurrence × detectability and is a number between 1 and 100 that indicates the priority that the improvement and prevention team must give to each error in order to eliminate it. With an RPN (risk priority number) over 100, prevention or correction actions should be undertaken to prevent errors from occurring.

Part no.:	1231-C		Date of last review	11-nov-06
Article:	*Andon board* for control of *takt time*			
Company:	Lean Shop Inc.		Division:	Hardware
Project:			Prepared by:	Luis Socconini
Process:	Manufacture of *takt boards*			

Figure 12.1

			FMEA													
											RESULTS					
			1			**2**		**3**	**4**					**5**	**6**	**7**	**8**
#	Function/ Process Step What is the function of the process?	Potential Failure What could go wrong?	Effect What is the consequence?	SEVERITY	Potential Causes	OCCURRENCE	Existing Controls	DETECTION	RPN	Recommended Actions	Person Responsible	Implemented Actions	SEV	OCC	DET	RPN
	Cutting															
	Painting															

Figure 12.2

No.	Function of process	Potential failure	Potential effect of failure	GRAV	Potential causes of failure mechanisms	OCC	Current process control	DECT
1	Cut	Cut too much	The cabinet cannot be assembled	8	Operator carelessness, training failures	4	Final inspection	4
1	Cut	Cut with wrong die	Slight bumps on the edges of the board	4	Lack of order and standardization	6	Operator experience	6
2	Paint	Use wrong color	Product out of specification	8	Operator carelessness, training failures	4	Check with pantone colors	2

Score	Detection
1	**Very High** probability of detecting the defect
2	
3	**High** probability of detecting the defect (almost always)
4	
5	**Moderate** (the defect may be detected)
6	
7	**Low** (the defect probably won't be detected)
8	
9	
10	Cannot be detected

Figure 12.3

With an RPN over 30 and under 100, it should receive second-priority attention.

Although the RPN is the value that indicates the priority level, it is very important to also consider the most serious errors within the priorities.

Take preventive, corrective, or improvement actions

To reduce errors, we must decide whether we will take prevention, corrective, or improvement actions. This information can be found in the "recommended actions" box in the table in figure 12.4.

Recommended actions are presented by assigning people specific action and dates , so that the actions are followed up and fulfilled. Finally, an evaluation is done to establish the new RPN and determine if further action will be taken or to simply document improvements.

Potential causes of failure mechanisms	OCC	Current process control	DECT	RPN	Recommended actions (required if RPN> 30)	Responsibility and completion date	Actions taken since that date	GRAV	OCC	DECT	RPN
Operator carelessness, training failure	4	Final inspection	4	128	Filter change and water test periodically	J.P. (10/10/05)	Reorder point min. x max.	5	3	8	120
Failure of order and standardization	6	Operator experience	6	144	Training program	L.S.					
Operator carelessness, training failure	4	Check with pantone colors	2	64	Periodically check the expiration date and batch	J.P. (10/10/05)	The supplier is asked for a substitution plan at each expiration date	7	1	10	70

Figure 12.4

Chapter 13

Poka-yoke error proofing

Background

In the 1960s, Japanese engineer Shigeo Shingo created this quality assurance technique as for him it was almost essential to use statistical methods for quality improvement, but he realized that no matter how rigorous the inspections were, the goal of zero defects would never be reached.

When he realized that a large part of the defects were generated by human errors, he thought that the best way to ensure quality was by creating it from the operations that transform the products, testing each product with elements that detected the error before the defect occurred and thus creating quality processes rather than simply detecting defects in a reactive way.

Traditional quality states that to ensure a product has the quality desired by the customer, said product has to be inspected using statistical methods to ensure with a certain level of confidence that the specifications are met. However, this is hardly ever done because, by inspecting only one sample, defects are not always detected since they can occur in isolation or in series and thereby it is only possible to find a proportion in a sample that represents the population.

Traditional quality also seeks timely feedback to determine the nature and causes of defects but, there is not always such information to make decisions in the short term, but rather much later, when the problem can only be corrected.

Definition

Poka-yoke devices are methods that prevent human errors in processes before they become defects and allow operators to concentrate on their activities.

Poka-yoke systems allow 100% inspection and therefore immediate action when defects occur.

In the application of Lean Manufacturing a very important rule is that no operation sends defective products to the next operation because the continuous flow is interrupted and the production of excesses or *mudas begins.*

Translation from Japanese

Poka = unnoticed errors.

Yokeru = avoid.

What is Poka-yoke implemented for?

The following are some of the benefits of implementing Poka-yoke:

- It ensures quality in every workstation.
- Provides operators with knowledge about operations.
- Eliminates or reduces the possibility of making mistakes.
- Avoids accidents caused by human distraction.

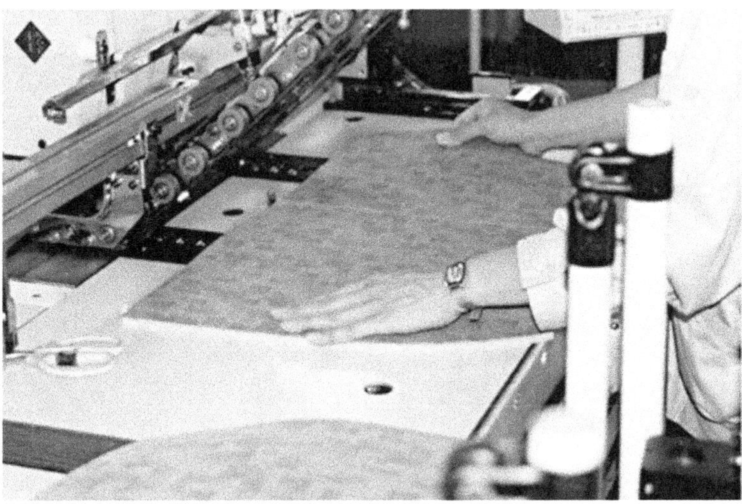

Defect-free production.

- Eliminates actions that depend on memory and inspection.
- Frees the mind of the worker and allows him to develop his creativity.
- Typically, Poka-yoke systems are inexpensive and simple.

Sources of defects

Materials
- Damaged.
- Wrong.
- That do not meet the specifications.
- Obsolete.

Manpower
- Bad training.
- Unnoticed errors.
- Mistakes.
- Oversights.
- Misuse of equipment.

Methods
- Incomplete.
- Unclear or complex.
- Obsolete.
- Lack of documentation.

Machinery
- Inadequate maintenance.
- Bad settings.
- Poor changeovers.
- Dirt and contaminants around products.
- Inadequate facilities.

Courtesy: Javier Masini.

Evolution levels of quality assurance systems

Level 0. The plant sends defective products to the customer frequently. At this level customers are dissatisfied with the service and constantly complain about the quality of the products.

Level 1. The plant uses many inspectors to find many defects, realizing that its processes are not suitable and that even if it does not ship defective products, the cost of non-quality is very high.

Level 2. The plant has largely reduced defects by using statistical process control but, although it knows the capacity of the processes and many inspectors are involved in quality assurance, the cost of these systems is high, and the inspection usually detects problems when the products have been finished.

Level 3. The training of operators and process leaders facilitates the detection of defects, which we attempt to eliminate by making operators participate as auditors of the previous process prior to carrying out their operation. This is done using fail-safe mechanisms that do not allow operators to make mistakes.

When is Poka-yoke used?

Poka-yoke is used:

- When there are processes that are continuously generating defects or are unsafe and can cause damage or accidents to the operators.
- When there are very serious errors in the Failure Mode and Effects Analysis that may cause accidents or defects in key customer requirements.
- When there are process controls that do not have a good level of defect detectability.
- When the occurrence of defects, errors, or accidents requires the establishment of fail-safe mechanisms.
- When the customer requests that Poka-yoke mechanisms be implemented to produce their products.

Categories of Poka-yoke elements

1. **Poka-yoke warning**
   The warning element notifies the operator or user before the error occurs. However, the fact that the mechanism warns him does not necessarily mean that the error is avoided.
2. **Poka-yoke prevention**
   With this type of element, we try to avoid errors by using mechanisms that make it impossible to commit them.

An example of Poka-yoke in everyday life is the SD memory card which has a standardized shape that prevents it from being inserted wrongly.

Poka-yoke levels

Level 1. Detects the defect when it has already occurred but usually makes sure it does not arrive at the next station.

Level 2. Detects the error at the time it arises and before it becomes a defect.

Level 3. Eliminates or prevents the generation of errors before they occur and generate defects.

Classification of Poka-yoke mechanisms

Richard Chase and Douglas Stewart have defined four types of Poka-yoke:

- Physical Poka-yoke.
- Sequential Poka-yoke.
- Grouping Poka-yoke.
- Information Poka-yoke.

Physical Poka-yoke

These types of devices are aimed at ensuring the prevention of errors in products or processes and are used to identify errors or physical inconsistencies.

Sequential Poka-yoke

When order is important, any change or omission in the order can cause errors, so specific ways are sought to restrict the sequence so that only one default order can be followed.

Grouping Poka-yoke

In these types of devices, *kits* or the surplus method are used. In the *kits* elements such as materials, parts, etc. are prepared in such a way that all are ready, and none are missing when performing the operation.

Information Poka-yoke

These systems provide feedback to the person with clear, simple, and complete information about what is needed to avoid mistakes.

Examples of Poka-yoke devices
- Guide rod or pin.
- Template.
- Microswitch / limit switch.
- Counter.
- Surplus/excess method.
- Sequence restriction.
- Standardization and solution.
- Key condition indicator.
- Detection and delivery slider.
- Block / flap.
- Sensor.
- Color code.

How long does it take to implement Poka-yoke?

A Poka-yoke improvement event lasts from four to eight days.

Procedure for implementing Poka-yoke

Before doing the Kaizen event (one or two weeks before)

The event should be planned based on the problem or system we want to improve.

- Use process Failure Mode and Effects Analysis (see Chapter 12).
- Identify the highest or most important RPN (risk priority number).
- Identify processes and/or operations with more serious errors.
- Establish the scope of the project.
- Choose the team leader.
- Identify team members.
- Four or five people with product, process, and control knowledge.
- Invite at least two operators.
- Set the date of the event.

During the Kaizen event (four to eight days)

- Identify the stages of the process.
- Identify the type of Poka-yoke elements to be used according to the error.
- Characterize inputs and outputs.

Identify the stages of the process

The stages of each process are identified step-by-step to know the operation sequence. For this step we should go to the site and carefully observe each operation to understand the specific mechanical movements, activities, environment, and transfers, as well as the location of the parts before and after processing, the means of transport, the workers' attention level, visual aids, etc. The purpose is to raise awareness and gain a complete understanding. It is also necessary to exchange views and experiences with the people who work there.

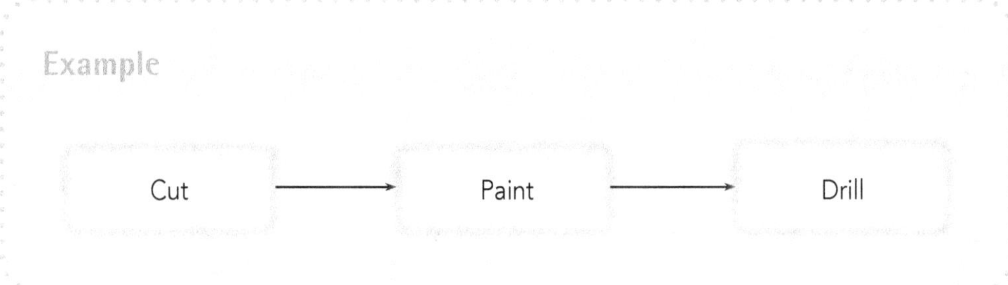

Implementation of poka yoke in a production plant.

Identify the type of Poka-yoke elements to be used according to the error

In general, when controls or fail-safe mechanisms are in key process inputs, preventive mechanisms are being applied, and when they are located in outputs, we are applying reactive mechanisms.

A good source of information for identifying stages in a process where a Poka-yoke mechanism needs to be applied can be a Failure Mode and Effects Analysis. For all potential errors with a low level of detectability and a high RPN, we can implement a mechanism that completely prevents the error from occurring.

Characterize inputs and outputs

The goal of identifying the inputs and outputs of each operation is to understand everything that can affect the operation and become failures, errors and therefore, defects.

After the Kaizen event

Monitor the effectiveness of the event, analyzing occurrence and detectability in the Failure Mode and Effects Analysis.

Basic principles

- Mistakes are inevitable, defects are not.
- The error must be detected before it becomes a defect.
- The best tool to prevent the defect is the one that isolates the source of the problem.

Bibliographical references

Zero Quality Control, Shigeo Shingo.

Chapter 14

8 D problem solving

Background

Ford Motor Company has combined several methods and tools for problem solving, among them is Team Oriented Problem Solving (TOPS), which is the fundamental basis of the 8 disciplines (8 D). Corrective action reports for Ford supplier companies require documentation of the 8 D.

This methodology, in addition to being used by the automotive industry, is used in many companies in different industries and has been recognized as one of the most powerful documented ways to solve problems.

Definition

The 8 D is a methodology to solve problems in a systematic and documented way by recording the actions undertaken in a series of 8 steps that are developed by a multidisciplinary team.

What is 8 D implemented for?

This structured method of troubleshooting serves to:

- Solve problems whose root cause is unknown.
- Document the entire troubleshooting process.
- Learn the process for solving specific problems in a team.
- Generate comprehensive and long-term solutions.

When is 8 D used?

8 D is used:

- When it is necessary to solve problems that have their origin in the past and whose causes are unknown.
- When a customer requires a structured and documented methodology for problem solving.
- When the symptom is known and quantified.
- When management undertakes to devote the necessary resources to solving the problem.
- When the complexity of the problem requires the skill of a team.

In Chapter 3, "Diagnosis and implementation", it was mentioned that the corrective action mechanism is used when there is a deviation in some indicator, which gives the signal to start a troubleshooting process, and for this the appropriate tool could be the 8 D.

How long does it take to implement 8 D?

Usually one to four days, although sometimes it takes longer.

Procedure for implementing 8 D

1. Define the problem.
2. Form the team.
3. Describe the problem.
4. Develop containment actions.
5. Define the root cause.
6. Develop corrective actions.
7. Develop preventive actions.
8. Recognize the work of the team.

To document the troubleshooting process, use table 14.1, "8D Troubleshooting and Analysis".

This table documents each step, as described below:

PROBLEM
1. DEFINITION OF THE PROBLEM:
2. EMERGENCY ACTIONS:
Person Responsible
Status
3. DESCRIBE THE PROBLEM:
IT IS
IT ISN'T
WHAT:
WHERE:
WHEN:
HOW MUCH:
4. CONTAINMENT ACTIONS
Person Responsible
Status
CAUSE
methods
material
manpower
machine
Initial definition
SOLUTION
6. PERMANENT CORRECTIVE ACTIONS
Person Responsible
Date
Status
7. PREVENTIVE ACTIONS
Person Responsible
Date
Status
Prepared by:
Revised by:
Approved by:
TEAM MEMBERS INVOLVED IN PROBLEM SOLVING:
Process and quality audits and records

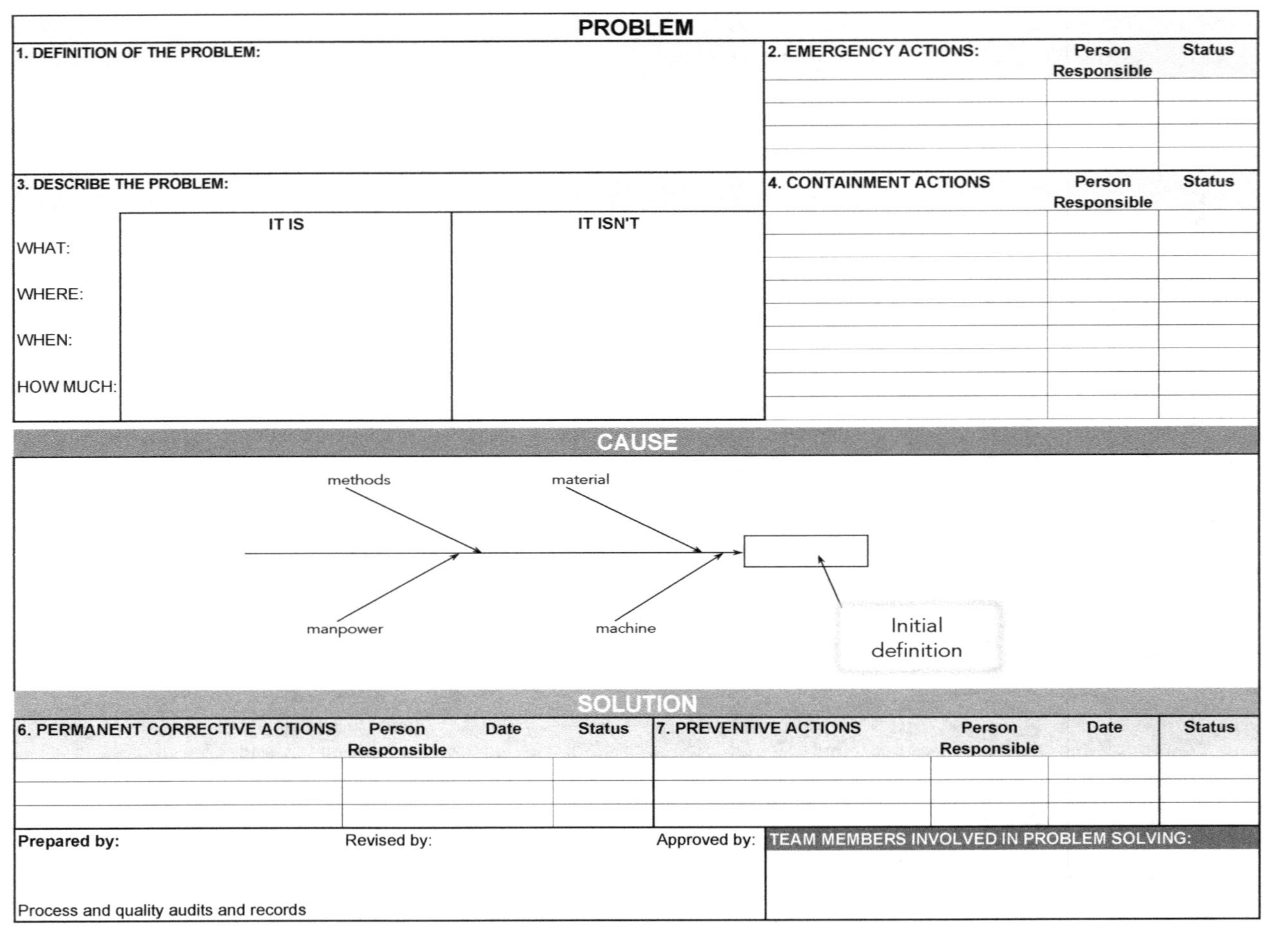

Table 14.1

Operation or machine: [ ]

No. of part: [ ]

Description: [ ]

Date: [ ]

No. of report [ ]

First, the header of said table should be filled out, noting the name of the operation or equipment where the problem occurred, followed by the part number, the part description, the date the resolution process starts and the consecutive report number.

It is advisable to keep track of all reports so that they can be quickly located if these problems occur again and to always have documented follow-up of corrective actions.

At the end of the table, it is specified who prepared the document, who reviewed it, and who approved the actions carried out.

Prepared by: Reviewed by: Approved by:

1. Define the problem

We first need to be sure of what the problem is before we begin looking for solutions.

Defining a problem is simple and consists of a subject and a predicate. It can be easily described by answering questions:

- What is wrong (defect)?
- With what or where (object)?

When defining the problem it is important to be clear that if it's not done well, only the symptoms will be attacked and not the problem itself.

1. DEFINITION OF THE PROBLEM			
EMERGENCY ACTIONS			
EMERGENCY ACTIONS	Responsible	Date	Status

If emergency actions need to be performed at this point, then said actions, those responsible for doing them, the date and status of the application are described.

2. Form the team

"Working as a team ensures success."

HENRY FORD

- Form a team of between four and five people.
- Members must have knowledge of the product and process involved.
- Members must have problem-solving skills.
- Members must have teamwork skills.
- Members must have complementary knowledge of the subject from which the problem arises.
- The team must decide the time and resources needed to resolve the problem.
- The team must have people who have the authority to make decisions.
- Members' communication and leadership skills should be considered.

Roles of team members
Sponsor

- Owns the process.
- Has authority to make changes.
- Provides resources for the team.
- Supports team decisions.
- Monitors the team's progress.
- Eliminates interference.
- Attend meetings whenever needed.

Leader

- Is the team representative.
- Directs the use of the methodology.
- Coordinates meetings.
- Guides the work of the team.
- Summarizes agreed decisions and actions.
- Documents results.

Members

- Provide knowledge and skills.
- Assist in the execution of the event.
- Generate ideas.
- Suggest solutions and implements them.
- Are involved from beginning to end.

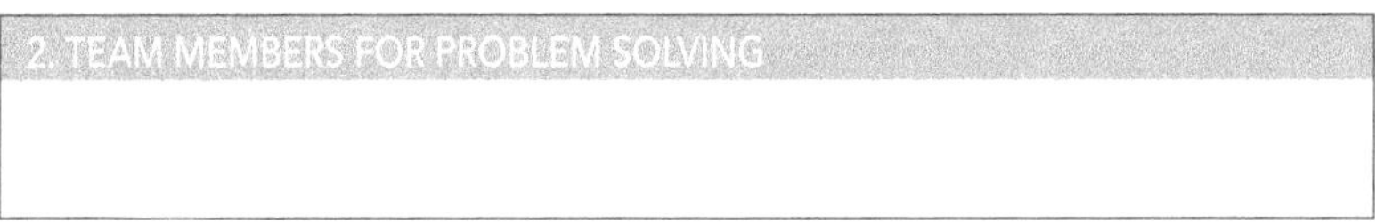

3. Describe the problem

This step sets the limits of the problem by organizing and collecting data in four dimensions:

- When the problem occurs and when it does not occur.
- Where the problem is and where it is not.
- How the problem happens and how it doesn't.
- How many problems are being generated or how many are not.

3. DESCRIPTION OF THE PROBLEM		
	It is	It is not
WHEN:		
WHERE:		
HOW:		
HOW MANY:		

It is very convenient to review the process where problems are being generated to detect the possible origin of the errors. table 14.1 provides a space for this purpose.

3 A. DESCRIPTION OF THE CURRENT PROCESS.

4. Develop containment actions

Containment actions are used to prevent the effects of the problem from reaching the end customer or the next link in the chain. We try to contain the problem from a cost, quality, and time perspective, as well as to gain time while finding the root cause of the problem.

Containment actions are documented in this part of the table but note that only the symptom is being attacked, as the cause is not known. Likewise, they should also be monitored continuously to verify their implementation and it should be remembered that they are temporary and must be replaced by actions that eliminate the root cause.

4. CONTAINMENT ACTIONS	Responsible Date	Status

5. Define the root cause

In this section, the problem should be written down as was done in the initial definition of the problem, from there, brainstorm to find the root cause among the different alternatives of methods, material, manpower, and machinery.

To establish the root cause, we need to identify all the possible causes that made the problem appear and compare them with the initial definition and description of the problem.

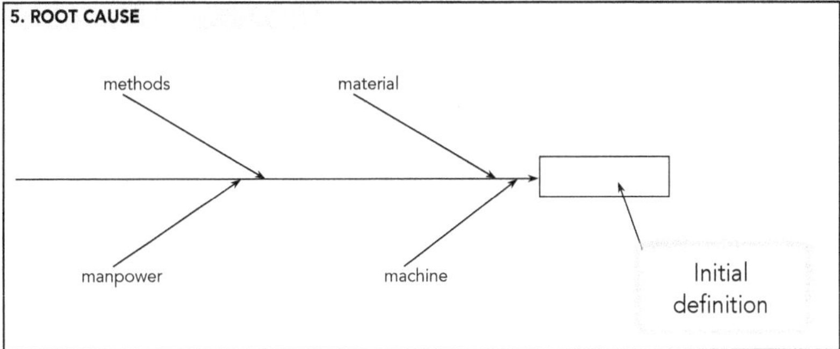

It is important to ask ourselves "Why?" several times until we can connect the causes and effects so that we can identify the root cause of the problem.

6. Develop corrective actions

This step consists of selecting the actions that will definitively eliminate the root causes and verifying that the solution to the problem really is successful.

6. CORRECTIVE ACTIONS	Responsible Date	Status

This section describes the actions taken and verifies that they work and do not generate undesirable effects; their application is planned by assigning a person responsible and noting the date when they will be carried out. The status of the implementation may be written down. It's necessary to monitor these actions, even in the long term, to verify their continuity and effectiveness.

VERIFICATION OF EFFECTIVENESS

7. Develop preventive actions

Here we establish actions that prevent the recurrence of the problem as well as the generation of negative effects during the implementation of such actions. Also assigned are a person responsible for these actions, the completion date, and the status of each preventive action is kept up to date.

7. PREVENTIVE ACTIONS	Responsible Date	Status

8. Recognize the work of the team

This last step is very important as it recognizes the goal that the team has achieved. But for this it is necessary for the team to present its results briefly at the end of the execution, in order to know the problem-solving process, and in this presentation all members must participate.

Finally, the highest-ranking person must recognize the team's contribution to the solution of the problem, which will create an atmosphere of respect and admiration for those who carry out a job with satisfaction and leadership.

> "Sometimes we don't have time to do things right at first but we should have time to repeat things two or three times because they went wrong."
>
> ANONYMOUS

Chapter 15

Six Sigma for variation reduction

Background

Six Sigma is a methodology for the improvement and solution of complex problems that was developed from a doctoral thesis by Dr. Mikel Harry in which he took total quality management concepts and problem solving mechanisms and turned it into a powerful way to make companies more profitable by reducing the variation in processes and products. The quality movement is much more than standards and awards; it is a system of knowledge and discipline that involves constantly renewing the way things are done.

People like William Deming, Joseph Juran, Philip B. Crosby, Armand V Feigenbaum, Kaoru Ishikawa, Genichi Taguchi, and others contributed with their effort and dedication to build the concept and philosophy of quality and marked the beginning of what is now known as Six Sigma, product of the constant evolution of methods and tools.

In the 1980s, Motorola was experiencing a competitiveness crisis and its results didn't provide a promising outlook. On one occasion, Bob Galvin, CEO of the company, said: "Our quality sucks." The problem was a quality level so low that it could even cause the company to close, so he summoned his staff to significantly improve the quality. He was looking to advance from three Sigma levels (93.3% of good products) to a level ten times higher, i.e. the equivalent of a four Sigma level (99.3 %). Several engineers from the company began working towards quality, including Dr. Mikel Harry. He caught Galvin's attention by proposing that they no longer use the average as a way of evaluating global results but rather the standard deviation, since when it's measured it represents the variation of a data set with respect to its mean. With this, it would be more important to consistently comply with the quality of the products rather than averaging good and bad results.

> "If we don't know, we can't act.
> If we cannot act, our risk of failure is high.
> If we know and act, the risk is controlled.
> If we don't know or act, we deserve failure."
>
> MIKEL HARRY

In the United States, Malcolm Baldrige, Secretary of Commerce, proposed to President Ronald Reagan to establish the National Quality Award, but shortly before handing it over for the first time, Baldrige died in an accident and the award was named after him. This award was given to Motorola not only for having achieved four Sigma levels, but for having some processes deliver an almost perfect quality of 99.9996%, equivalent to Six Sigma, so the project was renamed with this name.

Later, other companies such as General Electric, Lockheed Martin, Texas Instruments, and Honeywell, among others, followed Motorola's example and continued to develop their staff and projects to achieve a more efficient and productive industry.

> "Six Sigma is the best training we've ever done. It's better than going to Harvard Business School because it teaches us to think differently."
>
> JACK WELCH, CEO OF GENERAL ELECTRIC (SLATER 2000)

Definition

Six Sigma has several definitions:

- It is a measurement system that allows one to measure any process and compare it with any other one.
- It is an improvement methodology that is used to drastically reduce variation.

- It is a management system to achieve business leadership and maximum performance.

When the variations are measured statistically, the standard deviation represents the variation of the data from the average and is represented by the Greek letter sigma, hence the name sigma.

Six Sigma means that there can be six standard deviations between the average and the customer specification, which makes the variation so small that there are only 3.4 defects per million.

What is Six Sigma implemented for?

The following are some of the benefits of applying Six Sigma:

- It ensures quality in every workstation.
- It makes it possible to create an infrastructure of people capable of improving quality.
- It makes it possible to establish a work philosophy and a business strategy.
- It significantly improves the quality of products and services.
- It ensures the permanence of business and increases profitability.
- It enables the development of powerful products and processes.
- It ensures a clear understanding of customer requirements.

When is Six Sigma used?

Six Sigma is used:

- When we want to reduce process variability, i.e., improve the level of compliance with customer specifications if they present a variation that has gone out of control.
- When quality levels don't meet customer expectations and the existing variation obliges us to improve process performance.

Features of Six Sigma

- A training structure is established.
- The application approach is proactive.

- A structured methodology with various tools is used.
- It works on the key process variables.
- The principle is to work on the key quality characteristics.
- Quality is generated in processes and not in inspections.
- Process outputs are based on inputs.

What is Six Sigma's relationship to Lean Manufacturing?

Some experts estimate that a company that has 10% waste reduces its capacity by up to 40%. That is why speed (Lean Manufacturing) and quality (Six Sigma) are two sides of the same coin.

If we talk about agile companies, we need not only an improvement methodology but also a set of elements that help us reduce defects, improve delivery speed and therefore, achieve total customer satisfaction.

This book suggests methodologies and tools for creating agile companies. These methodologies work well when given the right approach. The following functions have been described:

Methodology	Application
Lean Manufacturing	Improve speed, quality, cost and delivery. Eliminate excesses.
Six Sigma	Reduce variation and solve difficult problems.
FMEA	Prevent problems.
8 D	Solve problems.

Therefore, agile companies must have tools which allow them to respond to the various situations they face daily.

How long does it take to implement Six Sigma?

Typically, the implementation of a Six Sigma Project takes between 3 and 12 weeks.

Structure for Six Sigma

The Six Sigma methodology, along with the applied tools, is very powerful but its power lies in the structure since different levels of training and certification are established for its effective application. The roles of the Six Sigma structure are detailed below.

Master black belt

This is the mentor or teacher of the black belts; he reviews and has the prestige and leadership because he teaches and carries out difficult projects. Master black belt is a black belt person who has demonstrated great experience by the results of their projects and above all, by the profits accumulated throughout the application of the methodology and tools in high value projects. It is a high-grade position in companies.

Black belt

This is an expert in the tools who guides teams on projects and trains others. He has studied the methodology and tools and has demonstrated his skills in the implementation of projects, achieving results in the reduction of defects and with considerable financial impacts, in some cases with annual savings of up to one million dollars.

The black belt is a kind of internal consultant dedicated to improving and solving difficult problems by reducing defects and costs. He usually works full-time on projects and training staff. He receives training of between 120 and 150 hours.

Green belt

Green belt people correspond to different levels in the company and are not engaged full-time in Six Sigma activities. However, they know the methodology and tools at an application level in the projects to which they are invited. They are trained for 48 to 72 hours in the methodology and are familiar with the tools in general so they can lead small projects or provide support when they are invited to participate in a project.

Sponsors

They are executives who know and believe in the benefits of Six Sigma application. In addition, they are key elements in its implementation. They sponsor training programs, set company priorities, and turn the Six Sigma initiative into a business strategy aimed at raising the company's competitive edge and ensuring tangible economic benefits. They support the projects in process with resources and means to achieve positive results.

Champions

These are high-level managers who allocate resources and prioritize the training of black belts, demonstrating that Six Sigma is a strategic program to achieve the company's goals. They receive training on the key concepts of Six Sigma's methodology and application to work on the best projects. They work with the black belts, giving them support and resources for the correct execution of their projects.

Procedure for implementing Six Sigma

Six Sigma uses a methodology called DMAIC (Define, Measure, Analyze, Improve, Control) which consists of:

- Define: the project to be carried out is defined.
- Measure: data and measurements are obtained.
- Analyze: data is analyzed and converted into information.
- Improve: improvement actions are carried out.
- Control: checks that improvements are maintained.

Define

At the initial stage of a project is known as the define phase, here we describe the objective, justification, scope, resources, team assigned, and a preliminary project schedule. This stage is the most important because it is where the basis for the implementation of the project is established.

Tools used in the definition stage (as necessary)

In the selection of the project

- Matrix diagrams and prioritization matrices to select projects that are aligned with the goals and objectives.
- Pareto charts to identify significant opportunities.

- Process maps as visual means to define processes and identify opportunities.
- SIPOC diagrams to identify activities in processes, key inputs and outputs, customers, and suppliers.

In the project scheduling

- Gantt charts to understand the program and monitor the progress of the project.
- Pert analysis to determine the key path.

Measure

The purpose of the measurement phase is to understand the current state of the process and collect reliable data on quality, cost, and speed.

Activities to be carried out

- Know the voice of the customer.
- Determine key process inputs and outputs.
- Know the process in depth.
- Obtain process data.
- Establish the necessary measurements for a baseline.
- Evaluate the measurement system.
- Validate the objective and scope of the project.

Tools used in the definition stage (as necessary)

In the process definition

- Flowcharts and process maps to get an in-depth understanding of the process and define the process level of the project to be worked on.
- Sampling techniques to collect the necessary data.
- Needs map to know the key quality requirements.
- QFD (Quality Function Deployment) to prioritize technical requirements.
- Kano model to understand, analyze, and classify our customers' requirements according to priority.

In the baseline estimate

- Control charts to investigate the stability of the process and evaluate its capacity.
- Histograms to display process-related outputs.

- Mean confidence intervals and proportions to estimate process performance when not statistically under control.
- Probability graphs to verify the distribution of the process.
- OEE (Overall Equipment Effectiveness) to know the total effectiveness.
- Sigma level to set error probability.

In the analysis of the measurement system

- R&R studies to quantify the measurement error associated with equipment, personnel, and procedures.
- Regression and linearity analysis to understand the measurement error.

Analyze

The purpose of the analysis phase is to assess the stability and ability of the process to produce within specifications as well as to establish the root causes that are generating variation.

Activities to be carried out

- Determine the sources of variation.
- Identify the bottleneck in the process.
- Analyze root causes.

Tools used in the definition stage (as necessary)

In value stream analysis

- Value stream map to know the processes in depth and validate the activities that add value.
- Flowcharts to identify all activities involved in the process.
- Spaghetti diagram to identify unnecessary movements of material or personnel.
- Mudas analysis to identify and eliminate waste.

In the process analysis

- Ishikawa diagrams to identify cause and effect relationships.
- Confidence intervals to check hypotheses presented.
- FMEA (Failure Mode and Effects Analysis) to identify potential errors in the process and/or product.
- Hypothesis testing to compare samples of different conditions.

- Design of experiments to detect factors and levels of variation.
- Control charts to differentiate common causes from special causes of variation.
- Histograms to graphically display process outputs.
- Multivariate graphs to categorize the variation and interrelation of factors.
- Pareto charts to focus on opportunities.
- Reality trees to understand the cause-effect relationships of diverse situations.
- Cpk to assess process capacity.

Improve

The purpose of the improvement phase is to implement the changes that are necessary to improve the process.

Activities to be carried out

- Determine the conditions of the improved process.
- Calculate the benefits of the proposed improvements.
- Investigate the failure modes for the new process.
- Implement and verify process improvements.

Determine operating conditions

- Future state value stream map to know the improved processes.
- Pert analysis to verify the cycle time reduction.
- Spaghetti diagram to identify unnecessary movements of material or personnel.
- Simulation of the process to know the behavior of the changes.

Lean tools (seen in other chapters)

- 5S to eliminate activities that don't add value.
- Continuous flow to reduce cycle times.
- Leveling to balance processes.
- SMED to reduce cycle time.
- TPM for maximum equipment effectiveness.
- Kanban to set pull flow.

Improve operating conditions

- Prioritization matrices to ensure solutions are aligned with customer needs.
- *Box-whisker* charts to graphically compare before and after.

- Cause-effect charts to generate a chain of assumptions that affect the identified solution.
- Design of experiments, regression analysis, residual analysis, and interaction graphs to determine where the maximum or minimum expected response is.

Control

The purpose of the control phase is to standardize new methods and ensure that improvements are maintained.

Activities to be carried out
- Document the improved process.
- Continuously verify the impact of improvements.
- Verify that improvements are maintained.
- Establish control methods.

Tools used in the control stage (as necessary)
In control activities
- Control charts to observe variations in the process.
- Failure Mode and Effects Analysis to document potential errors and prevent them.
- Control Plan to document controls and minimize process variation.
- Flowcharts to identify all activities involved in the process.
- Training so that everyone understands and applies new methods.
- Standard documentation for documented references.

Part VII

Tools for materials and production control

Chapter 16

Kanban for material and production control

Background

Many Japanese businessmen visited plants in the United States on several occasions to learn about their inventory control systems.

In an attempt to find ideas or systems to avoid overstocking, Taiichi Ohno and his colleagues visited several vehicle assembly plants and smelters. They didn't find what they were looking for, but they often visited supermarkets

The *Kanban* system is inspired by the way supermarkets work and *Kanban* cards symbolize banknotes that give a cue to the materials supply companies.

during their journey and were very struck by the way the items were replenished once the customer took them off the shelf and paid for them; that is, the recipe was a signal to the merchandizer that he had to replenish the product(s) that the customer had taken down.

Definition

The "pull system" is a communication system that makes it possible to control production, synchronize manufacturing processes with customer requirements, and strongly support production scheduling.

Types of Kanban

- Withdrawal **Kanban.** Specifies the class and quantity of product that a process must withdraw from the previous process.

Storage Rack #	F26-18	Part Code	A5-34	Previous process
Part #	56690-321			STAMP B-2
Part Name	MOTOR SUPPORT			Next process
Type of vehicle	SX50BC			MECHANIZATION
Box capacity	20	Type of box	B	

- Production **Kanban.** Specifies the class and quantity of product that a process should produce.

Storage rack #	F26-18	Part Code	A5-34	Process
Part #	56690-321			MECHANIZATION
Name of the part	MOTOR SUPPORT			
Quantity to produce	200			

What is Kanban implemented for?

The following are some of the benefits of implementing Kanban:

- It prevents overproduction.
- It makes it possible to work with low inventories.
- It guarantees customers that they will receive the products on time.
- It makes it possible to manufacture only what the customer needs.
- It is a visual system that makes it possible to compare what is manufactured with what the customer requires.
- It eliminates the complexities of production scheduling.
- It provides a common system for moving materials in the plant.

When is Kanban used?

Kanban is used:

- When it is necessary to structure the material control and production management system due to the high mix of products and the production volumes that tend to be lower.
- When the variables of equipment availability, good housekeeping, quick changeovers, and minimum batch quantities have been entered and the conditions lend themselves to applying Kanban.

How long does it take to implement Kanban?

Kanban implementation takes from one to twelve weeks.

Procedure for implementing Kanban

- Select the part numbers to be set in Kanban.
- Calculate the number of pieces per Kanban.
- Choose the type of cue and standard container type.
- Calculate the number of containers and the Pitch sequence.
- Do follow-up (WIP to SWIP).

Select the part numbers to be set in Kanban

Select part numbers that share the same product family. It is advisable to work with part numbers that are commonly used.

It is very important to work with part numbers where manufacturing flexibility has already been worked on, for example, where manufacturing cells have been established, change times have been reduced, and process machines have improved their availability.

Calculate the number of pieces per Kanban

The parts formula for Kanban is: D × TE x U x (1 + % VD).
   Where:

D   = weekly demand. The monthly demand is usually multiplied by 12 and divided by the number of working weeks or by 52.

TE = delivery time in weeks that the internal or external supplier has, which includes:

For purchased products

Order generation time + supplier delivery time + shipping time + reception, inspection, and stock time.

For manufactured products

Time to generate the work order + total processing time + reception/inspection time.

U   = number of locations. For example, at the start of the implementation it is advisable to have two full locations, one for the supplier and one for the customer.

Percentage VD = level of demand variability. It is the standard deviation of demand for the period divided by the average demand for the same period.

- **Delivery time:** is the total time of the value stream from the raw material to the finished product. This time includes activities that add and don't add value. Normally this time is defined on the value stream map.

- **Takt time:** is the time available for production divided by demand.

- **Units per Kanban:** is the batch size that each card will represent according to the capacity of the containers that a person can load or the logical amount of production given the operating conditions or simply the economic lot.

Example

Select the part numbers to be set in Kanban.
Part number: 2214. Engine bracket.

Calculate the number of pieces per Kanban
Monthly demand = 22,534 pieces.
Annual demand = 22,534 × 12 = 270,408 pieces.
Weekly demand = 270,408 ÷52 = 5,200 pieces.

D = 5,200 pieces.

TE = 1 Week.

U = 2 (to avoid problems at the beginning, it is advisable to start with one location with the supplier and another in the manufacturing area). In the future the quantities will be reduced but with this we ensure continuity in the procurement process.

% VD = standard deviation of demand for the period / average demand for the same period.

Part #	2214	Description	Motor Support

January	22350
February	28570
March	35514
April	25468
May	24515
June	20667
July	18422
August	14304
September	17209
October	19129
November	22345
December	21916

Average	22,534
Std. Dev.	5,608
Variance	25%

Figure 16.1

% VD = 25%.
Quantity of pieces = 5,200 ×1 ×2 × 1,25 = 13,000 pieces.

Another way to obtain the necessary Kanban in the processes is based on the covering of materials according to the process cycle time or the delivery time (obtained from the value stream map).

$$\frac{\text{Process delivery time}}{\textit{Takt} \text{ time}} \div \frac{\text{quantity of parts}}{\text{per Kanban}} + \text{safety margin}$$

For example, we have the following:

Process delivery time of 7 days = (450 working minutes × 7 days) = 3,150 minutes.
Takt time = 7 minutes.
Units for each *Kanban* card = 30 pieces.
Safety Margin = 20 pieces.

Delivery time *(lead time)*	3150	minutes
Takt time	7	minutes
Units per *kanban*	30	Pieces
Safety margin	20	Pieces
Number of *kanbans* required	35	kanbans

- **Safety margin:** is a quantity of materials that maintains a certain confidence in the system in the face of possible contingencies.

Choose type of cue and standard container type
It is important that the containers are easy to handle and identify. Make sure that the color for applying the visual cue to the parts is consistent with the color of the container.

One recommendation is to select the container capacity according to the operator's load capacity for it to be a manageable load unit.

The container can be a box, pallet, tray, etc.

Calculate the number of containers and the pitch sequence

$$\text{Number of containers} = \frac{\text{Quantity of pieces in Kanban}}{\text{Container capacity}}$$

If the capacity of each container is 100, then the number of containers is:

$$\text{Number of containers} = 13{,}000 \div 100 = 130.$$

Pitch is the production rate according to the quantity of products per package.

$$\text{Pitch} = takt \text{ time} \times \text{packing capacity.}$$

Do follow-up (WIP to SWIP)

The WIP to SWIP is calculated by dividing the amount of inventory within the cell by the amount of SWIP.

Standard containers.

Total inventory in the cell ÷ standard inventory of the cell.

The ideal result is 1, which means that the WIP is equal to the SWIP.

If the result is greater than 1, then we have a lot of inventory in the cell.

If the result is less than 1, then there is little inventory and there is a risk that the cell will fall short of production.

Chapter 19 shows how to calculate the WIP to SWIP.

During application:

- Determine the part numbers to be implemented in pull system.
- Determine the maximum number of inventories per part.
- Calculate Kanban quantities for the operations.
- Determine the standard container size.
- Determine storage locations (supermarkets).
- Determine the number of containers.

Kanban rules

1. Defective products are not passed on to the following processes.
2. A Kanban is withdrawn when a process withdraws parts from the previous process.
3. The above processes manufacture parts in the quantities specified by the withdrawn Kanban (the Kanban provides them with a production order).
4. Nothing is produced or transported without Kanban.
5. The Kanban acts as a production order attached to the items.
6. The number of Kanban's decreases over time.

Useful tools and concepts for the application

1. 5S is an essential tool for facilitating manufacturing cell implementation activities.
2. Consider implementing TPM before implementing manufacturing cells. This will make the calculations more realistic and the equipment more reliable for working in a cellular environment.
3. Certify operators in multiple operations and perform a training matrix in which the operators can operate, maintain and analyze quality in each workplace.

4. Ensure the procurement of materials in all stations using the Kanban system or other methods so that production is never stopped for lack of materials.
5. Perform visual checks to help workers understand their operations thoroughly using visual instructions.
6. Apply *Andon* or visual control (lights, sounds or other means) to communicate the need for material, maintenance, assistance, quality, etc. This way, the cell will remain productive.
7. Establish hourly job progress measurements where operators record the production they have done so far and compare it to the production they should have done.
8. If possible, set up single piece work. This is achieved by balancing the production cell and having operators move materials directly from operation to operation as the process progresses.
9. Consider applying SMED (quick changeovers) to ensure that the cell works to its full potential.

Chapter 17

Heijunka for production sequencing

Background

At Toyota, the means to adapt production to demand is called production leveling and it consists of minimizing quantity fluctuations in the production chain.

Stages of production leveling

- Leveling the total amount of production.
- Leveling the production of each model.

Leveling the total amount of production

The objective is to minimize the difference between the production of one period and the next. The goal is to produce the same number of products in each period (usually each day).

Although demand can change considerably depending on the season (affecting monthly production volumes), leveling allows daily production volumes to remain constant.

Let us look at the series production of vehicles A and B, in which the series production plan is prepared based on a monthly production plan, which in turn is established according to the forecast demand. This quantity is simply divided between the working days in the month, thus obtaining the volume to be produced each day.

Traditional system AAAAAABBBBBBBBBAAAAAAAA

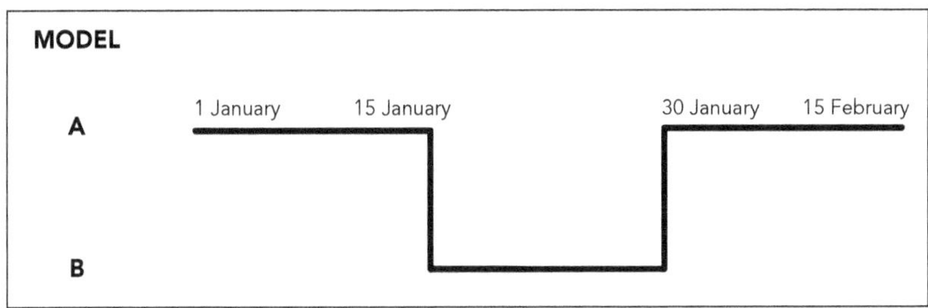

Figure 17.1 shows that traditional manufacturing sets long-term production priorities according to demand without that necessarily being the rate of sale.

Lean system (production level) ABABABABA

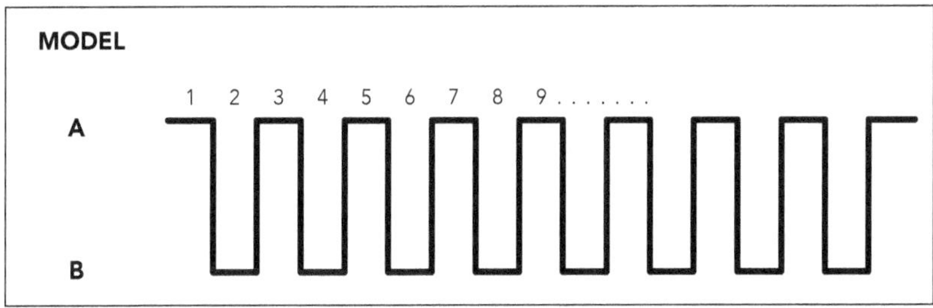

Leveling the production of each model

When the total production quantity is leveled, we can level the production level of each model by quick setup or product changeover and set the production sequence as the Kanban production cards arrive at the heijunka leveling box.

Definition

Heijunka production leveling is a control system that is used to level production to the end customer's rate of demand by varying the workload of the manufacturing processes.

What is heijunka implemented for?

The following are some of the benefits of implementing *heijunka:*

- It prevents overproduction.
- It fully establishes the pull system.
- It levels production in the line in production mix and production volume.

When is heijunka used?

When the Kanban system is mature, and more precision is required in production planning to avoid excessive inventories.

How long does it take to implement heijunka?

The implementation of heijunka takes four to six months.

Procedure for implementing heijunka

- Calculate takt time.
- Calculate the pitch for each product.
- Set the rate of production.
- Create the heijunka box.

Example

Available time = 27,000 seconds (8 hours – 30 minutes break).
Daily demand = 500 pieces per day.

$$\textit{Takt} \text{ time} = \frac{27{,}000 \text{ seconds}}{500 \text{ pieces}}$$

Takt time = 54 seconds per piece.

Calculate takt time

$$\text{Takt time} = \frac{\text{Time available}}{\text{Demand}}$$

Calculate the pitch for each product

Pitch represents the production and packing time of a production unit in its corresponding quantity of products per package.

Example

For this example, we have four products from a single family whose takt time is 54 seconds per piece.

Product W: 12 pieces per box.
Product X: 24 pieces per box.
Product Y: 10 pieces per box.
Product Z: 20 pieces per box.

Pitch:

W = (54 x 12) ÷ 60 = 10.8 min.
X =(54 x 24) ÷ 60 = 21.6 min.
Y = (54 x 10) ÷ 60 = 9 min.
Z = (54 x 20) ÷ 60 = 18 min.

Set the rate of production

To establish the sequence, we take the lowest value from the above calculations, which in this case is 9 minutes.

Assuming production starts at 8:00 h, the sequencing would be as follows:

8:00 8:09 8:18 8:27 8:36 8:45 8:54...

$$\text{Pitch} = \frac{\text{Takt time} \times \text{quantity of pieces per package}}{60 \text{ seconds / min.}}$$

Create the heijunka box

The heijunka box, also known as the production leveling box, is a matrix that can be made of wood or some other material and is used to establish how production will be sequenced in the periods calculated in the previous step.

This box is like a mail room that is used to schedule production. A runner is also needed to put the Kanban cards in the heijunka box in order to set production priorities and sequences as the cards move given the demand for the products.

The runner will introduce these cards, which will become a visual cue to know when and what to produce.

Part VIII

Integration and control of information

Chapter 18

Standard work

Definition

Standard work is based on operational excellence. Without standardized work, it is not possible to guarantee that products are always processed the same way in operations. Standardized work makes it possible to apply the Lean Manufacturing elements, as it defines the working methods in the most efficient way to achieve the best quality and the lowest costs.

To understand standard work, we only have to observe (by measuring) the work of the operators. Standard work consists of three elements:

- Takt time (speed of demand).
- Standard sequence of operations.
- Standard inventory in process.

What is standard work implemented for?

Standardizing operations establishes the baseline for evaluating and managing processes and evaluating their performance, which will be the basis for improvements. The documentation of standard work serves the following purposes:

- It ensures that the sequence of operator actions is repeatable.
- It supports visual control, thus creating an environment to detect anomalies easily.
- It provides help to compare documentation with the actual processes.
- It's a tool for initiating improvement actions.

- It makes the method of documenting improvements easier.
- It establishes an invaluable bank of information that can be consulted whenever necessary.
- It helps maintain a high level of repeatability.
- It ensures safer and more effective operations.
- It improves productivity.
- It helps balance the cycle times of all operations in accordance with the takt time cycle.
- It reduces operator learning curve.

When is standard work used?

The documentation of standard operations is used when relevant information on the processes such as operation times is obtained, or when we need to know the sequence of operations and their relationship to takt time, and once the process has been improved to document the new established methods and train staff in their new job.

When a Kaizen improvement event is done the standard documentation is prepared and used at different stages to have the processes and their improvements documented.

How long does it take to implement standard work?

Depending on the complexity of the process it can take anywhere from one to two weeks.

Procedure for implementing standard work

1. Select a specific process or a process operation.
2. Perform the corresponding time measurements and capture them in table 18.1 (p. 253), "Time measurement sheet".
3. Calculate the operating capacity and fill in table 18.2 (p. 254), "Operating capacity".
4. Design or document the optimized capacity sequence in table 18.3 (p. 256), "Standardized operations combo box".
5. Draw the process in table 18.4 (p. 258), "Standard work".
6. Document the operating instructions in table 18.5 (p. 259), "Operating instructions".

Process	LSSI — LEAN SIX SIGMA INSTITUTE	TIME STUDY DATA COLLECTION SHEET		Date		Process #	

No.	Work elements	Measure point	1	2	3	4	5	6	7	8	9	10	11	12	13	14	15	Lowest repeated time
Cycle Time																		

Table 18.1

Date:

Manager		OPERATIONAL CAPACITY		Part number		Product type		Section	
Assistant				Name		Parts / product		18.2	
								Time available	

| Sequence | Process name | Machine number | Manual | | Automatic | | Total | | Tooling changes | | Manufacturing capacity | Observations |
| | | | | | | | | | Change interval | Changeover time | | |
			Min.	Sec.	Min.	Sec.	Min.	Sec.				

Table 18.2

Time measurement sheet

The time measurement sheet identifies the time a job item starts as well as the time it ends. This sheet measures each job item and sets the standard times for each process operation.

In the time measurement sheet, we record some measurements of each operation's cycle times. We do this by writing down the number of the operation in the process, the description of the job item or the name of the operation and specifying at which point in the operation the operation cycles are completed.

Operating capacity

The operating capacity sheet (see table 18.2) describes the operating capacity at each stage of the process considering the standard manual and/or automatic time of each stage in the process. It also describes how long the changeover takes in each operation sequence. The result is the production capacity of each operation, and this data is given in units of time per piece.

This sheet is used to determine whether the process can work at the takt time rate and to confirm system constraints.

It will also be useful to establish system constraints which will mark the rate of production and be used to feed the value map.

Standardized operations combo box

The combo box (see table 18.3) makes it possible to view the production sequence graphically and design the sequence to optimize capacity. It is also useful for balancing the workload of each operation according to takt time.

Let us take a closer look at the time of each operation to realize that there are activities that could be combined with others to optimize time given the conditions in a future state and assign specific task responsibilities to each operator.

In this table we can see that three activities are carried out in the cutting operation with a cycle time of 22 seconds and a takt time of 79 seconds. As a result, we have a waiting time of 57 seconds that could be taken advantage of to share some tasks from another operation when the continuous flow is set up.

Standard worksheet

The standard worksheet (see table 18.4) presents the process design *(layout)* with the operator and material flow to establish the most efficient movements

LSSI — LEAN SIX SIGMA INSTITUTE

STANDARD WORK COMBINATION SHEET

Project & Model		Date Prepared		Units per shift		Man
Area		Prepared by		Takt time		Auto
						Walk

Operation time (seconds)

Step	Operation	Time			1 5 10 15 20 25 30 35 40 45 50 55 60 65 70
		Manual	Auto	Walk	
	Totals				

Table 18.3

according to static and dynamic operations; distances can be observed and group operations are analyzed.

This diagram presents static and dynamic operations, operators' distances and paths and analyzes the entire process as a whole to have a clear view of the sequence of operations and their flow.

To strengthen the creation of this document it is necessary to generate and validate it together with the operators who will work daily in the area.

Operating instructions

Operating instructions (see table 18.5) must be performed by process engineers or value stream leaders so that each step of the process is properly understood, and any operator may quickly and clearly understand each step of the operation. The generation of instructions strengthens the standardization of processes because with visual aids any process can be understood even an administrative one, and it is an element of the visual control system (see Chapter 8 of this book).

It is recommended that operators, engineers, and personnel from quality and human resources participate in the creation of process instructions so that as a team they consider all relevant aspects of process development.

Aspects to consider when applying standard work

- The standard work documentation is made up of live documents so it must be continuously reviewed and validated.
- These documents should be considered in the implementation of:
- Kaizen events.
- Cellular manufacturing.
- Quick product changeovers (SMED).
- Productive maintenance.
- Kanban.
- Ergonomic and safety improvements.
- These documents must always be made in cooperation with the operators.

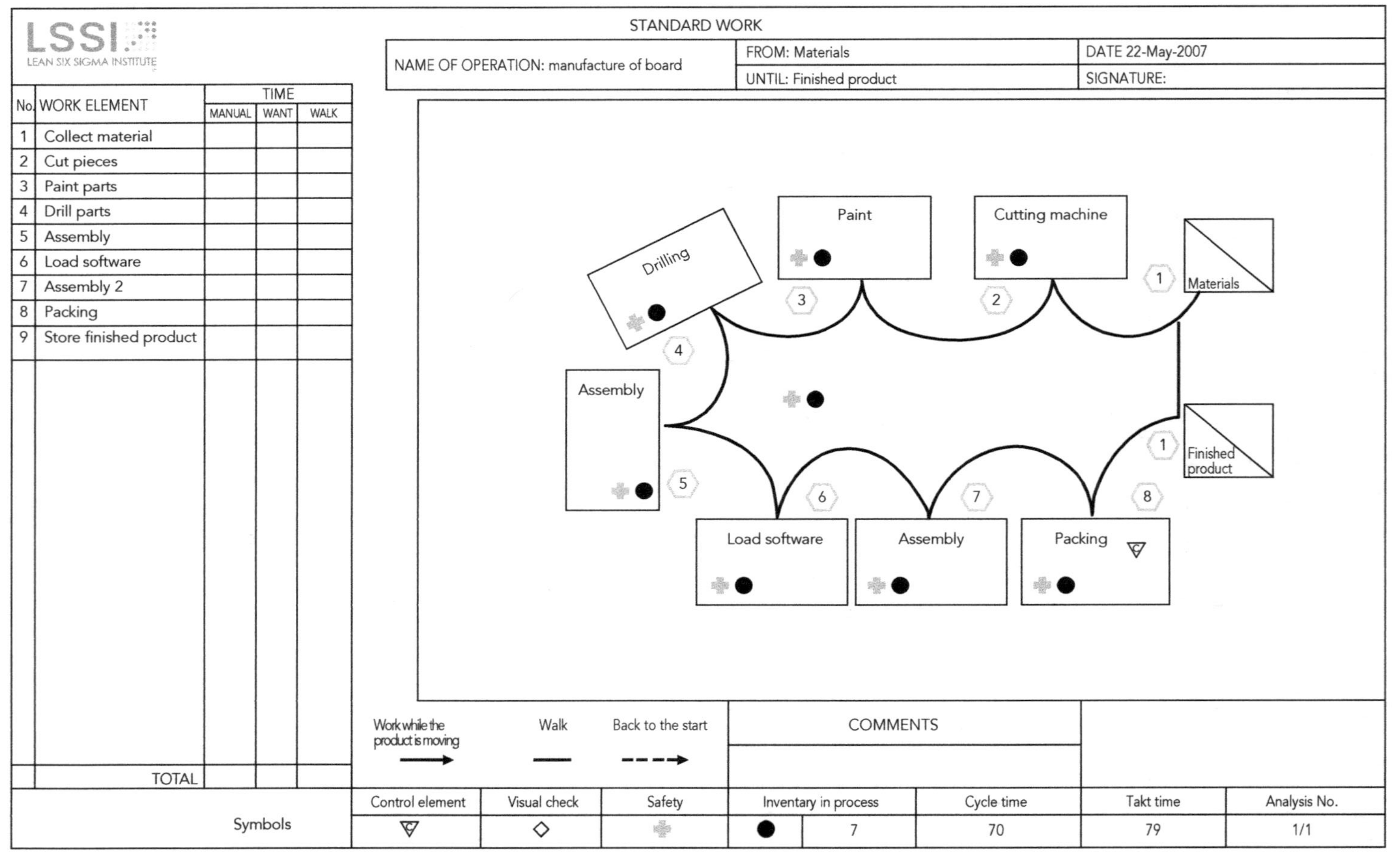

No.	WORK ELEMENT	TIME		
		MANUAL	WANT	WALK
1	Collect material			
2	Cut pieces			
3	Paint parts			
4	Drill parts			
5	Assembly			
6	Load software			
7	Assembly 2			
8	Packing			
9	Store finished product			
	TOTAL			

Table 18.4

WORK INSTRUCTION					
Department:	Area:	Operation:	Type of product:	Made by:	Pg. 1 of 1

NO.	SEQUENCE OF OPERATIONS	KEY POINTS	ILLUSTRATIONS
1			
2			
3			
4			
5			

CHANGES					SAFETY CONSIDERATIONS	SIGNATURES			
Date	Rev	Description of Change	Elim.	Approved		Date	Shift	Supervisor	Operator

Table 18.5

Chapter 19

Lean accounting for decision making

Background

Often times, companies that have initiated a Lean change and have not considered the application of Lean accounting from the outset find that the change appears to have no tangible benefit on their financial and accounting results so they sometimes wonder whether Lean Manufacturing will actually have a tangible benefit in terms of economic profits. It is also common to see that the accounting and financial team is not actively involved in the Lean transformation process and that it appears to be only a manufacturing initiative. That is why Lean Accounting seeks to analyze from a very critical point of view the advantages of Lean changes, not only in terms of economic profits but also in behavior modification.

> "Tell me how you measure me and I will tell you how I will behave."
>
> ELI GOLDRATT

In traditional accounting there are no methods to understand the benefits of Lean changes and sometimes accountants and financiers do not have simple methods to transform Lean changes into financial improvements.

Decision-making must also be agile, so Lean accounting provides better ways to know the benefits in costs, expenses, and changing conditions of business activity which a traditional system don't let us see.

Definition

Lean Accounting is an innovative method to obtain data, turn it into valuable information and generate indicators that support the company's strategic plan and to understand the world of costs and key indicators in the company.

Lean Accounting provides:

- Lean measurements that replace traditional ones.
- Methods to identify the financial impacts of Lean improvements.
- A better understanding of product cost and *value stream* cost.
- New ways of making decisions related to price and profitability.
- Better ways to decide whether to buy or manufacture.
- A way to focus the company on the value created by customers.

What is Lean Accounting implemented for?

Some of the reasons for implementing Lean Accounting are as follows:

- It provides information for taking better Lean decisions.
- It reduces time, costs, and waste by eliminating unnecessary transactions and systems.

Lean Accounting provides:
a very simple way
to understand where
the costs are and
where the value is.

- It identifies the potential benefits of Lean improvement initiatives and focuses on the strategies required to achieve these benefits.
- It motivates long-term Lean improvements by providing information and statistics with a Lean approach.
- It directly adds value to the customer by linking performance measures to the means of value creation and managing changes to maximize that value.
- It provides methods to identify the financial impact of Lean Manufacturing improvements.
- It provides a better way to understand costs, product costs, and *value stream* costs.
- It provides methods to eliminate a large amount of waste from accounting, control, and measurement systems.
- It provides free time for finance staff to work on Lean improvements.
- It provides new boards to make administrative decisions related to pricing, profits, making or buying, nationalization of products, and customers, etc.
- It is a way to focus the company on the value created for customers.

When is Lean Accounting used?

Lean Accounting is applied during all stages of Lean Manufacturing implementation. In the first stage, which refers to the creation of pilot cells, the implementation of the basic operational indicators for manufacturing cells is carried out; in the second stage, the maturity stage, a results table (box score) is implemented that allows operational and financial indicators to be kept for decision-making and in the last stage, key indicators are incorporated to measure the performance of the corporation.

How long does it take to implement Lean Accounting?

Phase 0.	Preparation	1-2 months
Phase 1.	Application of Lean measurements in pilot cells	2-3 months
Phase 2.	Value stream management.	6-12 months
Phase 3.	Maturation	Continuous

Procedure for implementing Lean Accounting

Phase 0. Preparation

In the preparation phase, finance staff and implementation leaders should be trained on the following topics (this preparation takes 40 to 80 hours):

1. Introduction to Lean Accounting.
2. Lean Accounting Diagnosis.
3. Importance of measurements.
4. Box score.
5. Financial statements.
6. Operational accounting.
7. Administrative accounting.
8. Cost accounting.
9. Implementation.

It is also important to establish a baseline for the start of Lean Accounting so that we can realize the benefits that Lean Manufacturing is generating in accounting terms. We can understand the above if we set the values before and after on a support such as table 19.1.

Phase 1. Application of Lean measurements in pilot cells

A company that has started this stage can take the following actions:

- Calculate the benefits of Lean changes.
- Eliminate multiple reports.
- Identify value streams.
- Eliminate waste.
- Implement continuous flow.
- Reduce changeover times.
- Implement productive maintenance.

At this stage, the following measurements are established in the pilot areas:

Daily hourly report

The fundamental measure of Lean performance is the daily hourly report which monitors the success of the cell in achieving the takt time.

Lean Manufacturing project measurements			
Line or processes			Date:
Tangible benefits			
	Before	**After**	**Comments**
Number of operators			
Area	m²	m²	
Current demand			
Delivery time	sec.	sec.	
Inventory			
Inventory turnover			
Product in process			
Changeover time			
Cost of non-quality			
Conversion cost			
Batches			
Parts per operator			
Production capacity			

Table 19.1

Lean cells are designed to achieve a predetermined cycle time for the manufactured product. This time is determined by the takt time required by customer demand.

The daily hourly report monitors the cell's ability to achieve takt time and provides quick feedback when problems occur.

This information is summarized on a dashboard located within the cell and shows the amount of production required each hour to meet the customer's takt time.

First time through production report

The purpose of this report is to monitor the cell for obtaining good products the first time through.

It is a measure of the effectiveness of the cell in standardized work.

Standardized work is an essential feature of Lean Manufacturing.

TIME	PLAN	REAL	DIFFERENCE	TOTAL PLAN	TOTAL REAL	ACCUMULATED DIFFERENCE
8:00 - 9:00	20	13	– 7	20	13	– 7
9:00 - 10:00	20	10	– 10	40	23	– 17
10:00 - 11:00	16	21	+5	56	44	– 12
11:00 - 12:00	20	10	– 10	76	54	– 22
12:00 - 13:00	20	22	+ 2	96	76	– 20
13:00 - 14:00	20	0	– 20	116	76	– 40
14:00 - 15:00	16	25	+ 9	132	101	– 31
15:00 - 16:00	18	12	– 6	150	113	– 37

Figure 19.1

The two main purposes of standardized work are to ensure that the product is made correctly and that the cell production cycle time is met.

Cell operators are trained to complete the production process exactly according to the standardized work.

The "first time through production" report in the cell shows the percentage of product made in the cell without rework, repair, or waste.

Obtaining measurement of first time through production

$$\frac{\text{Total units processed - rejections or repetition of tasks}}{\text{Total units processed}}$$

Example

Total units = 40
Reworked units = 3

$$\text{First time through production} = \frac{40 - 3}{40} = 92.5 \, \%$$

WIP to SWIP

The WIP to SWIP report displays the inventory level in the cell.

WIP is the work in process and SWIP is the standard work in process.

The cells are designed to have a certain amount of inventory. Frequently, this inventory is determined by the number of Kanban's among the work centers of the cell.

The purpose of Kanban is to protect the production process within the cell from delays or problems as well as to maintain the single piece production flow.

Calculation of the WIP to SWIP report

As we saw in Chapter 16, the WIP to SWIP is calculated by dividing the amount of inventory within the cell by the amount of SWIP.

Total inventory in the cell ÷ standard inventory of the cell

The ideal result is 1, which means that the WIP is equal to the SWIP.

If the result is greater than 1, then we have a lot of inventory in the cell.

If the result is less than 1, then there is little inventory and there is a risk that the cell will fall short of production.

Overall Equipment Effectiveness or OEE

See Chapter 9, "Total productive maintenance".

$$OEE = availability \times efficiency \times quality.$$

WIP to SWIP report

Week 22

	SWIP	WIP	Result
Monday	10	11	1.10
Tuesday	10	9	0.09
Wednesday	10	10	1
Thursday	10	7	0.70
Friday	10	14	1.40
Saturday	10	16	1.60

Table 19.2

This measurement represents the truly effective time in a production day or period which is affected by the big equipment losses that occur, such as the following:

- Breakdowns.
- Changeover times.
- Speed reduction.
- Minor stoppages.
- Quality defects.
- Repeat tasks.

Example

Availability = 80 %
Efficiency = 92 %
Quality = 95 %

OEE = 70 %

Overall total performance

The total performance represents a way to measure all the steps in the process considering the quality performance of each one of them and seeking to understand the overall performance of the process.

Calculation of the RTG report

Step 1	1000 enter process	980 leave	Yield = 98 %
Step 2	980 enter process	950 leave	Yield = 97 %
Step 3	950 enter process	900 leave	Yield = 95 %

Total Performance = Performance 1 ×performance 2 × performance 3

$$RTG = .98 \times .97 \times .95 = 90 \ \%.$$

This means that there is a 90% probability that a part will complete each step with zero defects.

Multi-skills Matrix

Name	Register	Get info.	Diagnose	Fix	Testing	Invoice	Check out	Total	Ranking
John Smith	1	3	4	0	2	1	1	**12**	C
Bob Hope	5	5	5	5	5	5	5	**35**	G
Robert Mills	3	4	2	1	5	4	2	**21**	E
Dave Jones	1	0	4	4	2	2	1	**14**	C

Table 19.3

Cross-training

A requirement for cell manufacturing to function satisfactorily is that operators know the operations to be able to balance the work and exchange functions. This measurement will help operators to be aware of their level of preparation in the different jobs and implement a powerful training program.

Performance measurement system

Now that the production cells are already functioning, we need a way to measure the performance of the team and not that of the people. One of the main contributions of Lean Accounting is to stop measuring people and instead, measure team processes.

For this purpose, it's proposed to use a performance evaluation system based on group and individual results as shown in table 19.4.

This example shows an evaluation where the first four indicators evaluate team performance while the last two evaluate individual work. As can be seen, the focus is on teamwork and the goals set mainly modifying the behavior and attitude towards work, because now staff will not only seek the individual good but also the participation of their colleagues to achieve the results.

With this evaluation system we can establish a system of incentives that translate into benefits for the people who work in this scheme.

Some of the benefits of implementing Lean Manufacturing in pilot cells are:

- Lean production cells successfully implemented.
- Extensive training in Lean principles.
- Pull flow in pilot areas.
- Quick product changeovers
- Standardized work.
- Quality at source and inspection carried out by the operator.

Indicator	Objective	Value
Production	100 pieces	30 points
Defects	0 defects	20 points
OEE	68%	15 points
On time deliveries	100%	10 points
Work station audit	0 cautions	10 points
Attendance	0 absences	10 points
Punctuality	0 lates	5 points
	Total	**100 points**

Table 19.4

Some of the benefits of implementing Lean Manufacturing in pilot cells are:

- Lean performance measurements in production cells.
- Calculation of the financial impact of Lean improvements.
- Elimination of many of the transactions.
- Identification of primary cost and performance indicators.

Phase 2. Value stream management

At the beginning of the stream management phase, all members of the company fully understand cellular manufacturing. So, it can be said that we have learned good lessons on improvement from applying it first in pilot areas. We also have an impeccable plant for the application of 5S and with the visual controls it has been shown that all the key indicators of the production cells can be quickly understood.

At this stage, the Kaizen improvement teams already understand the importance of organized and well-focused work and are ready to start a company-wide transformation.

The Kanban system has been integrated into the pilot cell and we can start with the preparation of the information to implement it in other areas. Inventories are relatively low and consistent.

In the value stream management phase, a results table called the box score or results table, is introduced, which is a key element in decision-making and a tool that connects strategic planning (see Chapter 4, "Hoshin kanri strategy") to short-term execution and decision-making.

This tool consists of three sections, one for operational indicators, the second for capacity use and the third for financial results.

The following is an example of a *box score* used in decision making.

The yellow area contains operational indicators that should give information on the progress of initiatives related to operations. In the green area there are fulfilment percentages for demand, production capacity, and available capacity. Finally, in the Blue Area there are financial indicators that make it possible to do a simple balance sheet to know the profitability of the value stream without having to obtain the accounting information monthly or quarterly.

The role of finance staff

The financial and accounting team moves from a passive state in operational decision-making to a proactive state in which it largely leads the way towards a world-class company by analyzing the measurements made and making short-term decisions. In the implementation of Lean Manufacturing, accounting staff spend at least half of their time analyzing trends and indicators and charting the direction of the company as this process has a strategic approach.

Why is Lean costing so simple?

Value stream costing is simple because detailed current costs of jobs or products in production are not collected. Costs are collected for the entire value stream and added up in weekly periods. Staff costs are simply added to salaries and direct benefits paid to people working in the value stream, and this data is easily obtained from the payroll system.

The summary of material costs is also obtained weekly. All purchases are assigned to the value stream cost center, as are supplies, tools, and other costs. These are simply applied to the value stream cost center and are obtained from the accounts payable process.

It's a very simple process when operating conditions allow for a continuous flow and the cost and engineering effort can be better focused on teamwork to detect variations in cost since the decision on prices also depends on this.

Standard Costing is a complete and correct method for calculating the cost of products for companies that are involved in mass production methods. Standard Costing is structured based on assumptions about production processes. These assumptions may be valid for traditional manufacturing done in production batches.

In traditional manufacturing, each product has its own unique path of production.

In Lean, products that have similar production flows are grouped in a value stream. These groups greatly simplify the costing process because we will see the cost of the value stream.

Typically, the flow rate through the value stream is determined by the flow rate of the product through the bottleneck operation within the value stream. The number of units that can be shipped is constrained by the number of units that can be processed through the bottleneck operation.

The cell or value stream can only work as fast as the slowest operation or bottleneck.

For the cost of the products, we need the following data:

Conversion cost

These are the expenses incurred during the period and include salaries, energy, administrative support expenses, rent, etc., that is, everything that must be paid for even though nothing is produced. Generally, they are obtained weekly and divided by the hours worked during the week in order to obtain an hourly conversion cost.

To keep track of the conversion cost, a table like 19.5 should be prepared to have an accurate and short-term control of the costs of each value stream:

Material costs

These are the costs incurred in materials and any other totally variable cost each time a product is produced and sold.

Production rate

This is the rhythm of the whole system or cell to produce a certain part number.

Phase 3. Maturation

In the maturation phase, metrics such as costing by objectives are introduced, many transactions are eliminated, and financial indicators are used to drive improvement and change. At the beginning of this phase, the company is already organized by value streams, there is extensive cooperation between customers, and suppliers and continuous improvement is already a way of life.

In the Lean Accounting aspect, costing by objectives will be used to understand customer value and in product design to link value to business objectives.

Value stream mapping already extends across the supply chain and many of the administrative processes are being simplified or made more agile. Routine accounting activities have been automated.

Conversion costs

	Material cost	External cost	Employee cost	Employee cost	Other costs	Conversion cost
Customer service			$ 12,108			$ 12,108
Purchases			$ 16,145			$ 16,145
Logistics	$ 358,512		$ 17,080	$ 16,956	$ 20,000	$ 54,036
Assortment of materials	$ 25,608		$ 23,485	$ 2,016		$ 25,501
Testing and reworking			$ 17,080	$ 3,528		$ 20,608
Assembly	$ 128,040		$ 10,675			$ 10,675
Shipment			$ 2,669			$ 2,669
Quality assurance			$ 8,073			$ 8,073
Manufacturing engineering			$ 8,073			$ 8,073
Maintenance			$ 8,073			$ 8,073
Accounting			$ 8,073			$ 8,073
Information systems			$ 4,036			$ 4,036
Design engineering		$ 7,760	$ 4,036			$ 11,796
TOTAL	$ 512,160	$ 7,760	$ 139,606	$ 22,500	$ 20,000	$ 189,866
Hours per week						40
Conversion cost per hour						$ 4,747

Table 19.5

Example

Let us take a look at an example to illustrate the concept of production rate.

In the Lean Shop company, they have two products and these are manufactured in the same value stream.

The conversion cost for this process unit is $ 7,000 per hour.

	Product 1	**Product 2**
Material cost	$ 435 per unit	$ 553 per unit
Production rate	16 parts / hour	35 parts / hour

Cost of product 1

Material	$ 435
Conversion	$ 437.5 (i.e. $ 7,000 ÷ 16)
Cost	$ 872,5

Cost of product 2

Material	$ 553
Conversion	$ 200 (i.e. $ 7,000 ÷ 35)
Cost	$ 753

If we want to make decisions about the utility or profit of the products, we could stop taking the profit margin for making decisions about the price and profitability of each product. We should use the generation speed as the primary indicator, for example.

We have three products: A, B and C, whose prices and costs are as follows:

		Margin analysis by product					
Product	Selling price	Cost of materials	Direct labor	GIF	Total cost	Margin	Priority
A	$ 300.00	$ 174.00	$ 17.05	$ 40.80	$ 231.85	$ 68.15	1
B	$ 95.00	$ 62.00	$ 5.30	$ 12.69	$ 79.99	$ 15.01	3
C	$ 195.00	$ 140.00	$ 7.58	$ 18.14	$ 165.72	$ 29.28	2

We can see that the best positioned product is A because it has a margin of $ 68 but in the Lean system we will analyze an additional concept: the speed of the bottleneck, i.e. production or sales capacity.

For the same example we will use the decision process based on the speed of the system to generate profits.

			Analysis of the actual contribution			
Product	Selling price	Cost of materials	*Throughput*	Time per part (sec.)	*Throughput por second*	Number
A	$ 350.00	$ 170.00	$ 180.00	45	$ 4.00	2
B	$ 120.00	$ 78.00	$ 42.00	20	$ 2.10	3
C	$ 198.00	$ 122.00	$ 76.00	10	$ 7.60	1

In this case the only data we require are the selling price and the totally variable costs of each product, bearing in mind that the operating expenses have to be covered regardless of the decisions we make on the products.

Now we have C as the best product because it gives the highest generation speed at 7.6 dollars per second, followed by A at 4 dollars per second and finally product B at 2.1 dollars per second.

In the maturation and excellence phase it is also very important to use the ROI indicator (return on investment), which explains in a single number the result of the company.

The ROI is obtained by multiplying the profit margin for the period by the rotation of goods, which are shown in the diagram on the next page.

With this diagram it is possible to understand the progress of Lean changes from a systemic approach in which we can see the components of the return on investment.

When carrying out a Kaizen activity aimed at reducing or eliminating waste or excess, it is important to analyze the impact on costs, operating expenses, and inventories. The simulator we present in a spreadsheet can be used to observe the financial impact; for example, if we reduce inventory as a result of an improvement event (Kaizen), this amount affects the return on investment and we will have an objective assessment by taking a systemic point of view, i.e. an improvement is reflected in the entire system.

In the branches of the operating profit margin the components and the relationship between them can be observed. We see that the sum of materials plus the cost of manpower plus indirect costs gives the cost of product which added to selling costs plus administration costs plus taxes gives the cost of sales. And if the cost of sales is subtracted from sales, then the profit is obtained. Finally, the division of profits by sales gives the profit margin on sales.

In the branch on the right, corresponding to rotation (see figure 19.4), it is observed that the sum of inventories plus accounts receivable plus cash minus current liabilities gives the working capital and this added to the permanent investment minus the initial debt, gives us the net investment; and if sales are compared again with net investment, then rotation is obtained.

Finally, if we multiply the profit margin on sales it's possible to obtain the return on investment which, in a single number, indicates the overall performance of the business.

In the mature state of Lean accounting, we find that administrative aspects in areas of financial, operational and administrative accounting will evolve as the fundamental changes are introduced. Such changes will allow for more streamlined accounting processes. Some examples of these changes are:

- **Accounts payable**
  Go from many payment processing procedures to releasing materials directly to the production line and paying the supplier directly for them by electronic means.

- **Accounts receivable**
  Go from complex processing procedures to payments made directly by electronic transfers related to the actual consumption of the product.

- **Administrative authorizations**
  Go from releases and authorization reviews to a point where each level of the chain has authority and responsibility in capital management.

- **Monthly closings**
  Change monthly closings that represent major adjustments for financial statements that show the actual situation at any time.

ROI
7%
RONA
29%
% Profit/Sales
24%
Net Investment
$ 17.356.000
Sales
$ 5.000.000
Working Capital
$ 15.090.000
Permanent Investment
$ 2.300.000
Initial Debt
$ 34.000
Accounts Receivable
$ 90.000
Inventory
$ 15.000.000
Cash
$ 4.000
Current Liabilities
$ 4.000
Profit
$ 1.180.000
Sales
$ 5.000.000
Cost of Sales
$ 3.820.000
Sales
$ 5.000.000
Cost of Sales
$ 180.000
Administrative Cost
$ 500.000
Taxes
$ 90.000
Production Costs
$ 3.050.000
Overhead
$ 800.000
Materials
$ 2.000.000
Labor
$ 250.000

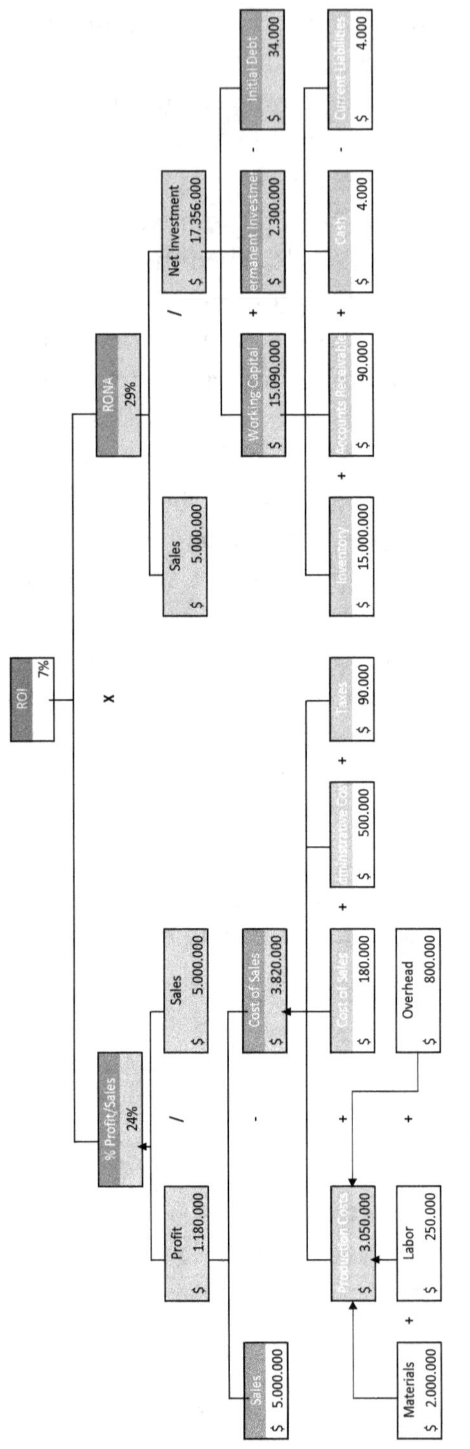

Figure 19.2

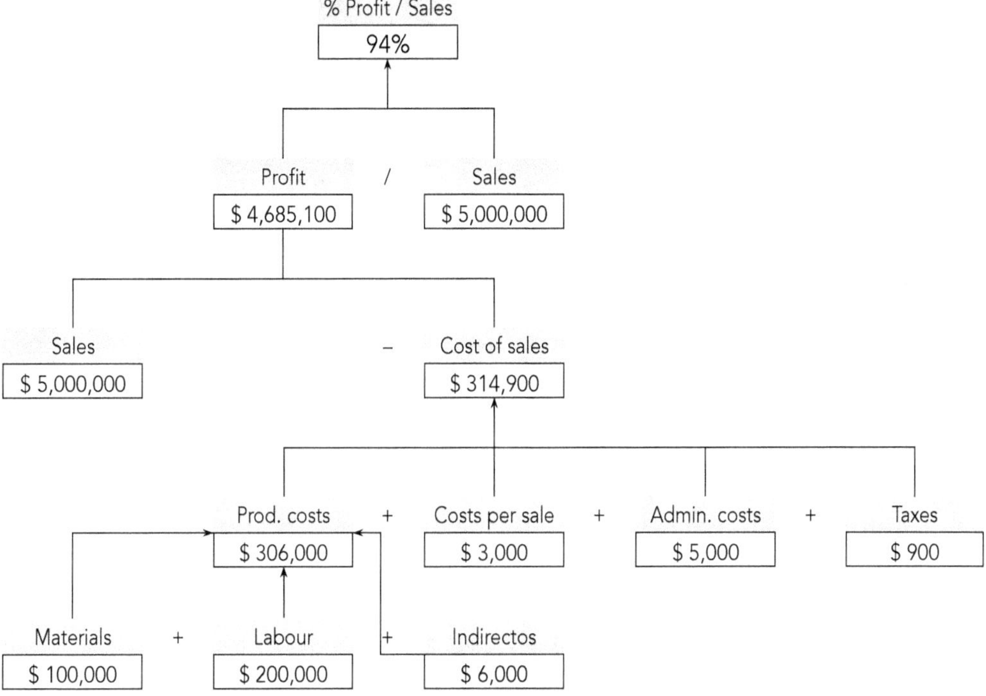

Figure 19.3

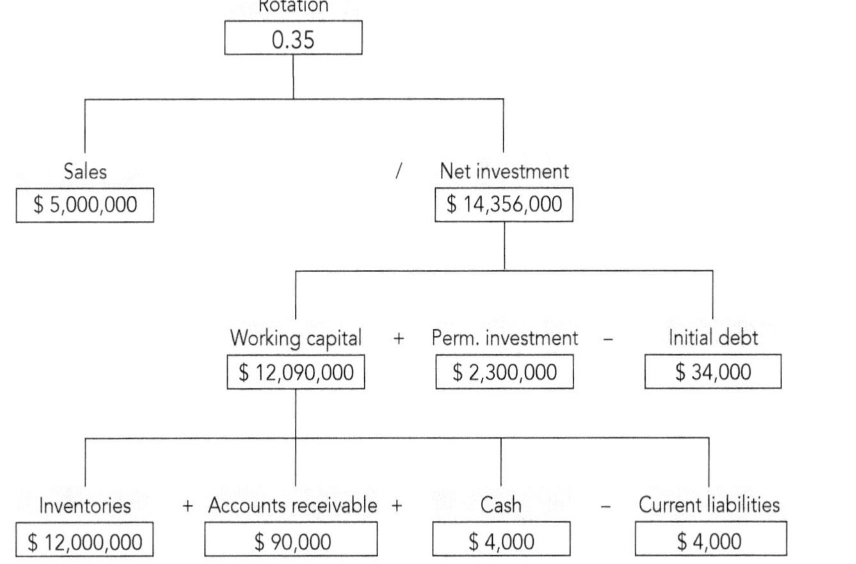

Figure 19.4

- **Material costs**
  Set aside the allocation of accumulated material costs to the product and transfer material costs directly, thus reducing inventory and cycle time.

- **Labor and indirect costs**
  Change the monitored tracking and control of manpower for each operation by charging the work done directly to the value stream production.

- **Inventory traceability**
  Increase the reliability of information by eliminating the need for physical inventories.

- **Cost of product**
  Stop assigning indirect manufacturing expenses to cost and assign the costs directly to the supply chain.

- **Alignment of company strategy and goals**
  Go from assessing efficiency based on objectives and measurements, especially financial ones, to a statistical analysis that allows an accurate understanding of variability in results.

- **Performance measurements**
  Go from results obtained by historical analysis to a statistical analysis of the process in order to measure performance by incorporating Six Sigma objectives.

- **Budgets and planning**
  Stop managing budgets for each department and manage the objectives at cell level.

- **Product utility management**
  Transform the passive use of historical costs into an integral use of the characteristics of the product to link it directly to the customer.

- **Role of accounting staff**
  Transform the concept of accounting staff from performance evaluators into integral members of the supply chain.

- **Continuous improvement**
  Move the waste, no longer hiding it within the indicators of the financial statements, to a place that positions it as the first goal of work and improvement.

- **Faculty and learning**
  Rethink the use of performance metrics, turning them into a tool that enables employees to learn and improve, succeeding and expanding available capacity proactively and creatively.

- **Financial benefits of Lean changes**
  Stop seeing only isolated benefits of Lean changes in reducing costs and improving efficiency, using information on financial advantages in sales and the approach to business strategies.

- **Organization by *value stream***
  Stop being an organization that functions departmentally, reorganize the company along the supply chain and eliminate functional departments.

- **Customer value and costing by objectives**
  Stop managing by product and move beyond Lean goals, modifying our product features to the customer's specific needs and requirements.

- **Rewards and recognition**
  Go from performance by cost-cutting initiatives to a profit-sharing program that financially rewards each person for achieving Lean goals.

Part IX

Tools for energy reduction

Chapter 20

Energy saving

Background

Normally, energy saving is not considered a usual project among traditional companies since the bill is normally passed to the payment department and they cover the expense.

Few people know their electricity bill in detail and far fewer do a detailed analysis of consumption and above all, the detection of energy waste.

We simply do not know the cost of energy added to the products and services that are produced. Hence the importance of introducing in this chapter the subject of energy saving and its multiple alternatives for reducing consumption and therefore, conversion costs.

Definition

An energy saving event is a task carried out by a team that understands the concepts related to the consumption and use of energy as an integral part of Lean Manufacturing projects. Just remember that Lean's goal is to reduce or eliminate waste wherever it is found. Energy saving is a factor that has gained momentum globally and is expected to become increasingly more important.

The objective of this chapter is to provide a practical approach to taking simple steps without the need to invest in specialized equipment. The electricity bill will already give us useful information to begin to take corrective action and reduce consumption and the amount of money paid for each bill.

Energy consumption data

- Global energy consumption has grown exponentially in recent decades. The world's largest energy consumers are consuming more and more. According to the report of the World Economic Forum, the energy consumption of countries such as China, India, Japan, Russia, and the United States far exceeds the consumption of the twenty nations with the best energy architecture.
- Today, fossil fuels are consumed at a rate 100,000 times greater than the time it takes to generate them.
- Currently 95% of companies waste energy in some way; only 1% do anything about it.
- Energy expenditure accounts for between 10 and 30% of the operating costs of companies and institutions.
- In a period of 7 to 20 years the energy that Mexico produces will not be sufficient to meet national demand.
- Just using energy-efficient "ready-to-use" technologies could reduce the cost of heating, cooling, and lighting homes and workplaces by 80% (U.S. Department of Energy and Maryland Energy Administration).

Introduction

To avoid getting into subjects that are too technical for most people, let us look at a simpler approach (some may consider it oversimplified but, for what we wish to exemplify this is enough).

It should be borne in mind that, for this explanation the example presented is made with Mexico's HM tariff (for general service at medium voltage with a demand of 100 kW or more), which is the most common in companies and in industry and the one that allows most savings if it's properly managed. With this rate schedule, electricity varies in price depending on the time of day. On the CFE website (www.cfe.gob.mx) for example, more information can be found.

Time-of-use rates

This company operates three times, each of which charges a different price for electricity consumed. The times are:

- Base.
- Intermediate.
- Peak.

Although it is true that the price of electricity changes every month, suffice it to say that when consuming 1 kWh at peak time, it costs 3.8 times more than consuming it at base time and three times more than consuming it at intermediate time. This is because during peak time the CFE must provide electricity to turn on street lighting throughout the country.

What the electricity supply company is trying to do is to influence the companies' consumption habits so that they shift the electrical loads to another time and leave more slack to fulfill the supply at the time with the highest load.

Peak time changes in winter and summer since it gets darker earlier during the winter and the street lighting must be turned on earlier. For this reason, during the months from April to October, two electricity bills are received because one part of the month is charged at daylight saving time and the other at winter time.

- **Summer:** summer is the period between the first Sunday in April and the Saturday before the last Sunday in October.
- **Winter:** winter is the period between the last Sunday in October and the Saturday before the first Sunday in April.

Figure 20.1 shows the times for the Central, Northeast, Northwest, North, Peninsular and South regions (available on the CFE website).

Important metrics

I) consumption (represented as "Energy charge" on the bill)

a) **Kilowatt-hour (kWh):** are the kilowatts consumed by each device, multiplied by the number of hours it has been operating throughout the month. Separate readings are recorded at the different times already mentioned (base, intermediate, and peak).

b) **Unit price:** is the amount to be paid for each kilowatt-hour consumed. The price varies according to the time at which it's used, be it base, intermediate, or peak.

| Central, North East, North West, North, Peninsular and South regions | | | |
| From the first Sunday in April to the Saturday before the last Sunday in October | | | |
Day of the week	Base	Intermediate	Base
Monday to Friday	0:00 - 6:00	6:00 - 20:00 22:00 - 24:00	20:00 - 22:00
Saturday	0:00 - 7:00	7:00 - 24:00	
Sunday and public holidays	0:00 - 19:00	19:00 - 24:00	

Del último domingo de octubre al sábado anterior al primer domingo de abril			
Day of the week	Base	Intermediate	Base
Monday to Friday	0:00 - 6:00	6:00 - 18:00 22:00 - 24:00	18:00 - 22:00
Saturday	0:00 - 8:00	8:00 - 19:00 21:00 - 24:00	19:00 - 21:00
Sunday and public holidays	0:00 - 18:00	18:00 - 24:00	

Figure 20.1

II) demand (represented as "Demand charge" on the invoice)

c) **Kilowatt (kW):** is the maximum amount of energy required by the company during an interval of 15 minutes throughout the month.

III) Power and load factor

d) **Power factor:** is the fraction of power used by electrical equipment compared to the total apparent power supplied. It is expressed as a percentage. The power factor indicates that a piece of electrical equipment (or a group) causes the electric current supplied at the point of use to be out of phase with the voltage.

For practical purposes, the important thing here is that the section where it says "Power factor" should be 90.00% or higher, since the CFE penalizes with a "Power factor charge" those users whose factor is below 90% and gives discounts to users whose power factor is over 90%.

e) **Load factor:** unlike the power factor, in this case there are no penalties or discounts; this measurement only informs about the balance of loads in our company. It is simply a division of the average consumption for the month by the maximum. For example, if we normally consume an average of 70 kW per month and the maximum reached was 100 kW, our load factor is 70%.

A low load factor means that during a certain period in the month several pieces of equipment whose consumption far exceeds the average are put to work simultaneously. This is an invitation to analyze which pieces of equipment really need to operate simultaneously and which ones can stay off during that period and be turned on before or after.

What is an energy saving event for?

The following are some of the benefits from performing an energy saving event:

- Obtain economic savings by eliminating waste and inefficiencies in the use of energy resources.
- Help preserve non-renewable energy resources.
- Know the energy consumption patterns of the company.
- Identify areas of opportunity to carry out studies in more detail later on.
- Instill interest in creating an energy-saving culture.

When is an energy saving event used?

An energy saving event can take place at any time.

How long does it take to hold an energy saving event?

One to two weeks.

Procedure for conducting an energy saving event

1. Obtain the electricity bills for the last twelve months.
2. Look for trends, patterns in consumption, and/or areas of opportunity.
3. Apply corrective measures.

To increase the load factor (and therefore, reduce the maximum demand used in the month and the amount payable), a detailed study is made to achieve a better load balance. In other words, we are looking for ways not to use all the pieces of equipment at the same time but to "stagger" their use when possible.

Example

1. All bills are taken in the proposed format.

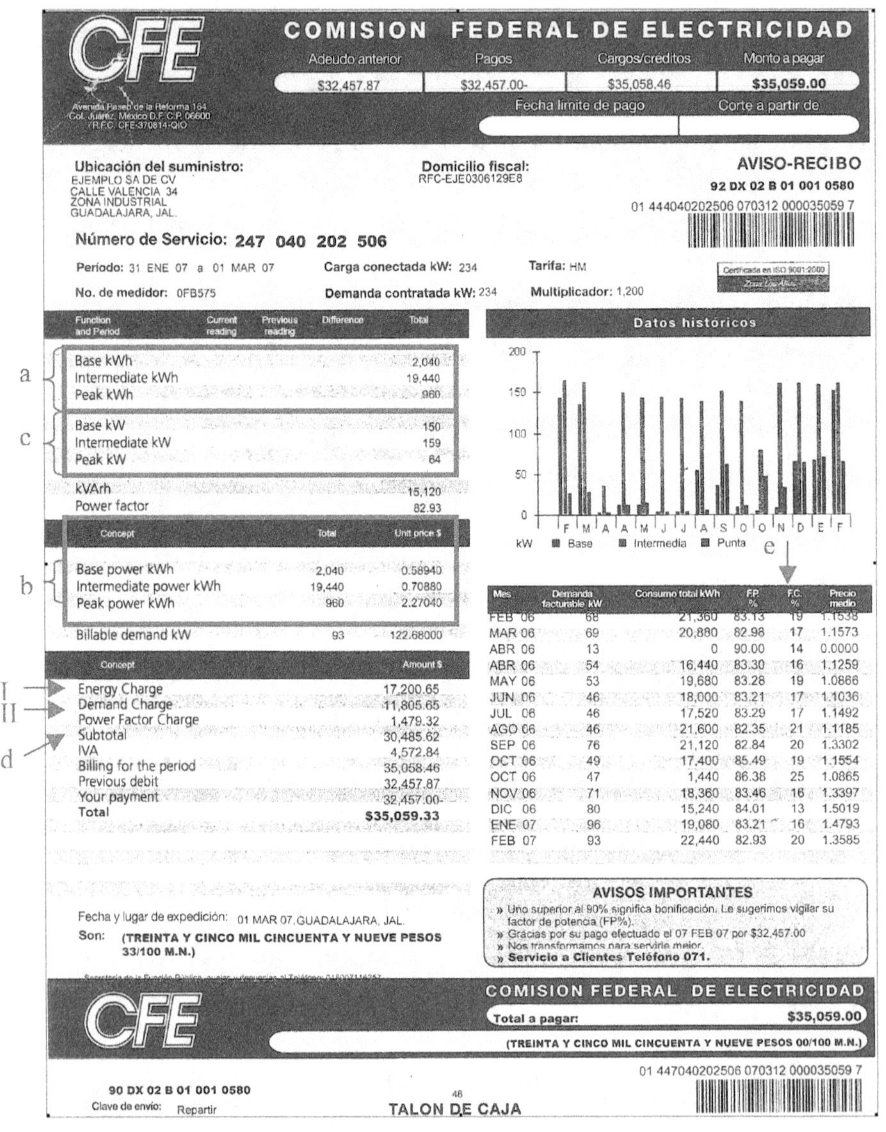

Mes	Demanda facturable kW	Consumo total kWh	F.P. %	F.C. %	Precio medio
FEB 06	68	21,360	83.13	19	1.1538
MAR 06	69	20,880	82.98	17	1.1573
ABR 06	13	0	90.00	14	0.0000
ABR 06	54	16,440	83.30	16	1.1259
MAY 06	53	19,680	83.28	19	1.0866
JUN 06	46	18,000	83.21	17	1.1036
JUL 06	46	17,520	83.29	17	1.1492
AGO 06	46	21,600	82.35	21	1.1185
SEP 06	76	21,120	82.84	20	1.3302
OCT 06	49	17,400	85.49	19	1.1554
OCT 06	47	1,440	86.38	25	1.0865
NOV 06	71	18,360	83.46	16	1.3397
DIC 06	80	15,240	84.01	13	1.5019
ENE 07	96	19,080	83.21	16	1.4793
FEB 07	93	22,440	82.93	20	1.3585

Figure 20.2

Electric power consumption record (2019)

	Jan	Feb	Mar	Apr	May	Jun	Jul	Aug	Sep	Oct	Nov	Dec
Base kWh	648	1,560	720	720	720	600	480	720	480	700	600	1.080
Intermediate kWh	18,324	19,560	20,760	15,480	18,720	17,820	17,040	20,760	19,560	17,880	17,400	13,800
Peak kWh	384	240	120	480	240	120	0	120	1,080	480	360	360
Total consumption kWh	19,356	21,360	21,600	16,680	19,680	18,540	17,520	21,600	21,120	19,080	18,360	15,240
Base kWh price	$ 0.5940	$ 0.5843	$ 0.5785	$ 0.5673	$ 0.5797	$ 0.6026	$ 0.6288	$ 0.6403	$ 0.6358	$ 0.6354	$ 0.6232	$ 0.6211
Inter. kWh price	$ 0.7146	$ 0.7029	$ 0.6967	$ 0.6825	$ 0.6074	$ 0.7249	$ 0.7564	$ 0.7702	$ 0.7648	$ 0.7643	$ 0.7496	$ 0.7471
Peak kWh price	$ 2.2884	$ 2.2509	$ 2.1983	$ 2.1859	$ 2.2333	$ 2.3215	$ 2.3894	$ 2.4666	$ 2.4493	$ 2.4478	$ 2.4008	$ 2.3929
Base kWh	12	143	54	12	12	4	4	54	36	4	8	64
Intermediate kWh	149	165	137	149	143	143	141	137	150	78	159	159
Peak kWh price	62	26	6	12	14	4	4	6	62	46	33	63
kvArh	12,924	14,280	14,880	10,920	13,080	12,000	11,640	14,880	14,280	11,400	12,120	9,840
Power factor	0.83	0.83	0.82	0.84	0.83	0.84	0.83	0.82	0.83	0.85	0.82	0.84
Load factor	17.46%	19.26%	21.19%	15.55%	18.50%	18.01%	16.70%	21.19%	19.56%	32.88%	16.04%	12.88%
Billable demand (kW)	89	68	46	54	53	46	46	46	89	56	71	92
Unit price kW	$ 123. 66	$ 121. 63	$ 122	$ 121.54	$ 120.68	$ 125.45	$ 130.89	$ 133.29	$ 132.36	$ 132.40	$ 129.74	$ 129.31
Cargo o bonificación por % FP	4.9%	5.0%	5.6%	4.5%	4.8%	4.3%	4.8%	5.6%	5.2%	2.9%	4.7%	4.3%
Base kWh price	$ 14,357.99	$ 15,200.45	$ 15,143.81	$ 12,022.55	$ 14,008.70	$ 13,557.86	$ 13,190.88	$ 16,746.36	$ 17,909.92	$ 15,289.12	$ 14,281.25	$ 11,842.21
Inter. kWh price	$ 11,005.74	$ 8,270.84	$ 5,592.68	$ 6,563.16	$ 6,396.04	$ 5,770.70	$ 6,020.94	$ 6,131.34	$ 11,780.04	$ 7,414.40	$ 9,211.54	$ 11,896.52
Power Factor Charge	$ 1,250.66	$ 1,163.25	$ 1,155.68	$ 844.35	$ 978.41	$ 835.81	$ 928.24	$ 1,275.01	$ 1,539.41	$ 659.68	$ 1,105.29	$ 1,015.52
Low voltage charge	$ 532.29	$ 492.69	$ 437.84	$ 388.60	$ 427.84	$ 403.29	$ 402.80	$ 483.05	$ 624.59	$ 467.44	$ 491.96.29	$ 495.09
Subtotal	$ 27,146.67	$ 24,634.54	$ 21,892.07	$ 19,430.06	$ 21,392.15	$ 20,164.37	$ 20,140.06	$ 24,152.71	$ 31,229.37	$ 23,372.20	$ 24,598.08	$ 24,754.25
VAT	$ 4,072.00	$ 3,695.18	$ 3,283.83	$ 2,914.51	$ 3,208.82	$ 3,024.65	$ 3,021.01	$ 3,622.91	$ 4,684.41	$ 3,505.83	$ 3,689.71	$ 3,713.14
TOTAL	$ 31,218.67	$ 28,329.72	$ 25,175.99	$ 22,344.57	$ 24,600.97	$ 23,189.02	$ 23,161.07	$ 27,775.62	$ 35,913.78	$ 26,878.03	$ 28,287.79	$ 28,467.39

Figure 20.3

2. The graphs obtained from entering the data are analyzed.

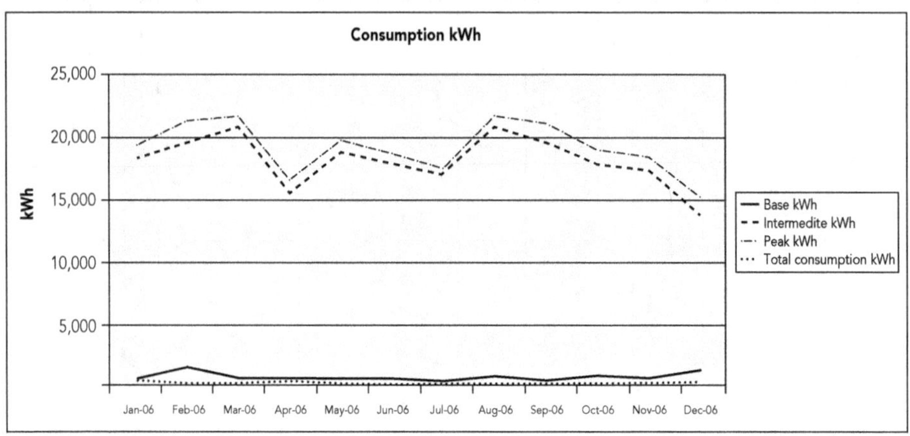

Figure 20.4

- It can be seen that consumption levels are going down as the end of the year approaches. The time when most work is done is by far the intermediate.

- As shown in figure 20.5, both load factor and power factor levels are very low, resulting in more expensive electric power bills.

- In the search for areas of opportunity, below are some ideas that could significantly reduce energy consumption.

Air leakage detection.

Electric power consumption record (2019)

	31	28	31	30	31	30	31	30	31	30	31	30
	Jan	**Feb**	**Mar**	**Apr**	**May**	**Jun**	**Jul**	**Aug**	**Sep**	**Oct**	**Nov**	**Dec**
Base kWh	648	1,560	720	720	720	600	480	720	480	700	600	1.080
Intermediate kWh	18,324	19,560	20,760	15,480	18,720	17,820	17,040	20,760	19,560	17,880	17,400	13,800
Peak kWh	384	240	120	480	240	120	0	120	1,080	480	360	360
Total consumption kWh	**19,356**	**21,360**	**21,600**	**16,680**	**19,680**	**18,540**	**17,520**	**21,600**	**21,120**	**19,080**	**18,360**	**15,240**
Base kWh price	$ 0.5940	$ 0.5843	$ 0.5785	$ 0.5673	$ 0.5797	$ 0.6026	$ 0.6288	$ 0.6403	$ 0.6358	$ 0.6354	$ 0.6232	$ 0.6211
Inter. kWh price	$ 0.7146	$ 0.7029	$ 0.6967	$ 0.6825	$ 0.6074	$ 0.7249	$ 0.7564	$ 0.7702	$ 0.7648	$ 0.7643	$ 0.7496	$ 0.7471
Peak kWh price	$ 2.2884	$ 2.2509	$ 2.1983	$ 2.1859	$ 2.2333	$ 2.3215	$ 2.3894	$ 2.4666	$ 2.4493	$ 2.4478	$ 2.4008	$ 2.3929
Base kWh	12	143	54	12	12	4	4	54	36	4	8	64
Intermediate kWh	149	165	137	149	143	143	141	137	150	78	159	159
Peak kWh	62	26	6	12	14	4	4	6	62	46	33	63
kvArh	12,924	14,280	14,880	10,920	13,080	12,000	11,640	14,880	14,280	11,400	12,120	9,840
Power Factor	0.83	0.83	0.82	0.84	0.83	0.84	0.83	0.82	0.83	0.86	0.83	0.84
Load factor	**17.46%**	**19.26%**	**21.19%**	**15.55%**	**18.50%**	**18.01%**	**16.70%**	**21.19%**	**19.56%**	**32.88%**	**16.04%**	**12.88%**

Figure 20.5

- Detect leaks. Every time we hear an air leak, we might not think it is a major loss but, if we consider that each one could cost between $ 300 and $ 1,000 a year and if we add up all the small leaks that might exist, the sum could be between $ 50,000 and $ 150,000 for medium to large companies.

  To measure and quantify gas leaks, it is advisable to use ultrasound equipment which admits a sound range of between 20 and 100 kHz and at these frequencies we will find a world of opportunities.

- Do not use the equipment at peak times. It is almost 3.5 times more expensive to use the equipment in two or three hours considered as peak hours because during those hours homes and other applications require more electric power, usually between 19:00 and 22:00 hours, depending on the time tariff.

  If we stopped using most appliances during this time, especially if capacity is greater than demand, we could achieve considerable savings in electricity expenditure.

- If we analyze the value stream map and the balance chart we find that if there are processes slower than takt time and we use them to produce more than what is needed, we start generating inventories in process or finished products; these inventories include an energy charge because machines, lights, etc. were used for processing them and they may even have been generated during peak hours. Therefore, the power consumed to produce those inventories can be

Load balancing

An electric charge within a system can be defined as any element that consumes power. Some examples are motors, elements (ovens), spotlights, air conditioning units, refrigerators, and power tools. On the "Demand" section of an electric power consumption bill it is necessary to clarify that what is charged is simply the maximum peak recorded during the entire billing period. It is very important to point this out because it means that if during the month the usual consumption of electric power in the peak

saved if we balance operations and establish continuous flow, or those resources can simply be used if necessary to meet demand.

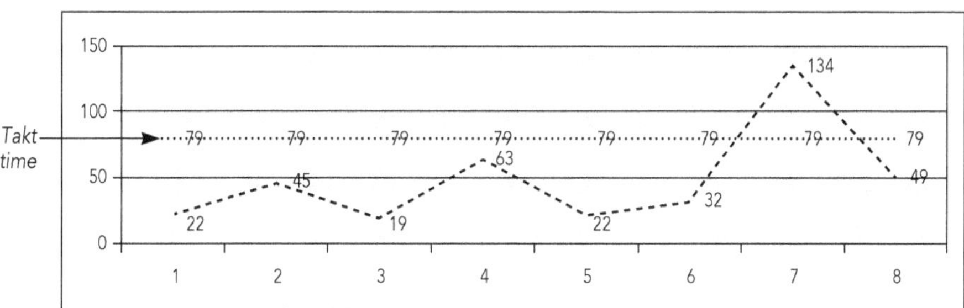

Figure 20.6

3. Corrective measures are applied. To improve the power factor, it is suggested to consult experts who, by an analysis with specialized equipment, will be able to determine the requirements for installing the capacitor banks. In some cases, these will dramatically increase the power factor. It should be noted that the investment made in capacitor banks is recovered in less than a year due to the discounts that are received from the CFE for having a power factor over 90%.

hours (20:00 to 22:00 hours in summer and 18:00 to 22:00 hours in winter) was 50 kW, but just one day for an interval of 15 minutes and for some unusual reason consumption was 100 kW, then the amount billed is 100 kW.

'Iherefore, it is necessary to be aware of the demand used. Below, we present a spreadsheet provided with this book where the impact of having better management of electric power demand can be tested by trial and error (see figure 20.7).

Demand Charge (Summer)
Summary of maximum peaks
Balance graph
Demand distribution
The colors indicate which time we are working in
The numbers in red indicate maximum consumption peaks within each time-of-use
Total for concept of demand

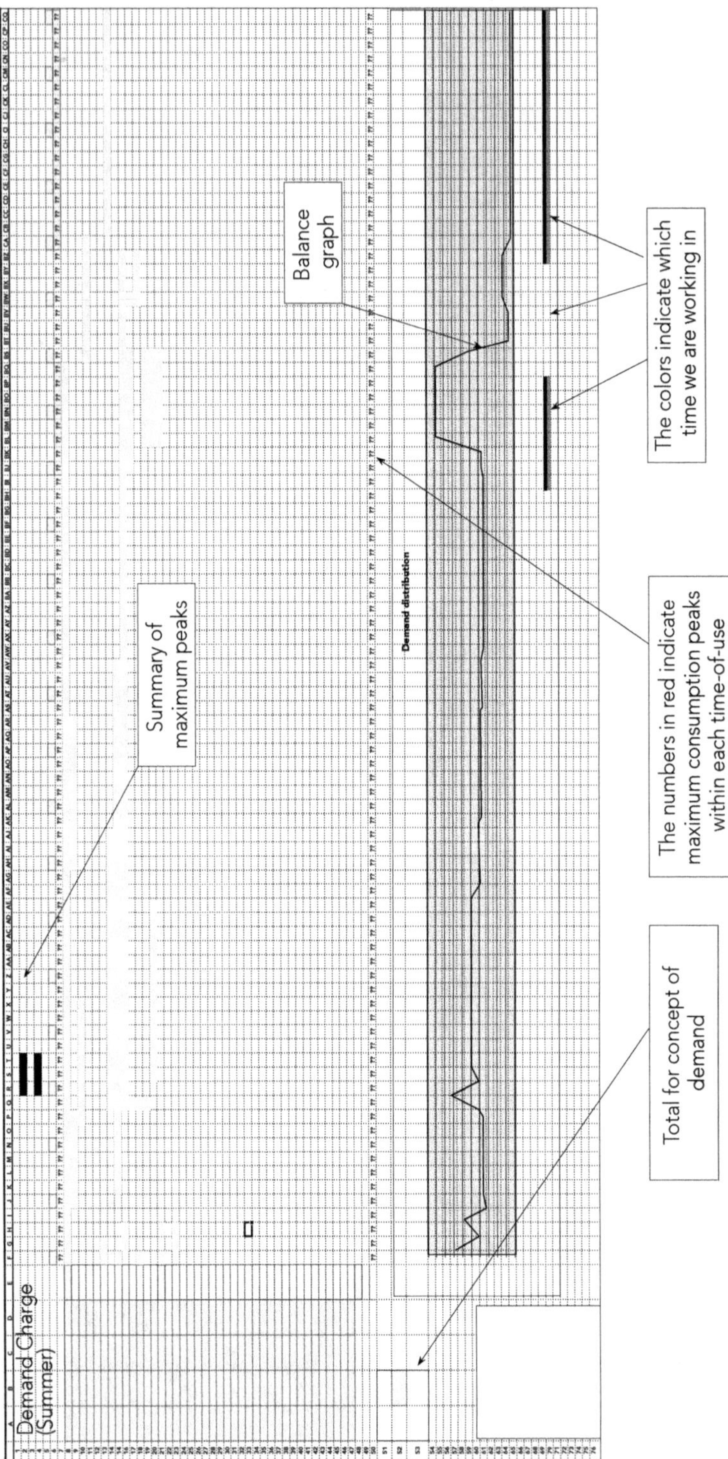

Figure 20.7

Glossary of terms and definitions

Activity that does not add value
It is any activity that generates a cost and consumes time but does not bring value directly to the process or product.

Andon
Japanese term meaning "lamp"; represents a visual or auditory cue that makes it possible to detect a quality problem in the process, the status of the process, or to quickly recognize an abnormal situation.

Automatic machine time
The time a machine takes to produce a unit, excluding loading and unloading times.

Basic time
Time set for a specific operational stage in standard work.

Black belts
They are leaders in the implementation of Lean Six Sigma with technical and leadership qualities to implement improvement projects in the organization.

Bottleneck
Is any aspect that prevents a system from reaching its full potential. It's used in operations to denote the slowest resource constraining the production of the entire system.

Box score
Results board in which operational, capacity, and financial indicators are established. It is used to monitor the results of a company or value stream in the short term and to make good decisions based on reliable results.

Cellular manufacturing
Is an arrangement of machines and workstations in the process sequence, which allows operators to work within the cell, thus balancing loads, improving communication, and achieving single piece flow or very small batches. Mate-

rials are delivered and handled outside the cell.

Change agent

Person devoted to making changes in processes, information and above all, culture.

Continuous improvement

Is a systematic process to improve processes, products and the work environment. It requires the commitment of managers and staff throughout the plant.

Cycle time

The time an operator takes to complete a work cycle. In general, it's the time that elapses before the cycle is repeated. (See Machine cycle time and operator cycle time.)

External setup

Elements of tool setup that can be done safely while the machine is running.

External time

Is the time for changeover activities that is used while the machine or equipment is working.

Five S's (5S)

Is a discipline to establish good housekeeping conditions in any work area. The 5S are *seiri* (sort), *seiton* (set in order), *seiso* (shine), *seiketsu* (standardize), and *shitsuke* (sustain).

FMEA (Failure Mode and Effect Analysis)

Is a technique for assessing reliability and for determining the effects of equipment failures.

Gemba

Japanese term meaning "crime scene".

Global production system

Expansion of the Toyota Production System; this is the strategy that enables Lean manufacturing using Kaizen methodology.

Green belts

They are employees from different levels in the company who are not devoted full time to Six Sigma activities and who know the methodology and tools at an application level in projects to which they are invited.

Heijunka

It is the leveling of production to the end customer's rate of demand.

Hoshin

Direction in which the compass needle points.

Hoshin kanri

Is a strategic planning technique that helps companies to focus their efforts as well as to establish strategies and projects that support the implementation of their guidelines.

Internal setup

Elements of tool setup that must be done while the machine is stopped.

Internal Time

It is the changeover time that should be used only when the machine is not working.

Jidhoka

Japanese term that means automation. It is a mechanism that allows the machine to detect and warn of a problem in the product.

JIT (just in time)
Production system that consists of manufacturing what is needed, when it is needed, in the quantity that is needed.

Kaizen
Combination of the Japanese words *kai* (change) and *zen* (for the good) which means continuous improvement. It consists of performing improvement events to implement Lean tools.

Kanban
Is an information system in which cards are used to inform the processes that the internal or external customer has withdrawn products and notifies the time and quantity to be produced to replenish in time and quantity.

Kanri
Management, control.

Lead time
Is the time necessary to produce a single product, from the moment the customer places his order until the delivery of the product.

Lean Manufacturing
Continuous and systematic process of waste identification and elimination.

Machine cycle time
The time a machine takes to produce a unit, excluding loading and unloading times.

Master black belts
They are mentors or teachers of black belts. They review and have the prestige and leadership because they teach and carry out complex projects.

Mission
The mission describes the raison d'être of the organization.

MTBF (Mean Time Between Failures)
Approximate period that a machine runs without failures.

MTTR (Mean Time Through Repair)
The estimated time that a machine will be idle while it is being repaired.

Muda (waste)
Activity that does not add cost but neither does it add value to the product. There are seven wastes or excesses: 1. Overload. 2. Excess inventory. 3. Defective products. 4. Transport of materials and tools. 5. Unnecessary processes. 6. Waiting. 7. Unnecessary movements of the worker.

Mura (variability)
Is the variation generated by the process itself, materials, methods, people, and machines.

Muri (overload)
Occurs when there is a workload that exceeds the members' capacities.

Nagara system
Run two or more activities with a single movement.

OEE (Overall Equipment Effectiveness)
Indicator obtained by multiplying availability by efficiency by quality.

Operator cycle time
The time that an operator takes to complete a predetermined sequence of operations, including loading and unloading and excluding time out.

OTC (One Touch Change)
The setup time to change over from one product to another or start an operation with a single touch of a button.

Poka
Unnoticed errors.

Poka yoke
Japanese term meaning "error proofing". A *poka yoke* device prevents human errors from affecting a machine or process and an operator's errors from becoming defects.

Process stock (WIP)
Stock waiting between steps in the operation.

Production
Quantity produced for which the system earns money.

Production leveling
Method for scheduling production in such a way that, for a certain time, the buoyancy in customer demand is eliminated from manufacturing, producing every piece every day.

Productivity
Is the relationship between the outputs of a process and its inputs.

QFD (Quality Function Deployment)
Also known as the house of quality. It is a process of spreading out customer needs in different matrices to know the design, process and control requirements for a product or service.

Restriction
A workstation or process that constrains the capacity of the entire system.

Seiri
Sort.

Seiketsu
Standardize.

Seiso
Shine.

Seiton
Set in order.

Sensei
Master or respectable teacher.

Setup reduction
Reduction in idle time that runs from the changeover from the last piece until the first good piece in the next operation.

Shitsuke
Sustain.

Single piece flow
Production system of a good or service that allows operators to move material from one station to another in a single piece without the need to make batches between processes, thus creating a continuous flow.

SMED (Single Minute Exchange of Die; Single-Digit Minute Tool Change-over)
The setup time for changing over from one product to another or starting an operation, achieved in less than 10 minutes, using a methodology for reducing setup times through continuous improvement events.

Spaghetti diagram
Drawing of the path of materials through all the production phases that is used to

understand the flow of production from the material warehouse.

Standard operations
The best combination of operator and machine, using the least amount of manpower, space, stock, and equipment.

Standard process stock
Minimum material requirement for the operator to complete a work cycle without delays.

Standard work
Default sequence of tasks that the operator must complete in takt time.

Standard worksheet
A diagram showing the sequence of operations and a drawing of the workstations to indicate how the work should be done.

Standardized operations combo box
A document that shows the sequence of production steps and graphically illustrates the sequence and times when workers and machines work together.

Stock
In general, this is the highest cost category; the *stock* consists of all raw materials, purchased parts, process *stock,* and finished products that have not yet been sold to a customer.

Suboptimization
Optimization of each piece of equipment; keep all machines running regardless of cost or consequence. It is normal that this increases the main cost of production: materials.

Supermarket
Premises on the factory floor next to the production line where the parts are sorted and made available to operators.

Takt time
The speed at which the customer buys and the time to which the production system must adapt to meet the customer's expectations. It's obtained by dividing total time available by customer demand.

Tool changeovers
The time that elapses from the last good piece of a previous batch to the first good piece of the next batch and consists of the changeover of tools, components and procedures needed to produce different part numbers.

Toyota Production System
Based on some of the principles of Henry Ford, the system presents the philosophy of one of the most successful companies in the world. The bases of TPS are: production leveling, *just in time,* and *jidhoka* supports.

TPM (Total Productive Maintenance)
An improvement methodology that allows the continuity of the operation in the equipment and plants.

Value added
Any activity that transforms a product or service to meet the customer's need.

Value analysis
Evaluation of the operations in a process to detect and quantify activities that add value and determine their contribution to the total delivery time.

Value Stream Map or VSM

Is a graphical representation of a process from the generation of customer requirements, passing through production and material control, up to arrival at the supplier companies. This diagram draws the entire process with operations and inventories in process and finally quantifies all value-added time and non-value time to determine delivery times.

Values

Within a company's set of beliefs, those that the company considers most important or valuable.

Vision

Vision is a statement of the possible and desirable future state of the organization.

Work sequence

The correct steps that the operator takes in the order that he must take them.

Yokeru

Avoid.

**Sales and operations
planning.
S&OP in 14 steps**
Cristina Peña Andrés

**Practical guide to the
Incoterms 2020 rules**
David Soler

**Estrategia = Ejecución.
El método para mejorar,
renovar e innovar
en la era digital**
Jacques Pijl

**Inteligencia directiva.
Manual para liderar
equipos**
Jaume Llopis Casellas

**Cómo gestionar la cadena
de suministo**
Ed Weenk

**Economía circular.
Un enfoque práctico para
transformar los modelos
empresariales**
Rozanne Henzen, Ed Weenk

**Sincronización y sinergia
empresarial**
Matías Birrell Rodríguez

**Tecnologías para liderar
el futuro**
Marc Busom

**Plan de marketing.
Diseño, implementación
y control**
Ricardo Hoyos Ballesteros

Lean Six Sigma White Belt. Certification Manual
Luis Socconini

Lean Six Sigma Management. Certification Manual
Luis Socconini

Lean Service. Certification Manual
Luis Socconini

Lean Six Sigma Yellow Belt. Certification Manual
Luis Socconini

Lean Six Sigma Green Belt. Certification Manual
Luis Socconini

Lean Six Sigma Black Belt. Certification Manual
Luis Socconini

Lean Six Sigma. Management System for Leaders
Luis Socconini, Carlo Reato

5S Practical guide to improve quality and productivity
Luis Socconini, Marco Barrantes

Lean Energy 4.0. Guía de Implementación
Luis Socconini, Juan Pablo Martín

Brutau, 160 – 08203 Sabadell (Barcelona) – Tel. +34-931 429 486 – marge@margebooks.com – www.margebooks.com